power up

power up

Transforming Organizations Through Shared Leadership

David L. Bradford and **Allan R. Cohen**

authors of the bestseller

Managing for Excellence

JOHN WILEY & SONS, INC.

New York • Chichester • Weinheim • Brisbane • Singapore • Toronto

Copyright © 1998 by David L. Bradford and Allan R. Cohen
Published by John Wiley & Sons, Inc.

Library of Congress Cataloging in Publication Data:

Bradford, David L.
    Power up : transforming organizations through shared leadership /
David Bradford and Allan Cohen.
      p.   cm.
    Includes bibliographical references and index.
    ISBN 0-471-12122-3 (cloth : alk. paper)
    1. Leadership. 2. Organizational change. I. Cohen, Allan R.
II. Title.
HD57.7.B697 1998
658.4'092—dc21   97-35610

In memory of our parents,
Lee and Marty Bradford
and
Ben and Frances Cohen.
They were our teachers about
leadership and followership by instruction
and example. They offered vision about how
to live, the chance to join in family decisions,
and every so often, mutual influence.

PREFACE

For two decades we have been asking what it takes to achieve organizational excellence. The research for our first book together, *Managing for Excellence,* unearthed a surprising finding: Poor leadership was not, by and large, the barrier to outstanding performance. In fact, most of the executives we studied were good at their jobs, but the harder they tried to be good leaders, the more these smart people blocked excellent results. We concluded that *good was the enemy of excellence.*

The problem was the fundamental heroic assumption underlying the concept of leadership, that it is the leader who is responsible for determining the right answers and managing the unit assigned. But what was the alternative? Although we had observed moments where employees demonstrated great leadership, we found few fully developed leadership models. Groping to articulate a better way, we constructed a new model we called Post-Heroic Leadership, which combined the best features of many different managers. Central to the model is the belief that managing is the responsibility of everybody in the unit, not just of the designated leader.

As this shared leadership model was introduced, we encountered strange reactions from the managers we worked with. Perhaps half of them folded their arms across their chests and said, "no way, this is too far out." Another group were intrigued but thought that it would be too hard to implement, either because they didn't have the skills to do it, or believed their organizations weren't ready. Only a handful were sufficiently intrigued to begin putting the ideas to work at once.

Now, a decade and a half later, the reactions are quite different. We see almost no managers who reject the concepts. Instead, they want to know how fast they can learn what is needed, since they are pressured by their organizations for a much higher level of performance. Managers realize that they can't have all the answers, and are dependent on making full use of every employee's abilities. Almost no one has a routine managerial job in which they only administer the status quo; all managers must initiate change and become leaders. (Thus, in this book we use the terms *leader* and *manager* interchangeably, since both sets of skills are needed at all levels of the organization.)

This doesn't mean that resistance to post-heroic leadership has vanished; we still get ambivalent responses when we explain the model. Someone will say (often in the same breath), "Oh yes, I know all of this and already do it," and, "No, this is way too hard for me to do." How can the model be at once too obvious and too difficult? Perhaps it represents a change more profound than it first appears to be, yet one that is easier than it seems if the leader has the courage to launch it.

Part of why post-heroic leadership sounds obvious is because the language of leadership has been corrupted, with everyone claiming to be participative, empowering and even post-heroic. Post-heroism made a cover story in *Fortune,* though the article mentioned that there was more talking about the ideas than practicing of them.[1] But we have found that to achieve the extraordinary results possible, the seemingly simple ideas must profoundly overturn deeply ingrained assumptions about leaders and followers that persist in the face of rational acceptance that they are limiting.

Observing outstanding leaders in action, refining and spelling out the new model, helping leaders put it into practice, even taking leadership roles ourselves to understand the difference between verbal acceptance and actual usage, is what we have been doing for the last 15 years. In this period we have found that the basic concepts in *Managing for*

Excellence were right, but that they needed considerable re-finement to make them fully accurate and usable.

The important new insight is obvious only in hindsight, that leadership is meaningless as a concept without looking at the reciprocal behavior of followers. That hasn't stopped most of those who study leadership from overlooking this connection, and focusing too much on leader behavior with-out examining the ways followers must also change. In *Managing for Excellence* we showed the need for a change in leader mindset, but we have since discovered that this can't be sustained unless members also unhook their heroic as-sumptions. Otherwise they pull the leader back into heroic responsibility. In *Power Up* the leadership system is the focus, not just the individual leader, and we show how lead-ers or followers can change the systemic interactions that bind them together. And we now remind leaders that leadership is not just about managing subordinates, but is also about dealing upward and laterally in the immediate organization.

We have learned that what we first called overarching goals, and later renamed tangible vision, is more than a nice-to-have idea; it is an essential part of the new leader-ship. Despite the widespread cynicism about vision, we know how to create passionate commitment to what the or-ganizational unit stands for and where it is going.

A critical component of effective leadership is the capacity to encourage and exercise mutual influence, which is the key ingredient in the continuous individual development highlighted in our earlier work. We have been surprised to discover that too many leaders, in the name of being tough, are less tough than they need to be. They can crack down when needed, but have trouble dealing head on with those, including higher level leaders, who need direct feedback on their behavior. And they too seldom encourage and help re-solve the conflict needed to utilize differing expertise and perspective.

Implementation of the post-heroic system is more complex than we had assumed, though we have uncovered examples of rapid transformations in situations where the participants had been despairing of real change. In this book are two extensive case studies of actual leaders. The first illustrates how a very heroic manager made the change to shared leadership. The second case explores how an executive team created a sense of collective ownership and turned around the organization. We have included numerous other actual examples that help show how to release full potential by transforming the leadership system.

As a result of all of these changes in our thinking, this is a new book, not just an updated edition of *Managing for Excellence.* If you have digested that book, there will still be a great deal of benefit from this one, but it is not necessary to have read the previous one to profit.

In our training programs we have come to think of learning the knowledge and skills as the "flat forehead" program: managers learn the ideas, think they have them, then are confronted with a more complex problem that seduces them back into heroic behavior. The sound you hear is the slapping of palms against foreheads, as in "Dammit, I trapped myself again!" Then the cycle repeats. By the end of 3–5 days, however, the concepts are embedded, and they can take them right onto the job.

Partly as a reflection of our experience with this interplay between concept, practice, feedback and deeper concept, the book is organized in a spiral pattern. The concepts are briefly laid out in the first chapter, taken further in the next three chapters, a complete leadership transformation example is offered for application, then the concepts are revisited with more complexity, and an extended implementation example is used in the final four chapters. We think this comes close to replicating the way leadership ideas are best absorbed.

DAVID L. BRADFORD
ALLAN R. COHEN

ACKNOWLEDGMENTS

We have had more than the usual amount of editorial advice and encouragement, due to the vagaries of the publishing business. Our original editor John Mahaney provided support for the concept of the book, and Jim Childs, Janet Coleman, and Renana Meyers all contributed useful suggestions. Richard Luecke excised the water from our meandering stream of words and forced us to be clear about what we meant.

Many friends and professional colleagues read the manuscript and provided sage advice. For their help on the whole manuscript we thank Harry Bloemink, Dennis Gallagher, Eric Larsen, Robert LeDuc, Kent Nethery, and Richard Strayer. Reactions to chapters came from Alan Briskin, Andrea Corney, John DeShano, David Diggs, the members of the Catalyst Consulting group in Santa Cruz, Esther Hamilton, Susan Harris, Lynne Rosansky, Phyllis Schlesinger, Peggy Umanzio, and participants at the Museum Management Institute. Several people at Wilson Learning Corporation—Linda Antone, Abby Cantlon, Kalen Hammann, Velma Lashbrook, Michael Leimbach, Alex Muller, Dave Patrick, Tom Roth—provided helpful observations about the book based on their experience with training program clients. David is particularly grateful to Stanford MBA students and especially the executives in the Sloan and Leading and Managing Change Programs who raised many challenging questions and provided useful examples of how these ideas applied. Similarly, participants in numerous Babson executive education programs made the connections between our concepts and their managerial experiences.

We were able to apply our ideas in and learn from a range of organizations over the past 15 years, including Allergan,

Autodesk, Berkeley Art Museum, Cambridge School of Weston, Colonia Insurance, Digital Equipment, General Electric, Lafarge, Levi Strauss & Company, Mitre, Paul Revere, Polaroid, Raychem, Siemens-Nixdorf, and Stanford Medical Center.

We are especially grateful to Bill Glavin, former vice-chairman of Xerox and recently retired president of Babson College, who patiently helped Allan learn about leadership from the action perspective, and provided many wonderful incidents from corporate life. Allan's faculty and administrative colleagues at Babson were remarkably good-natured about his blunders in the leader and colleague roles, and gave humorous but pointed feedback that was highly instructive. The formal upward feedback provided by faculty at his request was thoughtful and a good guide to the leadership needs of competent and independent professionals.

David also had wonderful executive mentors, Robert Haas, CEO of Levi Strauss & Company and Robert Saldich, former CEO of Raychem. As long-term clients they provided wisdom, counsel, and an openness to learning that were inspirational.

Linda Bloom, Marge Holford, Dee Stonberg, and Beverly Balconi, along with the refreshingly competent Nancy Marcus Land and her team at Publications Development of Texas, all helped at one time or the other with the manuscript production, providing good cheer when everything looked most bleak.

We particularly thank our wives, Eva and Joyce, for patience beyond their usual remarkable endurance, good humor, and astute suggestions when we were wrestling with particularly difficult passages.

Finally, however, no matter how much we advocate shared responsibility, only we can be held accountable for the final product.

D.L.B.
A.R.C.

CONTENTS

PART THREE

ESTABLISHING A SHARED-RESPONSIBILITY SYSTEM

Introduction: A New Relationship for Leaders and Followers

This is a book about a radical new approach to leadership. In countless books and articles, pundits have described how business has become global, fiercely competitive, and characterized by the need to cope with breakneck change. You have heard the story. Many organizations have responded by becoming leaner and by broadening the span of control between management layers. They have also attempted to extend the base of leadership and responsibility through well-intentioned programs such as Total Quality Management (TQM), worker participation, participative management, self-directed work teams, and empowerment. Chances are that your organization has adopted or experimented with one or more of these initiatives. Implementation confronts executives, managers, and employees with a complex issue that few have resolved although it is critical to superior organizational performance—the relationship between leaders and followers.

The traditional relationship of the leader and the led in the business world is undergoing a fundamental change. Indeed, postindustrial competition drives us to it. Greater complexity and work specialization, greater task interdependence, more demanding customer requirements, and better educated employees have transformed a world in which leaders were expected to make all the decisions and others were expected to carry them out to the letter. If this relationship ever worked well (and there is ample evidence that it never did), it does not work well today. Today, the bulk of market and technical knowledge is not at the top of the organization but at all levels, where managers and employees interact with customers, competitors, allies, suppliers, and each other. To be effective, these managers and employees must take greater responsibility for thinking, planning, initiating, and doing. The day when everyone could look upward for direction is over.

Worker empowerment and participative management programs should have recast the system of leadership and followership, but they have not. They have gotten people to think and experiment, but have not achieved significant reform. Outmoded assumptions about the roles of the leader and followers block transformation. Most organizations find themselves in a painful and inconclusive transition between eras of *heroic* and *post-heroic* leadership.

The concepts in this book provide a practical bridge between those two eras.

THE CONCEPT OF THE HEROIC LEADER

We first presented the notion of heroic leadership in our book *Managing for Excellence.*[1] We described the heroic leader as a person who (whether or not it was still true) was supposed to:

- Know more than anyone else what was going on in the company, in his or her department, or in the marketplace of customers, competitors, and suppliers.

- Have greater technical expertise than any subordinate.

- Be able to solve any problem faster and/or better than anyone in the organization.

- Take primary responsibility for everything that the organization or the department did or failed to do.

The appeal of the heroic leader has a long history in Western culture. From ancient times through the Renaissance, heroic leaders were celebrated in epic poems, sagas, and histories. Ajax and Achilles, Moses, Alexander the Great, Julius Caesar, Beowulf, El Cid, and dozens of others, both real and mythological, were held up as examples. It was the "great leader" who shaped the world. All others—advisers, captains, confessors, and lesser followers—revolved around such leaders like minor satellites, playing bit parts in the dramatic unfolding of events.

Alexander the Great is the archetypal heroic leader in this tradition. For 17 centuries, ambitious young European men considered chronicles of his life and campaigns to be essential reading: He was the perfect model of inspired ambition, decisiveness, and bold action. Alexander was both a thinker and a doer. His tactics were often brilliant in their design and executed with skill—usually by Alexander himself. He repeatedly threw himself into the fray at the most decisive point in any battle. This courage inspired his followers to greater ferocity and eventual success.

For such a person, the term heroic is not an overstatement! Yet, how many executives and managers of sizable companies measure up to these criteria? Very few. Even those who are celebrated in the press, like Jack Welch, Bill Gates, or Lee Iacocca, are far more dependent on the contributions of others than is usually acknowledged. Sales managers almost always know more than CEOs about customers and competitors. Every department has specialists—in taxes, information systems, production, and many other areas—on whom company leaders depend for accurate data and advice. In the area of technology, the person at the top is generally the *least* likely to know which end is up; and front-line employees can usually solve immediate problems quicker and better than anyone at headquarters.

For all leaders, a legitimate part of their role is to serve as the symbolic figurehead, representing the organization to the world. This is necessary, but often causes problems because so much of what happens is credited to the leader and overlooks the contributions of others. Nevertheless, the concept of heroic leadership continues to define the leader-follower relationship in most corporations and shape how business is done. The negative consequences of this anachronistic concept are intuitively obvious:

- Organizations depend on a few individual leaders for their insights and vitality.
- The knowledge and talents of the many are untapped.
- No one else learns to lead—except by outdated example.
- The powerful leader smothers initiative and induces passivity.

It is time to discard the notion of heroic leadership that once worked and adopt a more timely and effective leader-follower relationship—*post-heroic* leadership. In the following chapters, we describe how this new collaboration of leaders and followers produces better decisions, more learning, more and better ideas, greater employee participation, and higher morale.

The benefits of post-heroic leadership are more obvious than the means to attaining them. If it were easy to change the leader-follower relationship, everyone would be doing it, and "employee empowerment" would be more than an empty business buzzword. The managers we study know that they need to share greater responsibility with their subordinates, but almost none of them do so. The reason: Like all significant change, the move to post-heroic leadership is difficult and often painful. Traditional leaders fear the consequences of losing control; some would equate it with putting the inmates in charge of the asylum. Even when leaders are personally willing to give ample latitude to subordinates, out of trust in their competence or sheer overload from today's flatter, leaner organizations, the subordinates may run their own areas well, but do not feel obligated to pull together. That is seen as the province of the leader, pushing responsibility for coordination back up. When there is complex, interdependent work to be coordinated, the leader cannot do it alone, but followers sense the danger in taking that kind of responsibility and accountability.

Power Up!

The need for a new relationship between leaders and employees is neither a figment of our professorial imaginations, nor a theory applicable to only a few unique industries. It is real and it matters for just about every company that operates in modern competitive markets. Writing in *Fortune* recently, John Huey put it this way:

> *Call it whatever you like: post-heroic leadership, servant leadership, distributed leadership, or . . . virtual leadership. But don't dismiss it as another touchy-feely flavor of the month. It's real, it's radical, and it's challenging the very definition of corporate leadership for the 21st century.*[2]

Paul Fribourg, new CEO of $16 billion Continental Grain, recognized the need to bring wider expertise to bear: "In the past, we could be run by one individual. . . . Now it takes a team." His vice chairman and CFO, James Bigham, explains, "Paul's job is forcing consensus."[3] Heroism is being replaced by new assumptions that release the talents and energy of everyone.

This book will tell you what you need to do to make the transition from the old model of the leadership to the new. That new model is applicable at any level, from top management to divisions to departments to even smaller units. Wherever people define themselves as either leaders or subordinates, the concept offered here will help them *Power Up* the work they do.

THE OLD AND THE NEW
WORLDS OF LEADERSHIP

The chapters in Part One explain the core ideas of the book. Chapters 1 through 3 describe the trap that restricts so many leaders, widely shared but outmoded concepts about leadership, and a new model of shared leadership that can transform organizational performance. These ideas are revisited later in the book with greater richness and context. The concepts come together in Chapter 4, which is an account of a leader who was able to learn to share leadership, despite his own resistance and his team's doubts. Chapter 5 describes the ambivalence that both leaders and subordinates feel about the new leadership and how to get past it.

THE LEADERSHIP TRAP

$\mathbf{A}$sk any manager about leadership today, and you are likely to hear much the same answer. Leaders should build teams, get everyone to pull together, develop vision, inspire extra effort, seize opportunities, encourage openness—and do other wonderful things. Almost everyone knows what leaders are supposed to do, but few leaders do them.

- Why do so many subordinates still complain about their bosses?
- Why do so many employees feel their abilities are underutilized, even as their managers feel overworked?
- Why are critical issues so seldom raised and resolved at team meetings?
- Why is there so much wasted energy?

Here's an example of an actual, all-too-common situation.

Example at Pharmco

Bill Boyer, a divisional VP at "Pharmco,"* a $900 million agribusiness company, was venting his frustration to Bob

---

* To protect confidentiality, we often use a pseudonym for a company or individual; the first use of the pseudonym is in quotation marks. Although

Mitchell, the President and COO, after an exasperating meeting of the firm's operating committee (OpCom).

"This isn't a team," he complained. "This is a disaster! We make almost no important decisions, but when we do, Gene feels free to change them. What's the point? Sure he's the CEO, and sure he started the company, but he causes as many problems as he solves."

Bob nodded his head sympathetically as Bill fumed.

"I know you try to protect us from him, Bob, but Gene's a loose cannon. He comes to our staff meetings unannounced, and leaves when he gets bored. What drives me crazy is that when he is there, he picks some minor issue and takes us off track. I think we should just disband this group!"

Bill would not be consoled. Gene, the CEO and founder, had just thrown cold water on one of Bill's pet projects. Other members of the OpCom team had been too afraid of Gene to come to Bill's support. Bob had jumped in to deflect the argument and keep Gene from making a knee-jerk decision. Failing that, he hoped that he could explain Bill's position outside the meeting and get Gene to change his mind.

After his discussion with Bill Boyer, Bob went to his office and stewed over his growing frustrations with running Pharmco.

"Gene is a great guy," he told himself. "He's responsible for the company's being where it is today, and he is tremendously creative. But sometimes he is uninvolved, and then suddenly he's jumping in and interfering, giving orders to people he doesn't directly manage, and making arbitrary decisions. And he's impossible to confront."

Bob recalled the many times he had seen the CEO rag on individual executives to the point that everyone,

---

we may alter details to disguise the identity of the company or person, we have not altered important evidence or concealed contradictory data. Quotations are as literal as possible, based either on notes taken at the time or recorded soon after the events.

including the hapless victim, just became silent and looked down at the table.

Working for Gene was difficult. In one breath, the CEO had complained that Bob's executive group was not working as a team. In the next breath, he griped about "groupie" stuff that never solved problems. "He's one of the main reasons we don't work together well," Bob concluded.

"He also says that I should be more aggressive and 'in charge.' But then he leaps in whenever he doesn't like what I'm doing."

Perhaps it was a hopeless situation. "I've been COO for more than 10 years now," Bob thought as he looked vacantly out the window, "and I still don't know if I'll ever get to be CEO. Will Gene ever let go? I don't know if I'll ever have the chance to really run this company. Maybe I should look elsewhere. I'm getting to the age where I have to move up or move on, or I'll be stuck."

Gene wasn't Bob's only problem. "The guys who work for me have lots of talent, but they just can't see beyond their own little empires or take the company point of view. They battle for dominance and compete instead of cooperate. They'd rather fight over which division's sales force owns certain customers than work together to provide better service. They're more interested in control and expanding their empires than doing what's best for the company.

"The VPs all think the CFO is Gene's spy and don't tell him anything they don't have to, which makes all of our jobs harder. As a result, our OpCom meetings are like a poker game with everyone holding his cards close to his chest."

Bob concluded that the OpCom was a good idea that simply wasn't working. Several major strategic and organizational decisions were coming up, but the team had demonstrated little ability to work on anything controversial.

"Maybe Bill Boyer was right," he thought. "OpCom isn't a team; its just a bunch of freelancers. If these people could forget their little fiefdoms for five minutes and think of what Pharmco needs, we would make real progress. And if I could get Gene to back off, to trust me to do what's right for the business, I could be a lot more effective. Why can't he understand that I'm as concerned about the company's success as he is?"

Pharmco has a leadership problem, but what is it? Gene's capricious interference? His intimidating style? Bob's way of dealing with Gene outside meetings? Bob's protection of Bill and the team? The team's willingness to be intimidated by Gene? The team's failure to address tough issues? Internal competition? All of the above?

Whatever it is, no company's leadership problem can be understood without looking at the behavior of *both* its leaders and followers. Without examining the behavior of those who are supposed to follow, any study of leadership is meaningless. All the managers at Pharmco are playing a part in the company's problems. As in a troubled family, each member is acting as an enabler of the others' dysfunctional behavior. Behavior does not occur in a vacuum, it exists in a *system,* with interacting parts.

How Systems Work

When dancers have been together a long time, the slightest pressure of the hand on the back, a raised eyebrow, or just a knowing glance can signal a clear response. It is easy to dance with a partner who knows the steps and wants to move together in time with the music. If each partner knows who should initiate and who should follow, if each understands who signals the turns and how the other should respond, there is little stumbling—even among new partners. A person who tries to turn the wrong way will be pushed, pulled, or guided into the correct steps.

In practice there are subtleties in dancing that only experienced partners notice. The designated follower may be more skilled and will covertly lead, moving into the next step just ahead of the designated leader. Though observers don't notice, the leader is actually being signaled where to move. All that the observers see is coordinated movement.

The dance is a metaphor for a system with connecting parts, where changes or actions in one component cause changes in others. Individuals are the elements of human systems such as teams, departments, and families, but they are linked together by feelings or beliefs, not the literal connections of a heating system or the braking system of a car. People have ideas about how things are supposed to work, how they and others are supposed to behave in particular situations.

A Vicious Circle

The leader-follower relationship is a *reciprocal* system. There is an intimate connection between what followers do, and how leaders act. Each responds to the other. When both assume that the leader has the answers and responsibility for decisions and results, there is tacit agreement that the contributions of followers are restricted and should await direction from the top. This reinforces the leader's belief that followers cannot initiate or contribute in a broad sense. This vicious circle creates a leadership trap from which escape seems impossible.

Most leadership theories make the same heroic assumption that there is a fundamental difference between the responsibilities of leaders and subordinates. The leader is responsible for achieving overall success, making the critical decisions, and coordinating the actions of staff, while subordinates are supposed to run their own areas, point out problems, and follow the boss's lead. Although this appears to be reasonable, it sets up mutually reinforcing interactions that limit everyone's potential contributions. The participants are caught in a dance that goes in circles (see Figure 1–1).

The assumptions of heroic leadership contribute to a mutually reinforcing system that causes and perpetuates the leadership trap of control and passivity. In assuming overall responsibility for the results of their units, leaders overmanage their subordinates. When issues are discussed, the topics are carefully restricted; the leader consults with subordinates when it seems appropriate but has the last say on critical decisions. This causes subordinates to feel less responsible, so they constrict their focus to their own areas, blame others, pass responsibility up to the boss, and protect their flanks. Observing this, the leader thinks, "Just as I expected, these people cannot accept responsibility or do

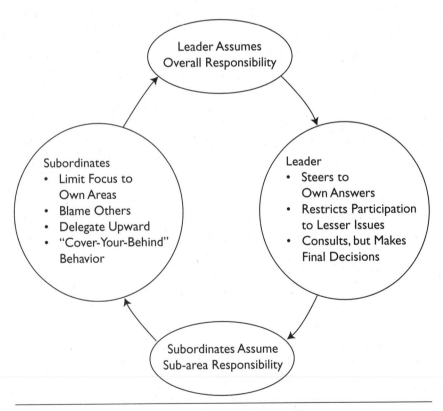

Figure 1–1. The Leadership Trap

more than stick to their own narrow assignments." This observation results in still greater control, which induces even greater passivity in employees. "The boss doesn't want us to take responsibility," they conclude, "so we'll do only what we're told—(or what will make me look good)."

No company can afford to repeat this cycle for long if they desire organizational excellence. That requires the active commitment of every employee at every level. Most people know this, but getting them to commit and to act is difficult as long as leaders and followers subscribe to traditional beliefs about their roles. That thinking locks them into a sad slow dance that keeps their feet shuffling to a tune from a bygone era. There are ways to stop the dance and to rearrange the steps, but neither party can do it alone. Neither can change without the cooperation of the other since each enables the other's inappropriate behavior. All of this is true at Pharmco. Its people are caught in a negative dance and have no self-corrective mechanism.

Cycles like the leadership trap perpetuate themselves until either the system breaks down entirely or someone recognizes the problem and does something to change the pattern. Unfortunately, the process of recognition is often obscured by the habit of blaming someone else for the problem.

THE BLAME GAME

Does Bob's litany of complaints about his boss sound familiar? His story may seem extreme, but it is real. Who hasn't heard variations of the following complaints about bosses? They are labeled:

- Arbitrary.
- Smart but interfering (or worse, less informed than they think they are, but still interfering).
- Demanding yet frequently unavailable.
- Teamwork poisoners who divide and conquer, setting team members against each other.

- Unsupportive.
- Manipulative.
- Unpredictable, changing direction without warning or explanation.
- Secretive, constantly leaving people in the dark about important issues.
- Not open to influence, or too intimidating to confront.

Bob's complaints about his subordinates should also have a ring of familiarity:

- Team members engage in bickering and rivalry.
- They are reluctant to share information or tackle conflict-laden issues.
- They have conflicting allegiances.
- They resist programs that require sacrifice but benefit the organization as a whole.

As he sees it, Bob is in a tough spot, squeezed between a difficult boss and a pack of self-serving senior managers. Like a good hero, he is sure he has to bear the burden of maneuvering around the problems alone. But before you develop too much sympathy for poor Bob, how do you suppose things look to Gene? Would Gene see himself as arbitrary or interfering? Would he say that he is unwilling to give up control? Let's hear another side of this tale of woe, this time from Gene's viewpoint.

> *"I brought Bob into the company with the hope that he could be my successor, but he still hasn't shown me that he can do it. He seems to be afraid to take charge, settling instead for endless, boring meetings that never come to clear conclusions. He's enchanted with all that soft-headed groupie stuff.*
>
> *"I don't know what his problem is—maybe he's afraid that someone won't like him if he makes a tough*

decision. But that's what's needed to run a company. You can't study everything to death. There are never any guarantees. You have to plunge in, get to the bottom of things, make the call, and take your lumps if you're wrong.

"Bob seems to be too detached from the action. When costs start to get out of line, or revenues slip, he doesn't move fast enough. If I didn't stay on top of the numbers, working closely with Ed, we'd get into a deep hole and never come out of it. When we did the leveraged buyout, I thought that would give Bob the incentive he needed to really drive the business for profit and market share, but we're barely holding our ground.

"Now we have to decide whether to sell off some of our divisions in order to concentrate on our main lines, or try to build on what we have. I don't see him grabbing hold of these issues and forcing us to decisions, whatever they are.

"Hell, I've bought businesses faster than he can make the decisions about how run them.

"If you're out talking to customers like I am, you get a feel for what to do, and all the fancy consultants and group meetings can't match what your gut tells you.

"I'll tell you what makes it hard for me to really let loose of the company, which I'd like to do if I could: I just don't know if Bob is tough enough to run things. He's too nice. When one of his people can't cut the mustard, he won't pull the trigger. In fact, he'd rather protect the weak person than have to fire him. If Bob were like me, I wouldn't have to get involved. When I ask an exec questions and get evasive or incompetent answers, I get all over him.

"I'd like to cut back time in the office to two or three days a week, and spend more time on charitable activities and with my grandchildren. But until I'm convinced that Bob can do the job—or until I find someone who can—I have to stay on top of things. Someone has to watch the store."

Gene's complaints about Bob seem as reasonable as Bob's did about him, and strangely parallel Bob's concerns about *his* subordinates. Gene sees Bob as not ready to address the needs of the business, just as Bob sees his team members as failing to do the same. Each locates the leadership problems of the company elsewhere—a curious displacement of responsibility for individuals who are eager to fulfill the leadership role of taking responsibility for everything.

The people on Bob's management team are also players in the blame game and prisoners in the leadership trap. Bill Boyer echoes the sentiments of fellow OpCom members when he says:

> *"Bob lets Gene interfere too much. There is no point in making tough decisions without Gene in the room, because he'll just decide what he wants anyway. Bob is too weak to stand up to him; we all wish that he would have the backbone to push back harder.*
>
> *"At the same time, Bob protects us too much from Gene. We are never sure what Gene is thinking, and we don't get the information we need to act sensibly. No wonder Gene took me apart at our last meeting; I didn't know how to shape my proposal to make him see its value.*
>
> *"I'll be the first to admit that our team isn't effective. It's less a team than a group of individual operators. And I suppose that I act like one myself. But I'm not going give up what I want for my division when I'm judged primarily on my results. It's Bob's job to get the team working toward common goals, but he hasn't done that. They'll take over the place if he doesn't crack a few heads."*

Here again, someone who professes a desire for responsibility displaces the problems of the company to others. He sees Bob's weak leadership as the problem.

The key managers of Pharmco are locked into the leadership trap and held there by attitudes and assumptions that prevent clear diagnosis and reform. The symptoms of heroic leadership are everywhere:

- Everyone expects the leader to assume responsibility.
- Subordinates delegate tough problems upward.
- Subordinates are concerned with their own territory, not the overall goals.
- Teamwork and coordination are weak.
- Leaders overmanage.

It is particularly difficult to escape the trap because the role of subordinates does not include obligations to take responsibility for the coordination of the whole unit. Even when the leader is not controlling and is eager to have subordinates take initiative, they act from the perspective of their own area. After a while, the competitor and lack of coordination upsets the leader, who feels the need to reassert control in order to assure coordinated effort. Taking responsibility for the whole reinforces the old division between the leader's and the subordinates' concerns.

From a single position in a system, one's own behavior seems reasonable. This makes it difficult to see the whole system and its patterns. This happens even though leaders are also subordinates to other leaders, and colleagues to their peers. The tensions and contradictions inherent in the heroic style blind the players in the system, whatever their positions, to the commonalties of their experiences. They see individual flaws, not their shared assumptions, as the actual cause of the problems.

Limited perspective is exactly the cause of limited results. As the old organizational maxim explains, "where you sit determines where you stand." When individuals are in subordinate roles—expected to initiate with great caution, make few mistakes, defer to the boss when the boss has strong views, be responsible primarily for the subarea assigned— they may work very hard, but use only a portion of their talents. New opportunities are pursued only under clear mandate. The first question is, "how will this help my area (and increase my bonus)?" rather than, "how could this benefit the wider organization?" Colleagues who are not performing may be a nuisance, but unless they directly impinge one's area, are considered the boss's responsibility. A boss who is wrong-headed about an issue should be told very carefully, if at all, so as not to invoke resentment or retaliation. Thus, the full potential of subordinates is seldom tapped.

Some way must be found to enlist everyone to give all that they can, take the wider perspective along with the restricted one. If where people sit determines where they stand, then every direct subordinate must be invited to share the throne, to see what the leader sees, so that full contributions are possible. This has been called wearing two hats, that of one's assigned role and also that of the leader, a willingness to speak up and fully engage when there are issues that affect the whole unit. Inducing this form of psychological ownership or partnership from below is the challenge for leadership in a complex, changing world.

THE ALTERNATIVE: POST-HEROIC LEADERSHIP

There is an alternative to the heroic system that releases the potential power of everyone: We call it *post-heroic* leadership. In this new system, team members share responsibility for managing the unit.

Post-heroic leadership begins with a new mind-set, in which both the leader and subordinates take on new obligations. Leaders must shift away from the traditional notions of sole responsibility and control to induce greater acceptance of responsibility and initiative by their subordinates. In turn, subordinates must not only remain responsible for their own areas, but become working partners in what is usually thought of as the leader's job: spotting problems, initiating action, pushing colleagues to do what is necessary to accomplish the unit's work—in short, sharing the responsibility for overall unit success. Their duties include holding the leader accountable for his or her behavior, just as the leader holds them accountable.

The implications of shared leadership are profound. Passivity is not tolerated. No one can say "That's the leader's responsibility, not mine." Everyone is expected to seize opportunities, correct problems, and hold others accountable for performance. This makes everyone a leader, responsible for initiative laterally and upward, not just for control over those below. It enlarges the psychological ownership of everyone.

Shared leadership does not eliminate the leader's role or deny hierarchy; leaders still have plenty of work and remain accountable for the unit's performance. But they must now encourage and build a shared responsibility system, where the leader and direct reports collaborate in the management of the unit. This is challenging, because subordinates used to a constrained role will not automatically believe that their full partnership is welcomed, nor will they step up to the new expectations without considerable testing. *Is the boss sincere? Is this for real?* It takes time for all parties to develop confidence in their altered relationships, to see that behavior must change, and to know that change is worth the effort. But when responsibility is shared, not only does the performance of the overall unit improve, but subordinates are more likely to deliver on their sub-unit responsibilities, because they have both more colleague support and pressure to perform. All are in it together.

BUILDING A SHARED RESPONSIBILITY SYSTEM

For shared responsibility to work, three main implementation elements are necessary beyond the new mind set:

1. *A setting in which shared responsibility can occur.* To make critical managerial and strategic decisions

together, the leader and members need to develop a strong, cohesive team where those issues can be raised, debated, and jointly resolved.

2. *Basic agreement about the purpose and direction of the unit.* This requires developing commitment to a *tangible vision* of what the unit does that makes it special and significant. If members buy in to the vision, they will pull together when sharing in overall decision-making.

3. *A dramatic increase in the extent to which team members influence each other and the leader, and are influenced in return.* Thus relationships between individuals must be based on *mutual influence* rather than dominance or avoidance. This makes it easier for the leader to share responsibility.

Figure 1–2 graphically represents the differences between heroic and post-heroic leadership. Put these three elements

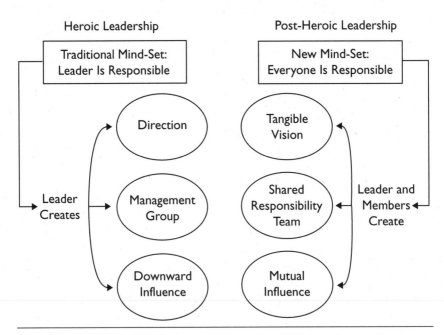

Figure I–2. Heroic versus Post-Heroic Leadership

together with the new mind-set and you will *Power Up* the performance of your organization. Later chapters explain the three elements in detail.

WHAT IS NEW?

Shared responsibility. A tangible vision. Mutual influence. Many executives who read this chapter will be tempted to say, "We already have these three elements working for us." But hold up a nondistorting mirror or ask your direct reports and you'll probably still see the old boss-subordinate relationship between people. Many managers and leaders think they are post-heroic, think they encourage teamwork and upward feedback, and think they are open to influence, but most are not.

There may be a stated vision, but:

- Do people agree on its meaning?
- Are they committed to using it regularly for decision making?
- Does it pull them past their individual goals?

There may be a group called a team that meets with the leader regularly, but:

- Do members say it is their team or the leader's?
- Are discussions fully open and passionate?
- Is debate based on honest differences rather than turf issues?
- Does the team make important decisions through consensus?
- Are there full contributions from everyone?
- Is it acceptable for the group to discipline those who don't come through, or advance personal goals at the expense of the overall unit?

The leader may influence members, but:

- How free are members to push back, especially if the leader signals strong views or starts to get hot?
- Are members expected to be responsible for each other and directly influence each other?

Even where there is reasonable consistency of direction, spirited meetings and fair give and take,

- Do team members really own the whole? Do they act like partners?
- Is the power potential fully realized?

Few leaders or organizations can answer all those questions in the affirmative. But for those that can, shared responsibility leadership has a substantial payoff:

- Leadership exists at every level.
- The organization taps the energy and knowledge of everyone.
- People from different units can tackle tough issues as a team, and not as a collection of warring parties.
- The burdens of responsibility are shared broadly; contributions come from many quarters; the organization can engage the full talents of every employee and obtain amazing results.

Amazing results: That's what the people at Pharmco were able to achieve within a year of the stressful scenes described earlier. The operating committee managed to break out of its self-destructive cycle and attack its most difficult strategic issues as a team. Not only did they turn "the disaster" into a strong team, they made decisions without nasty politics, fear of Gene the powerful founder, over-protectiveness of individual areas, or reluctance to say the tough things to each other. With new directness, they implemented a major reorganization, identified 10 percent strategic personnel reduction (instead of equal reductions across the board), and determined jointly which top managers, including some in the room, should leave or be moved. Reassignments of managers to new areas were done together, taking into account skills and needs, without possessiveness by current leaders. Managers began to collaborate, support each other, and put the interest of the company first.

Business performance improved dramatically in the wake of Pharmco's organizational improvements. Later chapters show exactly how this was accomplished and explain how almost any organization can do the same when it adopts a new system of leadership.

But what about Gene's imperial style? And what about Bob's problems as president and COO? As will be discussed later, even these troublesome problems were overcome. Confronted by the team, Bob learned to demonstrate that he could take tough action utilizing a shared responsibility team, pushed Gene hard, and earned his way into becoming CEO. Gene was persuaded by the top team and Bob's new leadership style that daily operations were in good hands and moved exclusively to the position of board chairman.

Any company can create comparable results if it changes to a leadership system based on shared responsibility. That new system isn't simply for top-level management teams, like Pharmco's OpCom. It can be applied to teams at all levels. The following chapters will show you how, beginning with an examination of the dynamics of the traditional system of heroic leadership.

2

HEROIC LEADERSHIP: WHERE THE BUCK STOPS TOO OFTEN

Years of experience have left most people with a deeply rooted belief that the main difference between managers and those who report to them is that *the manager is responsible for the group's success.* The buck may be passed around, but it always stops with the boss. When managers are talented or lucky, they have subordinates who pitch in, invest in the job, pull together, and shoulder more than their share. But in the end, managers remain fully responsible for the whole, while subordinates are responsible only for their own areas. That's the mind-set of heroic leadership. And despite all the books, articles, and seminars advocating participative management, this mind-set remains deeply anchored in the psyche of managers and subordinates alike.

Heroic leadership used to work. Its past success no doubt explains its persistence. It was useful when conditions were more stable, when employees were less educated, and when they performed routine tasks that required little interdependence. In those conditions, the leader was the expert who could provide needed coordination and control. Subordinates needed little initiative; to succeed, they stayed in their assigned roles and ignored other areas. Although work conditions of this sort have become increasingly rare, old habits die hard.

You can probably find examples of heroic leadership where you work. Think of the last meeting you attended at which the discussion wandered off the agenda. Chances are that more than a few people started looking up at the ceiling, or down at their notes, hoping that the leader would get the meeting back to the topic. And chances are that someone finally said: "Aren't we getting off track?"

What happened next? Probably, the designated leader sat up a bit straighter and took charge of the meeting, either pointing out the relevance of the discussion, or steering it back to the agenda. It is unlikely that anyone else at the table would do this—not the person who raised the objection; not the people looking at the ceiling. Typically, everyone waits for the leader to take charge and make things right. In the odd case that someone other than the leader moved in, how would others respond? Most likely they would look at the leader to get his or her reaction to being upstaged, usurped, or outflanked by the pretender to the leadership throne.

A system in which titular leaders take full responsibility for action and outcomes is fine if by some chance those leaders are perfectly knowledgeable, always know what to do, see everything, and can easily determine when to take charge and when to delegate. (We haven't met any of these lately. Have you?) Otherwise, too much depends on the leader's skill and initiative, and too little is asked of others.

That the leader is accountable for the ultimate success of the unit (whether it is a department, a division, a project, or an entire company), is a canon of organizational thinking. Managers and the people who work for them subscribe to this thinking, and they are right. The problem is that years of training and conditioning have led both to assume that accountability means that the manager also carries sole responsibility—and thus should know everything, control everything, and make the hard decisions. These duties are seen as the privilege—and the burden—of those who sit in the corner office.

These heroic assumptions can easily tempt managers to squash underlings with overbearing and arbitrary actions, although this is less true today than in the past. Thanks to people-centered management theories, changes in employee attitudes, greater spans of control, and growing evidence of the power of teamwork, the age of the managerial autocrat has largely vanished. But the underlying assumptions of that age linger on.

The boss may no longer be a tyrant, but heroism isn't dead. Instead, it has cloaked itself in the language of empowerment, consensus, and teams. The words may have changed, the degree of participation may have increased, and the boss may have found that soft talk is more effective than harsh orders, but everyone still assumes that the boss is responsible for the group's success.

Even participative management, as commonly practiced, is heroic. Subordinates have a say and some influence, but the manager makes the final decisions on important issues. Managers say they want to decide by consensus, which suggests equal sharing, but the boss is the person to convince. Likewise, when people sense what the manager wants they are subtly pressured to go along.

The pervasive assumption that the manager is responsible for the whole while others are responsible for their subareas reflects a traditional contract of leadership derived from culture and past conditions. Although seldom explicit, that contract is understood and deeply embedded. Until it is replaced, extraordinary performance will be an elusive goal.

THE TRADITIONAL LEADERSHIP CONTRACT

To show the traditional contract in action, we quote clients and colleagues—division managers, functional managers, and product managers—talking about life at work. Their words reveal their assumptions about who has responsibility for organizational success. Do any of these comments sound familiar?

Different Areas of Responsibility

Organizations divide up work and assign different tasks to different people and groups. Greater and lesser responsibilities are attached to these tasks:

> *As a manager, part of my job is to be sure that I've carved out the right assignments, and then I hold each person responsible for that. Clear goals and objectives make for real accountability; then I can oversee everything and make sure that the pieces fit together.*

> *I do my job as well as I can, and I expect the same from everyone else. Then it's up to the boss to pull it all together. That's why he gets the big bucks.*

> *If one of my colleagues isn't delivering the goods, as long as it doesn't negatively impact my area, that's the boss's concern. It's not my job to shape up people at my level.*

> *I don't stick my nose into other people's areas, and I certainly don't let them stick theirs into mine. Oh sure, I have my opinions about how they ought to do things, but I really don't expect them to listen, so I don't offer much. There's little enough I control around here, so I want to keep others off of my turf, small as it might be.*

Notice that the first component of the contract is the idea of superiors and subordinates. These terms are built into the hierarchical, structured way of thinking about organizations that has been around for a long time. The superior-subordinate dichotomy was created to help organizations control individuals with vast differences in competence and commitment. Today, it is hard to hear the words spoken without thinking that "superior" is *better* or *smarter*, and possibly even *more deserving*. "Subordinate" suggests *under, less able, dominated,* and *deferential.*

Subordinates are presumed to be responsible for distinctively different functions than are their superiors. Since organizations are arranged in a hierarchy of roles and responsibilities, subordinates are responsible only for the functions within their job descriptions; the superior's job description covers a much wider ground—seeing the larger purpose and being responsible for assuring the coordination of many subordinate activities. Subordinates should coordinate efforts with their peers, but the manager retains responsibility for overall coordination and for resolving disputes.

Decision Making

How decisions are made is a fundamental issue in every organization. The differentiation between leaders and followers shapes this issue:

> *The boss makes the big decisions. He's smart, so he listens to me and the other experienced people around here, but we all know whose hands are on the reins.*

> *I want to do well, so I let my manager know what I think she needs to know to make decisions, but I'm not going to be a martyr if she doesn't want to hear it.*

> *If I'm asked my opinion, I tell the truth, but first I try to see which way the wind is blowing to make sure that I don't ruffle any feathers. You don't have to poke anyone in the eye with a sharp stick to make your point; if they want to know, they'll get it.*

> *My job as leader is to make the tough decisions—that's what I'm paid for. While I expect every one of my people to tell me what I need to know to make good decisions, once they have spoken their piece, I expect them to get on board.*

> *I know how to mind my own business. There are a lot of things best left unsaid, especially if the boss is hot about something. Oh, I'll try to give warning signals if there are problems ahead, but after giving it my best shot, in the last analysis, it's her funeral.*

Although there are still a few autocratic leaders around who try to make all the decisions themselves, most leaders recognize the need for advice and counsel. They solicit and consider input, but if the problem is important, they see the decision as theirs. If they do not want to discuss a key issue, it isn't discussed.

Example at Biotekk

The CEO of "Biotekk" kept telling his executive team, all of whom opposed a major new business area being pursued by the company, "Sorry, the question of whether we should continue investing in 'Biochemline' is off the table." In his view, the team did not have the perspective to make the judgment (although several years and $200 million later, he realized the limited potential and cash drain on Biotekk, and agreed to retrench Biochemline and invest the funds elsewhere).

Team members are expected to share critical information and to cooperate with fellow members, but only in their own areas. They can initiate and attempt to influence decisions, but the manager has the final say. Similarly, team members are expected to respond to requests for advice and counsel, and get what they need from colleagues, but otherwise will not try to influence areas for which someone else is formally responsible. If a colleague feels strongly about something, he or she might say "Have you heard about this . . . ?" but if the peer shows no interest, the topic will be dropped. Unless a personal friendship is involved, people seldom feel obligated to be their brother's keeper.

Team Concepts

Despite the narrow, limited role of each employee, there is the expectation that individuals will work together as a team. In practice, this is interpreted in ways that make collaboration difficult:

We call ourselves a team, but we're really just a collection of representatives from our separate areas. Sure, we try to cooperate, but in subtle and not so subtle ways, we push our own interests.

Meetings are a big pain. We are asked to discuss things, and we do, but often we get the feeling that we can't end the discussion until we come up with the answer that the boss wants.

We never really talk about the issues that would make a difference. Those are too sensitive. Anyway, the big enchilada has an idea how he wants those to come out.

This is our manager's team; he's the real customer for what we do. We're there to give him advice when he wants it, but when discussions are off track, when we're wasting time or someone is blabbing too much, it's his responsibility to shape us up.

My boss tries to be nice and pretend that all of us are going to make the sticky decisions together, but when we're down to the match point on the issues he really cares about, the big guy will make it come out his way.

The most important thing in meetings is to be sure that no one screws up your area. You make your points to protect yourself, and watch to see that the others don't take shots that could make you and your people look bad. If there's a real disagreement, you try to work it off-line with the other guy or your boss; you don't want to expose yourself in front of the others.

I run the meetings and everyone knows it, but I try to keep a very light hand on the reins. If things aren't going well, I try to figure out how to fix them, which isn't always easy. Some people won't speak up, others say too much, and some challenge my authority all the time. It takes a lot of planning and some fancy maneuvering to keep things moving—and we still waste too much time.

In all these comments, it's clear that the team belongs to the boss. Despite the illusion of consensus decision making, the team members only play a consulting rule. In the end, the decision is determined by what the manager thinks is best.

The person in charge feels obligated to arbitrate disagreement and to make decisions whenever there is a lack of consensus. The team member's obligation is to provide information and ideas, and to avoid blocking behavior. But since each person feels primary responsibility for the area he or she manages, conflicts often occur, overtly or covertly, and the manager must find a way around them to a successful outcome. There is also an implicit understanding that subordinates should figure out just how much initiative and opposition the boss wants, and then be careful not to violate those limits.

Addressing Individual Performance

Correcting behavior and evaluating performance are touchy responsibilities that few managers enjoy. But they still see these as their job, whether or not they execute them well:

> *If there's a performance problem with one of my people, I talk to him in private, where he won't be embarrassed. If the others were present, the person would be too defensive to hear anything.*

> *I sure as hell am not going to tell a colleague to shape up when his style is getting in his way; that's the leader's job. If it's really bad, I might drop a hint to the boss. It's up to him whether or not to do anything about it.*

> *The only evaluation that really counts is the one your boss does. He who controls the purse strings calls the tune.*

> *Performance appraisals are a pain. You're subject to the most arbitrary stuff from your boss, who usually*

remembers one recent event and makes a big deal out of it. What the hell does she know about what I really do?

I hate doing performance appraisals. Half of the time, the subordinate is so defensive that he doesn't hear what I'm saying, and the other half of the time there's nothing the person can do about his weaknesses anyway. I just try to get through appraisals as fast as I can without doing any harm.

If one of my colleagues is a real jerk, I'll find a way to stick it to him with a humorous put-down in front of our boss, but that's always dangerous. I just live with most of my colleagues' weaknesses.

This "360-degree feedback" stuff is dangerous. You don't know who your accuser is, and the boss will insist on "confidentiality." If someone wants to get you, you're vulnerable to back-channel sniping.

Performance evaluation is the purview of the boss, who is expected to observe behavior and accomplishments and then determine each person's contribution. The manager might occasionally gather the opinions of a select group of subordinates, but this is done completely in private and never in the group setting. With the advent of 360-degree feedback, data are sometimes collected from peers about peers, or about the boss, but it is done once a year, and is considered to be highly confidential. Except for this special occasion, no one sees it as appropriate for subordinates to comment on or influence the boss's performance.

When one person's behavior is a problem, the manager is expected to deal with the individual off-line, not in the group setting, even if the problematic behaviors occur within the group. If the boss doesn't do anything about it, the unhappy team members feel constrained and may turn their dissatisfaction on the boss. Team members also avoid dealing directly with each other when behavior is annoying or obstructing progress. Some attempt to discipline members indirectly, through messages, often using humor aimed at the offender.

DIFFERENT FORMS OF HEROIC LEADERSHIP

Heroic management typically takes one of two forms, the *manager-as-technician,* and the increasingly frequent *manager-as-conductor.*[1] Technicians try to use the technical prowess that helped them reach the managerial ranks to stay on top of things, be it engineering, finance, sales, marketing, operations, information systems, accounting, or law. They favor an overt form of control in which they monitor all decisions.

When the leader is the most technically competent person in the unit, the manager-as-technician approach works reasonably well. The higher this person moves in the organization, however, the harder it becomes to sustain the necessary level of expertise since technology changes at such a rapid pace.

The manager-as-conductor, on the other hand, is usually less overt in control. This leader goes through the motions of subordinate involvement, consulting with others before making decisions, and often holds team meetings to get commitment and build team morale. Nevertheless, the manager-as-conductor often has a preconceived plan, inducing the use of strategy and manipulation to implement it. The conductor knows the score, and just when to call in the drum roll to achieve resolution.

Recent years have bought new approaches to organizational management such as empowerment, self-managing teams, quality, reengineering, transformational leadership, and vision. Each implies a less controlling form of leadership. However, without a fundamental shift from heroic assumptions (and without retraining), many managers have simply borrowed a few techniques from these new approaches and grafted them onto their deeply rooted approach to leadership. The net result is that little has changed. Managers continue to think and act in heroic terms.

HEROISM CAN WORK—BUT ONLY IN LIMITED CIRCUMSTANCES

Despite the weaknesses of heroic leadership, it can be effective for a stable industry, for employees lacking skills or education, and for routine, self-contained jobs. Even when these conditions do not prevail, an extraordinarily experienced and skilled manager can still employ the heroic style and get things done. These leaders are few, but they are a marvel to watch. Let's observe one of the best.

Example at Consultco: Jack Hawkins

Jack (Hawk) Hawkins, General Manager of "Consultco," the consulting division of a professional services firm, had just learned from his VP of Marketing, Martin Stanton, that one of their key marketing managers was being pursued by a struggling company in another industry. This manager, Tim Collins, did not want to leave, but the offer appeared to be too good to refuse. His pay would jump by 25% to 30%, and he would be given wider responsibilities—something he sought and was capable of handling.

Since Stanton was departing on a lengthy European trip and would be tied up in meetings most of the time, he asked Jack Hawkins to do what he could to keep Collins on board. This would clearly require a certain amount of direct courting from the top person.

Jack and Martin Stanton conferred by phone and discussed the problem. Stanton stressed that he wanted to keep Collins and would be unhappy if someone so competent were lost.

Jack was facing the kind of problem that is familiar to every top-level manager of a complex organization. The issues were multifaceted, there were personalities and

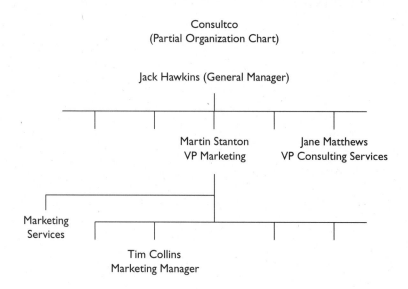

Consultco
(Partial Organization Chart)

Jack Hawkins (General Manager)

Martin Stanton
VP Marketing

Jane Matthews
VP Consulting Services

Marketing
Services

Tim Collins
Marketing Manager

politics to consider, a mistake would be costly, and there are no perfect precedents to guide action. But being an experienced and savvy pro, Jack Hawkins approached the question of how to keep Tim Collins as he did every organizational problem: He considered all his options.

"If I match the salary being offered," he told himself, "I'll distort the pay structure of the entire division. Chasing Collins with a better salary offer might encourage other people to go hunting for bigger salary offers from competing firms so they can demand huge raises." Instinctively, he ruled out this option. Perhaps he could offer an increase that was large enough to demonstrate Consultco's interest in keeping Collins, but not so large that it would throw a monkey wrench into the division's salary structure.

"What about a promotion?" he mused. "That's another option. Tim's a capable guy, and could handle more responsibility." But the division had just begun a major international expansion study, and it would be premature to make any moves now.

"Well, If I can't keep Collins with us, it won't be the end of the world. We have lots of capable people in the division, and losing one will create an opportunity for someone else to move up." Nor did he want to stand in the way of a good career move for one of his people, especially if that person would not be joining a direct competitor.

Like a chess master, Jack's mind thought ahead to the many possibilities created by the Collins situation. Years of managerial experience had trained him to view every move on the organizational chessboard as a part of a multidimensional situation, and to seek several outcomes at once. If the Collins situation forced him to make a move, he would try to use that move to remedy several other issues at the same time.

And other issues were simmering on the back burner that would eventually have to be dealt with. Martin Stanton was one of them. Since Jack was only in his late 40s, and likely to be General Manager for a long time, he knew that Stanton, a capable manager, would eventually seek a top executive position somewhere else. It was inevitable.

The one area in which Stanton had had problems involved the coordination of the division's large marketing services unit and the consulting services unit headed by Jane Matthews. These two units had never been able to operate on the same wavelength, to the detriment of the division's efforts to acquire and retain corporate clients. Jack had often wondered if the market services unit now directly managed by Stanton would be better run under Matthews.

As Jack mulled the complications of his situation, he wondered "Why not expand Tim Collins job to take on marketing services? That might solve several problems at once." The multiple payoffs raced through Jack's mind: Collins would get the greater responsibility he sought; he would be good at the job and solve a nagging problem for Jack. He would continue reporting formally to Stanton (with a dotted-line relationship to Jane Matthews' unit). The consulting services unit would be more effective. "If I could pull this off," Jack thought with a grin, "I could swoop down and kill two birds in one stroke." The hawk was ready to strike.

Jack knew that his plan would take a bit of selling. Stanton would likely resist for fear that the new arrangement would diminish his area. "Perhaps he could be persuaded to give up the service unit in exchange for some new and wider responsibilities," Jack speculated, "such as leading the hiring process for new consultants." Jack thought about how he could present this change to Stanton as a way to broaden his experience and better prepare him for a future General Manager job elsewhere.

With his usual careful plotting, Jack floated his idea past his most trusted subordinate, Jane Matthews. At first, she worried about the dotted-line reporting relationship with Collins, believing that Stanton would continue to dominate marketing services' philosophy and focus. But Jack convinced her that the task connection of marketing services was so much closer to her area than to Stanton's that she and Collins would naturally forge an effective relationship.

Jane Matthews accepted his hypothesis. Stanton required considerably more convincing, but in the end, he too was mollified.

"But what about Collins?" Jack asked himself. "How can I sell him on this plan?" Jack approached Tim. To keep the salary structure in line, the most he was willing to offer Tim was a 10 percent raise, significantly less than the competing offer. However, the money plus the marketing services unit job had Tim intrigued, though still uncertain. Jack perceived his uncertainty and began thinking of "sweeteners" that would quickly tip the younger manager's decision in his favor.

As they talked, Jack realized that Collins might well be interested in a new area that Consultco had been considering, namely the development of a proprietary software product designed to leverage the division's traditional consulting expertise. "This could be an enormous new opportunity for us," Jack told Collins, "but it needs real leadership to head a task force that can figure out the business opportunity and move it along. That could be you, Tim."

Collins was flattered by Jack's confidence in his abilities and by the possibilities that a successful new venture might hold for his own career. After considerable discussion and reassurance by his General Manager, Tim Collins agreed to stay.

Each of Jack's chess pieces had fallen into place!

THE BEST OF HEROIC LEADERSHIP

Whether Jack Hawkins's complicated game will work as planned or provoke unexpected countermoves and create new problems remains to be determined. Still, the intrepid General Manager has demonstrated skillful practice of heroic leadership. At their best, masters of heroic leadership:

- Seek multiple solutions when addressing an immediate problem.
- Think ahead several moves, anticipating possible actions and reactions.
- Put some opportunities on the back burner, reserving them as potential solutions to other problems such as the resignation of a key employee, a business acquisition, a new product line development, a corporate change program.
- Track individual strengths and weaknesses. They harbor no naive belief in individual perfectibility, but manage around weaknesses.
- Make tough decisions and take the consequences, but whenever possible maneuver behind the scenes to avoid playing the heavy.

- Have genuine concern for the welfare and needs of both subordinates and the organization.
- Hire smart people and give them substantial latitude once they've established their competence.
- Do their homework, and seldom come to a meeting unprepared.

There is little doubt that most managers would be thrilled if they could operate with the same finesse as Jack Hawkins. And even advocates of participative management who disdain heroic leadership would acknowledge that people who use these techniques effectively get things done.

Unlike a game of chess, however, organization life does not end after a series of skillful moves; instead, the game continues. Every move, even the most successful, has consequences that create the game anew. The next episode in the Consultco story provides an example.

Example: Jack Hawkins—Part Two

As he proceeded to implement his plan to keep Tim Collins, Jack Hawkins realized that he had a timing problem. Several weeks earlier, his executive committee had tentatively agreed on Neena Shah to head the software development task force—the same position Jack had used to lure Collins to stay with the division. The executive committee, which had no inkling of Jack's behind-the-scenes activities, was scheduled to finalize the appointment at its next meeting. Somehow, Jack had to shift the appointment to Collins without appearing dictatorial. With skill and luck, he reasoned, he would be able to do this in a way that didn't seem imperious or manipulative. And since Martin Stanton would be out of the country, he'd have to do it alone.

In retrospect, Jack wished that he'd had the time to confer with his executive committee before promising the job to Collins. He didn't want to upset them by declaring that he had unilaterally made the decision and the commitment.

"But if there were time to do everything," he consoled himself, "anyone could do this job."

So when the topic came up at the next excom meeting, Jack Hawkins employed skill and craft to get its members to reach the conclusion he supported.

"I've been thinking about the decision we made at our last meeting, and I wonder if it wouldn't be unfair to Neena to put the burden of this software venture on her shoulders. Health care consulting is facing intense competition right now, and I don't think we can spare her. Maybe we should use Tim Collins to run the software study team. Neena has a job-and-a-half already. Deflecting her attention now might be the wrong thing to do."

Some committee members looked surprised, and several exchanged glances. They had heard rumors about the possible departure of Collins, and Jack's suggestion triggered a visceral reaction: "The Hawk" was trying to overturn their supposedly collective decision process, something all had seen him do at one time or another.

Sensing that his colleagues had their defenses up, he nevertheless continued. "Tim is the logical choice for heading the task force. He has a strong interest in software and the assignment would be good career enrichment for him. We need to give people like him opportunities to learn and grow. Neena already has too much on her plate."

To Jack's dismay, the executive committee resisted. No matter how hard he argued for Collins's appointment (being careful to conceal his prior commitment), they wouldn't budge. A few excom members realized that they had finally caught Jack, the master of behind-the-scenes maneuvering, in a trap of his own making, and they made the most of the opportunity to make him squirm. Several resented the way Jack often created the appearance of consensual decision making while successfully pushing through his own agenda, and they used this opportunity to be difficult.

"You know, Jack, Tim is as busy as Neena."

"That's right, Jack, everyone is busy here. If we based assignments on who wasn't busy, we'd never get anything accomplished!"

"Doesn't Neena have more technical background than Tim? I would think she could develop the business plan much faster than Tim."

Feeling caught in his own machinations, Jack raced through his options, desperately looking for a new argument that could save the day. He was tap dancing as fast as he could.

As Jack's secret confederate in this game, Jane Matthews came to the rescue. "Maybe we can compromise. How about giving Neena another important assignment after her own situation is more stable? In the meantime, she could act in an advisory capacity to Tim."

Jack quickly supported Jane's idea, and breathed a sigh of relief when the executive committee agreed. He now saw the pieces of his plan falling into place. Thinking several steps ahead as usual, he told himself, "This arrangement would work better if Tim and the marketing services unit were officially moved over to Jane's area. But that can wait. The opportunity will come someday."

THE DEFECTS OF HEROIC LEADERSHIP

Skillful and effective executives like Jack Hawkins have elevated heroic leadership to high art. But few ever master this art form. Even when they do, they rely on their extraordinary personal talent, not organizational support. They succeed despite the system. Even in moments of success, however, they fail to create conditions in which they can tap the energy and talents of the many. Instead, they depend—to an unhealthy extent—on their own powers.

The core problem of heroic leadership is that it prevents the full contributions of each and every subordinate. Everyone—leader and subordinates—plays a role that reinforces

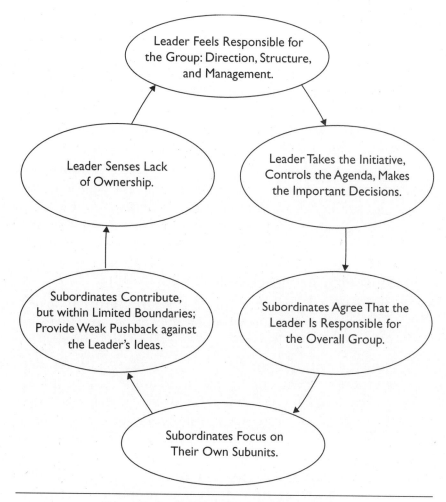

Figure 2–1. Self-Reinforcing Heroic Cycle

undesirable behavior in others, creating the vicious circle described Chapter 1. And because most people accept the traditional distinctions between leaders and subordinates, no one thinks of halting the game by saying "Stop the whirl, I want to get off." Figure 2–1 illustrates the self-reinforcing cycle that heroic leadership creates.

This cycle produces five major stumbling blocks to outstanding performance. All five occurred in the Consultco saga:

1. *The leader shares too little information.* As part of trying to be certain that the team will arrive at the right answers, leaders keep their own counsel, only revealing relevant pieces of information and plans as required. They use only select, trusted individuals to strategize, brainstorm, float trial balloons and carry out critical tasks, thereby restricting the contributions and development of the other direct reports.

2. *Collective problem solving is discouraged.* Deciding important issues in advance and then steering the group to a predetermined position restricts contributions, making it hard for everyone to bring knowledge and creativity to discussions. Trying to presell solutions may create resistance instead of open examination of ideas and full engagement.

3. *The leader is the only one to take the larger unit perspective.* Subordinates "know their place" and focus on their own subunits, delegating big issues upward.

4. *The organization has only one "sensing" unit.* Modern businesses need real-time information about customers, markets, technologies, and their own operating systems. The heroic system is overly dependent on a single sensing unit: the boss. Some executives understand "in their bones" how their organization works, the dynamics of their market, and the technologies that support their business. But these people are as rare as spotted owls. Seldom does a single person understand the many details that determine the success or failure of a business. There is too much complexity, too much reliance on specialized experience and knowledge, and too much rapid change.

   In fact, the people at the top may be *least* knowledgable about current markets, technologies, and the many different parts of the business. As Gary Hamel, a strategist and advisor to many top companies notes, the people *least* likely to have the latest information and be open to new ideas are the leaders, "Where are you likely to find people with the least diversity of experience, the largest investment in the past, and the greatest reverence for industrial dogma? At the top. And where will you find the people responsible for creating strategy? Again, at the top."[2] One of the most successful executives in the world, Andrew Grove, CEO of Intel, put it beautifully when he described his reluctance to rely on his own instincts about a new technology, "I don't believe that the Internet is about to reverse this trend [of pulling down intelligence from big computers to little ones]. But then again, my genes were formed by those same twenty or thirty years. And I'm likely to be the last one to know."[3] Grove believes in supporting organizational Cassandras, who provide early warning of sea changes in technology, markets and the industry.

5. *Being "in charge" and alone, the leader focuses too much on control, inhibiting initiative from below.* Subordinates respond with passive resistance or earlier-than-appropriate acquiescence. All leaders struggle with the tension between encouraging subordinate initiative and controlling subordinate behavior to be sure that organizational objectives are accomplished. Too much control is demotivating and debilitating; too much initiative lets the thousand flowers overrun the garden. Heroic leadership assumptions tilt managers toward the control side of this dilemma, especially when faced with a major problem.

   The problem is that even bosses who can let go of close supervisory control and encourage initiative, become frustrated when empowered subordinates still operating by the heroic contract pursue their own ends and do not feel overall responsibility. Eventually the leader will feel it necessary to take control, not of daily individual actions but of the coordinating, integrating process. So heroic assumptions pull overworked, less expert leaders back into the controlling role.

All five of these defects limit the effectiveness of the leader as well as subordinates. Heroic leaders seldom want to lose all the contributions of the people who work for them, so they try to figure out how to encourage people. That often results in the leaders holding back their own views, waiting to tag on to opinions that are in the direction the leader wants to go and pretending that the ideas have come from the group. In turn, subordinates focus attention on psyching out the leader's actual views, and all kinds of distortions of energy and communications arise. The atmosphere becomes one of manipulation and game playing rather than collaborative problem solving.

Despite the negative consequences, the heroic system keeps going because it is *self-reinforcing.* If the leader has overall responsibility and consistently acts to reinforce that idea, subordinates do not raise the larger issues. They stick to their knitting, confirming to the leader that control and initiative have to remain at the top. When subordinates do take initiative, but leave the coordination and control of their colleagues to the boss, this again eventually reconfirms the boss's responsibilities. Who will provide self-corrective feedback to the boss in this cycle?

In all of these ways, the Consultco executive team reinforced the inclination of Jack Hawkins to go it alone on the tough issues. Fortunately for the division, his skill and artfulness eventually produced a good result. But the "good" in this case stands between Consultco and organizational excellence.

Yet Some Stars Shine

The heroic system entraps both clever leaders and well-meaning subordinates. It's difficult not be to sucked into the black hole of the leadership trap. A few outstanding individuals nevertheless manage to embrace the larger unit perspective, step up to the tough decisions, take the initiative in finding opportunities that advance the organization and not just their own area, challenge the boss in a supportive way that prevents big mistakes, and push colleagues to do what is needed for overall excellence.

Star players break out of the leadership trap, but by extraordinary personal talent, not by organizational support. They do it *in spite of* the system. Unfortunately, their success reinforces the states quo. "If she can rise above parochial interests and do what's right, why can't everyone?"

No organization however, should depend on the abilities of extraordinary individuals; they are too rare. Instead, organizations should be designed to make it possible—even commonplace—for average people (on the average, that's who an organization will have) to perform extremely well. Management systems should tap the full talents of ordinary people and coordinate their efforts because, in the end, teams of fully engaged average employees create more value than an occasional superstar.

THE SEDUCTION OF HEROISM

Managing heroically may not enable your organization to achieve excellence, but it can be personally gratifying—and difficult to give up. There is great satisfaction in saving the day when the rest of the team is floundering. There's more glory in being the quarterback than in being the coach (even if one is occasionally sacked). Catching the mistakes that others miss, being the oracle from whom others seek guidance, and feeling the control that others never experience can be a fulfilling source of personal validation. Who doesn't like to go home and say, "I'm exhausted, but it was a great day; I was really needed, and I came through"?

Heroism is seductive, even to the authors. Though we developed the concepts of heroic and postheroic leadership and preach the limitations of heroism, we must confess to liking the feeling of being the ones who "know." When we teach, consult, make speeches, and manage, we get satisfaction from demonstrating our expertise and taking charge. There is no shame in enjoying the recognition that comes with authority and expertise. But in organizational life, leaders must learn to control the behaviors that minimize the ability of others to achieve outstanding results.

Leadership of the kind we explain in the rest of this book also feels good, but the pleasure is more subtle, less self-centered, and more vicarious—like the satisfaction of having built a winning team rather than calling every play and making every score. It is the mature pleasure of knowing that one played a role in the success of one's subordinates.

The next chapter will show how you and your organization can break free of the trap of heroic leadership and build a new and more effective leader-subordinate relationship in which all contribute their best.

3

POST-HEROIC LEADERSHIP

Jack Hawkins, the corporate leader in the previous chapter, has his own approach to creating success. But because that approach, which we call heroic leadership, is less potent today than in the past it often fails to optimize the performance potential of organizations and their members. In many industries, Jack's leadership style could sink a company.

Scott Cook is the cofounder and CEO of Intuit Corporation, one of the most successful enterprises in the computer software industry. Products like Quicken™ and Turbo-Tax/MacInTax™ have made it the leader in its field of personal financial software. This didn't happen because Cook and his cofounder Tom Proulx had a great new idea. Quite the contrary, when version 1.0 of Quicken™ was released in 1983, there were already 43 competing products in the market. But today Quicken™ is number one and commands 75 percent of the market for software of its type. Nor is Intuit successful because Cook is a master leader of the type described in the previous chapter.

"A truly entrepreneurial company," Cook contends, "has to feel entrepreneurial for all the people in the company." The leader cannot be the only entrepreneur. To be successful, a company must create an environment in which "entrepreneurship is something that is ultimately done by the hundreds and thousands of people in the company instead of just by one of them."[1] Intuit equates that environment with one in which the ability to make decisions rests with the people closest to the issues:

> *In this environment, we are surrounded with trust and given the latitude to be creative. We can talk openly about what needs to change, and we can see and make improvements happen. We feel energized by our work. We feel our full potential is not only being tapped, but is growing.*[2]

Though these terms may seem idealized—and perhaps the product of the corporate PR department—Intuit has matched its words with the behavior of its people. And that behavior has paid off for employees and shareholders alike.

Intuit exemplifies how our collective thinking about leaders and nonleaders is changing. Employees were once viewed as simple appendages of the mindless machines they served. Almost a century earlier, Henry Ford allegedly despaired about his workers' inability to follow directions without question. "Why, when I only want to hire a pair of hands," he complained, "do I get a whole person?" Today, that complaint has been reversed: "What does it take to get people to *think and to contribute* to the full extent of their abilities?" Modern economic life demands that everyone in the organization think entrepreneurially and take responsibility. To achieve continuous improvement and corporate renewal, people at all levels must be willing and able to spot new opportunities and then to exploit them by enlisting resources and providing the necessary teamwork. This is far different from the industrial age tradition of simply following directions. Any organization that puts its future into the hands of a few people at the top is unlikely to have a future. The world is too complex for business leaders, even with excellent advice, to make all the right decisions and provide all the needed coordination and control.

Just about everyone knows this. Yet the model of heroic leadership persists. Leaders work harder and harder while their subordinates park the most troubling issues at their doorsteps. Leaders still focus on control, stifling the initiative that everyone acknowledges as essential. Seeing power as a fixed commodity means that delegating any of it to others necessarily reduces one's own authority. In the hands of others, initiative, autonomy, or influence becomes a threat to control and coordination. Although leaders complain about subordinates being narrow-minded and shortsighted, they continue to reinforce the habit of subordinates to focus on the objectives of their subareas, leaving responsibility for overall outcomes to the people at the top. This heroic approach to leadership is outmoded and ineffective in the vast majority of contemporary organizations.

Extraordinary results require a new system of leadership and followership in which leaders and team members act more like partners. This approach fundamentally alters the traditional distinction between those who plan, organize, delegate, staff, control, and evaluate, and those who carry out plans and follow instructions. We call this system *post-heroic* or *shared responsibility* leadership. The post-heroic system has both its roots and its power in a new mind-set about shared responsibility.

A NEW MIND-SET

In 1996, Bob Weissman split Dun & Bradstreet into three separate companies. That in itself was a big change, but not big enough for the results this chairman/CEO hoped to gain. He knew that more than an organizational reshuffling was needed to obtain outstanding performance. People had to think differently about their roles and responsibilities. He recalled the first time he met with the top 15 managers of Cognizant, the one of the three reorganized companies he would run:

As we discussed incentives, I emphasized that we were building a "go for the win" incentive plan aligned with the long-term objectives of shareholders. We had reduced cash compensation for everyone in the room, and had added a market-priced stock option plan with six-year vesting.

In order to drive home the priorities, I took them through the numbers. I showed them that their personal financial leverage came from maintaining the growth rate of the corporation, and not from trying to get lower individual performance goals accepted. If everyone in the room achieved 100 percent performance against their budgets in every one of the next five years, their combined cumulative bonus would be about $23 million. If they could maintain the historic growth rate in earnings per share for the same period, the growth in potential market value for them was $163 million.

They got the message.

They started saying things like, "That means I should want investment to go to the place with the highest expected return, even if that isn't my unit." And, "If that's the case, I want a piece of the allocation decision process—I want to be involved." And "This is going to be hard, because I'll have to learn a lot more about the parts of the business I'm not directly responsible for." And "This is going to be harder than bringing you my budget and negotiating for the lowest acceptable result."

I am very excited about the outcome of that meeting and of the momentum that we are creating. But I'm not ready to declare victory in the battle to change attitudes. I have been advised by some very smart operating managers—people who have created similar programs—that continued selling and education will be needed. Even with obvious incentives, people tend to push the tough work upward to the boss. But we all need to be in it together and really share decision-making and commitment, or we'll never reach our potential.[3]

A new mind-set about sharing responsibility—as de-scribed by Weissman—is at the core of post-heroic leader-ship. Maintaining a dual perspective carries through all activities, individual or group. Even decisions made in the sub-unit must sustain the larger perspective. There is still a place for leaders in this mind-set, but the outdated idea of subordinates or followers, has been replaced by the no-tion of partnership. Concerns about how the leader can make the best decision and get it accepted shift to how team members and the leader can jointly make the best possible decision on critical matters. This new orientation is more likely to make full use of everyone's abilities and prepare the grounds for resolving the managerial dilemma of how to have high member initiative along with in-creased coordination and control. This is the way that excellence can be achieved in a complex world. We can contrast the old and new mind-sets as follows:

- *Heroic leader:* "It's my responsibility to determine the direction, to find the right answers, and to carry out the traditional management functions. It's your job to de-liver in your area."
- *Post-heroic leader:* "Everyone is a leader. My job is to build a strong team with a common vision and mutual influence, in which members share in the responsibili-ties of managing. It's your job to partner with me in this joint responsibility."

The shared responsibility mind-set turns the historic ten-sion that exists between ambitious, competent team mem-bers and their leaders on its head; it harnesses their ambitions and competencies to larger organizational goals in partnership with others. Leaders can divert their energy from control and mastery to developing and engaging the talents of team members around important problems. As-suring coordinated performance becomes the mutual re-sponsibility of those who best understand it is needed. This allows direct reports to tackle the most challenging issues without fear of overstepping their bounds; almost all issues are legitimate matters for discussion.

NEW ROLES FOR EVERYONE

Change is never easy, and the effort required to move from the heroic mind-set to the post-heroic model is no different. The new mind-set creates new roles for both leaders and their direct reports, and these, like a new pair of shoes, aren't always comfortable at first.

In the post-heroic world, the distinction between leader and subordinates is not as sharp as it used to be. Direct reports must assume the same sense of responsibility for overall organizational outcomes as the leader. They must become team members. Although each brings different capacities and views to the issues, and each contributes according to personal ability and experience, all should feel ownership for results. This does not mean that members have license to micromanage each other any more than a good leader would.

For Team Members

Creating shared responsibility requires subordinates to think and act like the leader by taking the perspective of the entire unit as well as that of their own areas. While these members retain responsibility for their own daily activities, they must also become a partner in their leader's team. Each person "wears the hats" of at least two teams, the leader's and the group or work area that the member represents.

Under post-heroism, many of the same team member obligations continue to hold. They must:

- Deliver on their subarea's obligations and commitments.
- Share relevant information accurately.
- Initiate ideas, reactions, and suggestions about areas for which they are responsible.
- Support their colleagues.

But there are new obligations: *to share responsibility for the larger unit's success and to make sure that everyone delivers on his or her responsibilities.* These obligations may appear to be minor, but they have profound implications for behavior. When the entire team owns the unit's success and shares responsibility for managing it, its members can no longer say, "That's the leader's job, not mine."

The post-heroic mind-set is something very new for most employees. They are so accustomed to acting as protectors/advocates for their own fiefdoms that taking the broader perspective, at first, is bound to feel unnatural. But they must make this transition if the shift to post-heroic leadership is to succeed. Otherwise, they are likely to think and act in ways that seduce all but the most resolute of leaders back into heroic behavior. It is, after all, hard to resist subordinates who say in words or performance: "You are the boss. Why can't you make the tough decisions they pay you the big bucks to make?" And many team members, skeptical about the sincerity or ability of leaders trying to adopt new behavior, are quick to conclude from insignificant events and comments that the leader does not really want to share control. They are primed to hear old whines in new battles.

For Leaders

Yes, there is still a role for post-heroic leaders, but it has changed in a substantive way. These leaders must *build a system* in which shared responsibility can occur. For the manager accustomed to rushing in to solve every problem, this new role is not easily adopted. Robert Haas, Chairman and CEO of Levi Strauss & Company, explained this in an interview with the *Harvard Business Review*:

> In the past, a manager was expected to know everything that was going on and to be deeply involved in subordinates' activities.
>
> I can speak from experience. It has been difficult for me to accept the fact that I don't have to be the smartest

guy on the block—reading every memo and signing off on every decision. In reality, the more you establish parameters and encourage people to take initiatives within those boundaries, the more you multiply your own effectiveness by the effectiveness of other people.

. . . It's a much tougher role because you can't rely on your title or on unquestioning loyalty and obedience to get things done. You have to be thoughtful about what you want. You have to be clear about the standards that you're setting. You have to negotiate goals with your work group rather than just set them yourself. You have to interact personally with individuals who you're dealing with, understand their strengths and shortcomings, and be clear about what you want them to do.

You also have to accept the fact that decisions or recommendations may be different from what you would do. They could very well be better, but they're going to be different. You have to be willing to take your ego out of it.[4]

To implement this new mind-set, leaders engage in three activities:

1. *Develop a mature, cohesive shared-responsibility team.* The shared-responsibility team is the forum through which direct reports share the management of the unit. Post-heroic leaders see to it that these teams address the important collective issues: the strategic and managerial questions that no single individual can adequately address alone. Ask the team to deal only with relatively trivial matters, and members will quickly lose interest in consensus decision making and return to their private estates. Only big questions can kindle energy and commitment to unit goals and make them at least as important as each member's individual goals. Working on key issues is what turns groups into teams.[5]

2. *Articulate a tangible vision and gain commitment to it.* The second core task of post-heroic leaders is to

generate articulation of a tangible vision of the group's ultimate purpose and see that it is accepted. Our work over the past decade suggests that nearly all leaders at all levels can lead the development of tangible visions for their units.

Tangible vision is a deliberately paradoxical term. *Vision* suggests a future state that may not be fully attainable. *Tangibility* suggests something that is vividly clear and direct, such as a three-dimensional holograph that appears to be touchable. A tangible vision provides a larger purpose that supercedes sub-unit and personal goals. It directs inevitable disagreements into productive channels. When there is agreement as to the purpose and direction of the group, then differences and disputes will be over means, not ends. And it enables greater individual initiative guided by the agreed overall direction.

Vision is more difficult to internalize than to articulate. Internalizing requires the concerted efforts of members as well as the leader. Vision comes alive when employees routinely use it to make tough choices about important issues and to guide their behavior.

3. *Establish mutual influence.* For effective shared responsibility, all participants—leaders and members— must be able to influence and be influenced by one another. The leader must be skilled at influencing direct reports (to have them take on shared responsibility and to help them acquire the necessary competencies that shared leadership entails). Team members, in turn, must be able to influence their peers and the leader to ensure coordination and excellent performance. Thus, the leader must be open to influence from members, otherwise they will back off at just those critical times that the leader most needs to be confronted, pushed, checked, stimulated, extended—or supported. Direct reports who are not skillful at influencing are not able to push back on the leader.

Team members must also learn to influence each other by applying their collective talents to solve problems, hold each other accountable, take the larger perspective, work creatively with each other, and in general behave as responsible leaders toward one another. Thus, they must learn to balance being influential with being influenceable.

These three activities reinforce each other. A shared-responsibility team is the instrument for tackling core problems and a venue in which members can influence each other (and the leader). A tangible vision pulls members above their parochial interests toward a common purpose and thereby aligns individual interests with the interests of the larger group. The vision serves as a standard for strategic decision making, coordination, and control. Greater ability to mutually influence each other is necessary for consensus decision making, for coordination and control, and for member, leader, and team development.

These three activities are developmental, reinforcing over time the post-heroic mind-set that, in turn, shapes behavior in favor of organizational excellence. The leader encourages members to take on more of the leadership functions, freeing the leader to spend more time on the lateral and upward aspects of leadership. None of this is easy to do, but the results are worth the effort. "When you start something like this," said Dennis Longstreet, President of Ortho Biotech ". . . you take a chance that employees may lead you someplace you don't want to go. But then you learn that most of them want the same things that you want. Everyone wants to succeed."[6]

CONTRASTS IN MANAGERIAL FUNCTIONS

The innocuous-sounding phrase "sharing responsibility for the management" has some radical implications for altering typical management functions.

Delegating

Determining work assignments is a delicate task that can occupy a good traditional manager's full attention. Which jobs are sufficiently challenging to increase motivation and development, yet within the existing capacities of subordinates? Who can be trusted? Who will know when to ask for help? Who has the political skills to pull off a delicate assignment? Answering these questions requires exquisite assessment skills, but the heroic selection process contains too little colleague input and few checks on the leader's biases or assumptions about people. Don't members collectively know more about each other's strengths and developmental needs than the leader? The people bypassed for assignments are seldom told the actual reasons and so must simply speculate.

The post-heroic leadership system creates a climate in which the delicate personal issues associated with new assignments can be openly discussed. Team members identify one another's developmental needs, acknowledge how each member would be affected by the assignment, specify ways in which a person has or has not delivered, provide assistance, and agree on what the team expects from the recipient of an assignment.

Control

Heroic leaders work hard to harness the work of team members to common goals. They cajole, reason, bully, plot, and lobby to prevent border warfare, enforce cooperation, and stimulate laggards. When someone shows that he or she can be trusted to work without close monitoring, the heroic leader is delighted, but never fully trusting, and always sleeps with one eye open.

Post-heroic members share responsibility for coordination and control with the leader, providing relief from constant vigilance. When goals are jointly determined, and mutual expectations clear and public, team members hold each other accountable. Instead of one trying to control all, *all control all.*

Performance Evaluation

Performance evaluation is problematic in most organizations, since it is hard for managers to give honest and constructive feedback to their direct reports.[7] They do individual evaluations, based on their best assessment of each person's performance. They might obtain input from other sources—trusted subordinates, peers, their own observations, and even 360-degree feedback systems—but evaluate in private. The process is considered too personal and too sensitive to share with others.

Post-heroic leaders, in contrast, use the power of collective performance feedback. Members let each other know about areas where performance has been strong and where it needs improvement. The result: better individual and team development. Eventually, they can make mutual contracts about desired behavior and reinforce these with each other.

Staffing

Staffing is traditionally seen as the leader's prerogative. A progressive heroic leader might have subordinates interview candidates and consider their recommendations, but in the last analysis, this leader would make the final decision.

Under shared responsibility, however, that decision is made jointly through consensus. This does not means that the post-heroic leader would accept someone that he or she could not live with, but the same standard would hold for the other members of the team. Consensus means that the decision is supportable by each team member, including the leader, even if it is not someone's first choice. Post-heroic leaders recognize that their new direct reports are also peers to the other team members, who depend on them for success. Heroic leaders expect to get their first choice, no matter how flawed; post-heroic leaders can always reserve the right to make any decision, but recognize that exercising it very often will undermine the building of shared responsibility.

OLD WINE IN NEW BOTTLES?

Our view of post-heroic leadership is very different from even excellent heroic leadership. Dubious readers, however, may ask, "Isn't this simply old wine in new bottles?" And their doubts have some justification. After all, our notion of shared responsibility can sound a great deal like empowerment and participative management. The defining characteristics are not to be found in the exact words, but in actual behavior. The seemingly small difference between the leader taking advice but retaining the final decision on important issues and the leader committed to joint decision making speaks much louder than any words. A leader may talk "teams" and repeatedly proclaim, "We are all in the boat together," but what really matters is how decisions are made and how responsibility is shared. Heroic managers also say they encourage risk taking, but too many are like one manager we interviewed, who declared with a straight face "Yes, I support risk taking. As long as my people don't make any mistakes, they can take all the risks they want!" James O'Toole aptly noted, "Ninety-five percent of American managers today say the right thing. Five percent actually do it."[8]

A critical difference is that post-heroic leadership engages team members not only in making particular business decisions, but in the management process for the unit. Sharing responsibility for management functions such as delegating, coordinating, controlling, evaluating, and staffing means that team members can not ignore important unit problems or discrepencies between the leader's words and actions by saying, "That's not my job." *Everything* affecting unit success is everyone's job.

Post-heroic leadership is not, then, old wine in a new bottle. Instead, it is an elixir for better performance. This new leadership system opens up the flow of information among

Preoccupations of the Heroic Mind-Set

Heroic assumptions create a logical, self-reinforcing system that works reasonably well when compliance is all that is needed from team members. But as conditions change and greater creativity and commitment are called for, this system becomes harder to sustain and leads to problems that can only be overcome with elaborate scheming. Heroic leaders spend a great deal of time puzzling about questions such as these:

- How do I want this discussion to come out? What is the right answer to push for?
- Have I done enough homework to establish myself as the best informed person on this issue?
- What will be the political fallout? How can I work around that?
- Whom do I need to take into my confidence or influence ahead of time? Whom must I neutralize?
- Whose opinion is likely to sway the group?
- How do I get the others to think that my solution is really their idea?
- Who is likely to bring up opposing ideas, and how can I minimize that resistance?
- Whom can I count on to champion my ideas?

leader and team members, enabling creative solutions to problems, more informed decisions, and early warnings about anticipated difficulties from those most in touch with employees, customers, and suppliers. By engaging everyone in management issues, greater total talent can be brought to bear on complex decisions. By licensing everyone to influence in all directions, each team member's strongest talents can be brought into play. Everyone can take initiative, with the assurance that colleagues will challenge them if they go astray. In turn, greater ability to influence sideways and upward frees anyone who sees an opportunity to pursue it without moping around and waiting for permission and formal authority.

Preoccupations of the Post-Heroic Mind-Set

The post-heroic leader shifts the locus of responsibility for problem-resolution from the leader to the team. Questions that naturally flow from the shared responsibility mind-set are suited to productive team actions:

- How can I make sure that everyone understands the complexities in this issue, including the political realities?
- How can I ensure that team members will contribute the richest information and ideas?
- What can I do to increase the group's ownership of this issue?
- Which decision parameters are absolute? Are team members aware of them?
- Is the team ready to tackle this issue? If not, how can I prepare them?
- Do we have sufficient expertise within the group to solve the problem, or should we seek outside help?
- What must be done to encourage free and open discussion of this issue?
- Do I need to do more to assure a top quality decision?
- How can I make my thoughts heard without inhibiting the views of other members?

The post-heroic mind-set keeps the leader thinking about how to share responsibility while seeking good decisions. Team members may not trust the motives or intentions of the leader at first, or leap at the opportunity to take responsibility, but the post-heroic mind-set makes it possible to simultaneously work on problems and team capabilities.

APPREHENSIONS

Some readers may see the new world of shared responsibility we have described as exactly how organizational life should be. Others may view it with apprehension, and the notion of responsibility sharing, consensus decision making, and a partnership with the boss may provoke extreme anxiety. Many leaders we have worked with were attracted to the benefits of post-heroic leadership but were either uncomfortable or doubtful about its application to their situations. Their reservations fall into three main categories.

1. *Fear that subordinates will not really take the larger perspective.* The first concern of senior executives is the ability and the willingness of their subordinates to rise above their direct interests and work toward the larger good.

2. *Concern that people might not operate as a mature, cohesive group.* The second executive concern is the ability and willingness of subordinates to act as a team instead of as a collection of warring tribes engaged in destructive conflict.

3. *The ability of people to operate with each other in ways that are direct, honest, and constructive.* This concern speaks to the interpersonal skills required for effective joint action.

Each of these apprehensions is legitimate. Leaders are properly cautious about abandoning a traditional system of leadership for one with which neither they nor their subordinates have experience. But rational conservatism should not dictate adoption of the pessimist's law that "every disaster that can be imagined will happen *to me!*" Yes, problems will arise, but most can be handled effectively as opportunities for advancing the new system.

Tackling the apprehensions about post-heroic leadership is the first step in the adoption of this new system and describes the responsibilities of the post-heroic leader. It is in tackling these concerns and the issues that underpin them that the leader and team members move the organization toward the post-heroic era. In fact, confronting each apprehension is an opportunity for thinking and acting in a new way.

The change we advocate is not achieved in a single stroke, but is the outcome of a developmental process (though one that takes months, not years). There is no on-off switch. Imagine what would happen at your company if the division general manager opened the next staff meeting this way.

> *Starting this morning, we are going to do things completely differently around here. We are going to adopt a program of shared responsibility, and we'll use that approach in solving key problems. And we might as well start with the three problems we need to solve today:*
>
> *Problem number 1 is our failing Eastern European operation. It needs immediate attention. One of you has to move to Romania to rescue it. Let's decide together who it will be.*
>
> *Problem number 2 is Ed's profit margins. Ed, you haven't lived up to your commitment to improve margins. You need to hear from all of us about how upset we are about this, and we need to agree on a new set of goals that you can meet and we can accept.*
>
> *Problem number 3 is the trouble I'm having with our colleagues in corporate new product development; I want you all to help me figure out how to get them to stop undermining me and our division.*

How likely is it that this group—or any group—would instantly rise to the occasion, share responsibility, take the larger perspective, and be open in their feeling about Romania, Ed's performance, and their leader's problems with corporate product development? Most would be totally confused.

Team Readiness

The leader who wants to move from a heroic approach to shared responsibility faces a Catch-22 situation: He or she would share responsibility if the group were ready for it, but the group is not ready because responsibility has not yet been shared. The way out of this dilemma is to think in incremental terms, asking, "How much can the team handle now—usually more than they think—and what can be done to stretch them to take more responsibility in the future?" This does not mean "development now for payoff later"; it is both at once. Thus, it is possible to achieve task success while dealing with the knotty team and member issues that face all leaders.

It is the leader's job to change the system from heroic to post-heroic. The leader must create the conditions where team members develop their ability and commitment to sharing management, where interpersonal and group problems can be resolved through open, creative, and tough-minded collaboration. This requires active leadership and high standards, not a passive "I'm just here to facilitate" approach. The new leader is active in building a process that invests team members in the unit's goals: They obtain the best information, follow appropriate problem-solving methods, make clear and strong arguments, work through differences without personal attacks, and commit to implementing their decisions. Whereas the traditional leader tries to manage around team member concerns, the post-heroic leader uses these matters as opportunities to develop member and team competence. The post-heroic leader can acknowledge member concerns openly and ask the team how they can work together to get past them: "I want to share more responsibility with this team, but I see how hard that is because we haven't developed traditions of rowing this boat together. What can we do to move us in that direction?"

A Tough Way to Manage

This style is directive and demanding, but demands less in terms of particular answers than that members take responsibility for the unit's work. And the leader can still make decisions. But where heroic leaders demand that the team come up with the leader's solutions to tasks, post-heroic leaders can demand that the team grapple with the unresolved, critical issue (as in "This meeting isn't over until we figure this one out").

This is a tough way to manage in the sense of facing difficult issues, in confronting individuals (and the team) when they are not doing their work or sharing responsibility for managing the unit, and in being willing to hear feedback about one's own behavior. This new leader, unlike most heroic leaders, can't hide behind a title or role.

No Abdication

Some managers have told us, "Sharing responsibility sounds like turning the asylum over to the inmates!" Abdication of responsibility by the leader would be inappropriate in any system of leadership, including the one we propose. In sharing responsibility, the post-heroic leader does not abdicate, but remains fully engaged as a partner in the managerial work of the unit. He or she may continue to provide technical, problem solving and interpersonal expertise, but in conjunction with the skills of team members working together to build consensus.

Despite shared responsibility, the leader never escapes formal accountability for unit performance or for the decisions of the unit, by whatever method they are made. It is never acceptable for the leader to say to his or her boss, "Sorry, I didn't want to make this decision but I had to go along with my team." And there may be times when the leader finds it necessary to make a decision autonomously, or to override a team decision that has been made without sufficient information or by a process that ignores critical considerations. Post-heroic leadership is not an excuse for the leader to avoid responsibility.

Leading post-heroically is both incredibly demanding and surprisingly easy. It is demanding because it requires skill and courage, and easy because once the new way of thinking about leadership is internalized, it shapes every managerial activity. Knowing how to proceed begins to come almost automatically.

Leaders and Team Members as Partners in Managing

The post-heroic world calls for a new system in which leaders and members must assume the same sense of responsibility for overall organizational outcomes. As has been discussed, this means that members are expected to take more initiative, make full contributions, and act more like partners to the leader. They too are responsible for doing what will make the whole unit successful. They are responsible for dealing with their colleagues and with the leader in a new way. (And don't forget that leaders are members to some other leader, so they too have to manage in all directions.)

Sharing responsibility in this way alters team member perspective, and has profound implications. It turns upside down the usual way of thinking about change in leadership style, that it is dependent on the leader deciding to proceed and encouraging everyone on the team to start acting in a new way. If team members share the responsibility, then while it might be easier to make changes when invited, they do not have to wait for permission from the top; they are obligated to initiate whatever is needed, including, if necessary, pushing the leader to be less heroic.

Certainly members have to take new initiative in identifying and contributing to solving overall unit problems, but if one of those problems is that the leader is blocking the full contributions of members, the responsible team member tries to figure out how to move the whole system. That might involve working to improve meetings, urging that a tangible vision must be agreed on or invoking it when making decisions, becoming more open about relevant data, confronting colleagues who are not contributing, or, most difficult, directly pointing out to the leader undesirable consequences of his or her current behavior.

Later chapters, especially Chapter 8 and Appendix A, "Power Talk: A Hands-On Guide to Supportive Confrontation," will show you more about how to step up to these difficult leadership responsibilities from any position in the organization. The ability to collaborate in all directions is a vital part of post-heroic leadership.

Does our picture of post-heroic leadership seem too idealistic? Is it realistic to expect that take-charge managers and underutilized subordinates can (or will) change their thinking and behavior without hypnosis or brain surgery? Yes, it is realistic. It requires a difficult personal transition, but it can be done, and it is worth the effort.

Chapter 4 tells the tale of one take-charge leader who made the change and improved his career at the same time with the partnership of his team members. It wasn't easy and it wasn't without pain. But it turned a division that performed reasonably well into an excellent one.

4

THE MAKING OF A POST-HEROIC LEADER

Peorle who worked with John Sloan thought his style of leadership could never change because it so strongly reflected his personality. Furthermore, he had produced outstanding results. So what would induce him to change the way he managed?

John Sloan was smart and effective, but the way he dealt with peers and direct reports was unacceptable for "Applico," the global firm that employed him as president of its Canadian division. Applico was a worldwide leader in household appliances, and widely recognized for its commitment to humane, people-oriented practices. John's approach to people was incongruent with that commitment. Something had to change. The description of what happened contains many lessons for those who aspire to build a shared leadership system.

JOHN'S PERFORMANCE APPRAISAL

John Sloan sat uncomfortably in the office of his boss, Ken Warner. He had traveled from Toronto to the company's U.S. headquarters in Westchester, New York, for a series of meetings, including this one: his annual performance appraisal. Like most people, he disliked this yearly ritual, but it went with the territory. In any case, Canada had made exceptional progress over the past 12 months so he expected his meeting with Warner to be perfunctory. But that is not how it turned out.

Ken Warner appeared to be tense as he joined John in the conference room adjoining his office. "John, you have produced incredible results in Canada over the past year—over the past *three* years for that matter—and for that we are very grateful. When you took over the Canadian division, no one in this building would have imagined that we'd see a doubling in return-on-investment. You've accomplished that already, and you seem headed toward a tripling of that measure."

Sloan was gratified that the company recognized his achievements and wondered if Warner's speech would now turn to something else: a promotion? a transfer to a division in need of help?

"Your vision and drive are great assets," Warner continued. "You are pushing the Canadian organization into the future. But I have to tell you that the way you get results just isn't acceptable."

Not acceptable! The words hit John Sloan like a punch to the belly. "I hate to tell you this, John, but the 360-degree performance evaluation I conducted is very critical of your style of management. Virtually every one of the fifteen people I interviewed said the same thing: They all respect your talents, but they think you're too controlling and disempowering. The staff people you deal with here at corporate describe you as angry, resistant, and uncooperative. The people you work with every day tell us you are argumentative and difficult to influence: 'Often wrong but never in doubt' is the phrase I heard."

John Sloan couldn't believe what he was hearing. But he could see that his boss had more to say.

"They say that you drive a stake into the ground and then won't budge from that position." He opened a file folder, adjusted his glasses, and found what he was looking for. "Here's a quote from one of your direct reports: 'Our meetings frequently end in arguments, and if John appears to give way, he will bring it up again until he wears us down.' Your managers also complain that they have trouble figuring out where you stand on many issues, especially when there is conflict, because you play your cards so close to the vest."

"People here at corporate appreciate your innovativeness, but see the same combativeness and are frustrated by what they refer to as a 'Fortress Canada' attitude." Looking again to his notes, he continued. "They say things like, 'He is unwilling to be influenced by external forces . . . he doesn't take direction . . . all he wants is autonomy . . . anything we suggest, he argues against.' They see you as interested only in 'the Canadian way,' which makes it difficult to achieve consistency across divisions. That's important to a global company with a brand name. We don't have to do everything identically, John, but there are areas where consistency is critical."

"I know this is tough for you to hear, John, but it's important that you take it to heart. This company has a tradition of teamwork. We say that people are our most important asset, and we want our managers to take that seriously. We can't have a senior manager who won't let his teammates get into the game."

Sloan's pride was deeply hurt, and he had to control the impulse to fight back. "Well, Ken, are you telling me that you want me out?"

"No, John, I'm not. You're a guy we want to keep. We want you to stay in the game for us. But we want you to change the way you manage. We want you to change from being a gunslinger to a team leader. I don't know if you can make that change, John, but we're prepared to help you with a training program, a consultant, whatever you want. But I must tell you that either you learn to manage in a way that fits our values, or you won't have a future here."

John was in a state of semishock during the flight back to Toronto that evening, both because his division had turned in outstanding performance under his leadership, and even more because he didn't recognize himself in the egocentric picture Ken Warner had held up to him. Sure, there was plenty of friction with the interfering staff people at headquarters, but they just didn't understand business conditions in Canada. Furthermore, he couldn't stand the insincere politics and buttering up that seemed to curry favor with them. There were problems with his subordinates also, but they were the problem, not him.

When John Sloan had moved to the Canadian organization three years earlier, he came with an open mind and a willingness to learn about country management. He had quickly seen that the division needed a major revamping in both manufacturing and in the way it related to its customers. For John, the shortest route between where the division was and where it needed to be was a straight line. His subordinates were less motivated to change and were, in John's view, constantly dragging their feet. "The company isn't ready for that just yet," they would complain. "We need to move more slowly." Their lethargy drove him crazy. Why couldn't they see the situation as he did? Especially since the results would be bigger bonuses for everyone.

Yes, he was firm, strong-willed and, at times, impatient, but he gave people plenty of autonomy as long as they kept sight of the end goal. While he didn't seek out conflict, he would deal with it directly by staking out a position and giving subordinates the job of persuading him otherwise. He was demanding but not impossible to influence, nor was he uncaring about his subordinates.

John thought back to his previous performance appraisals, and recalled other complaints about his management style that he had successfully deflected as the comments of one or more disgruntled subordinates. But this time, Ken Warner had personally interviewed over a dozen people, and their comments couldn't easily be dismissed.

Ken had been specific: A change of leadership style was a "must-do." Even so, John felt that his criticism was unfair. "Up to this point," he told himself, "the only thing that counted was making the numbers. Now he's changing the rules." At the same time, he realized that to save his career he had to set aside personal feelings. He couldn't continue with business as usual, and denying the problem wouldn't make it go away. Change he must. But how?

At first, John thought about going to a leadership training program, but he feared that he would forget most of what he'd learned as soon as he was back on the job. Better to bring in a good consultant, he concluded, someone who could coach him on the job and prevent him from relapsing into the habits of managing that seemed to be driving everyone crazy.

John's Track Record

John had begun working for Applico 12 years earlier, starting as an analyst in corporate financial planning. His first move was to a finance position in one of the key domestic divisions. There, his technical skills and hard work quickly earned him several advancements: Director of Operations; VP of Operations; General Manager; and ultimately, President of Applico Canada.

In just three years, the Canadian division had produced exceptional returns, even in the face of a stagnant general economy. There were casualties, of course. John had removed three of his direct reports: the human resources manager and the head of information technology—both because of poor performance—and the head of operations, whom John found resistant to his organizational reforms. Though most of the remaining subordinates agreed with John's decisions about these individuals, these terminations raised fear in the surviving managers. Would people be fired for opposing John's views?

John had then rotated three of the four remaining direct reports. Bill had been head of finance when John moved him to operations to replace the person he had sacked. Martha replaced Bill in finance as a developmental rotation

assignment from corporate finance. Darryl had been na-
tional sales manager, reporting to Wayne, but had always
been interested in information systems. John assigned him
there. Wayne, the only carryover, had been head of marketing and sales for years and performed his job extremely well.
In these assignments, John demonstrated a willingness to
move people cross-functionally, taking the risk that they
would grow and develop. Figure 4–1 shows the top tiers of
Applico's management team.

Paradoxically, John Sloan, the take-no-prisoners manager, did not obtain extraordinary results by cracking the
whip or by pressuring people to meet financial goals. Believing that there was already too much emphasis on "making the numbers," he aimed instead at changing the culture
and focus of the organization. Good results, he reasoned,
would follow. His approach to culture change was through
greater emphasis on teamwork and a more egalitarian climate. Employees soon found themselves attending more
meetings; reserved parking for key managers became a

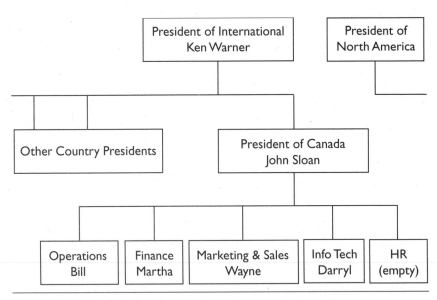

Figure 4–1. Applico Partial Organization Chart

thing of the past; free coffee was made available to everyone, not just the salaried office staff.

John was also one of the first Applico managers to initiate work on "vision and values," differentiating them from mission. The mission statement stressed the importance of financial success ("We are not a charity organization; we want to make a profit," John would often say). But the vision statement changed the focus of the organization from internal concerns to looking outward to the customer. And the agreed-on core values of openness, honesty, mutual respect, trust, and teamwork described how mission and vision were to be achieved. He used a series of workshops to push the program down through the organization.

Although John had originally involved the team in formulating the vision and value statements, he personally drove most of the ideas. Members later admitted that they had become engaged because they hoped their work on the values would help rein in John's dominance.

To implement these ideas, John championed a number of initiatives developed by team members and by him. They changed the manufacturing process from the rigid, high-control, piece-rate system to modular, team-based manufacturing with an incentive system that rewarded quality as well as quantity. To emphasize customer focus, they sent out a yearly "Customer Assessment Questionnaire" seeking feedback on how Applico was doing in Canada. They also established a Marketing Advisory Board made up of nine leading customers to get the company focused on changes in the marketplace.

John was quickly recognized for his high energy and willingness to get out in the field, visit plants and customers, and to create better relationships and communication. He was admired and liked in the plants, which he visited often, and he became known as "the people's president" because of his informal style and genuine interest in workers' ideas and concerns. The field sales staff, too, held him in high regard. Oddly, his direct reports painted a much different picture of the leader so many others revered.

JOHN MEETS HIS COACH

In response to his boss's directive to change his leadership style, John asked Ken Warner if he could recommend a good consultant. The next day he received a call with the name and number of Sam McIver. "We've worked with McIver before," said the message, "and I believe that he can be helpful to you. Give him a call." He did, and they arranged to meet in Toronto 10 days later.

At their first meeting, John described the going-over he had received from Ken Warner. "I realized long before my session with Ken that there were problems in my relationship with certain team members, but I always saw *them* as the problem, not my style of managing."

Sam listened with visible interest.

"It's not that I overmanage," John continued. "I believe in giving lots of autonomy as soon as we have agreement about direction. The trouble with this group is that if I stop pushing, they stop moving. There's a conservative streak in this division that resists change, and that makes my job harder. It means that I have to push *all the time.* If I don't, the wheels stop turning."

"Does that create conflict with your people?" Sam asked.

"Obviously. I don't particularly like conflict, but I do want the issues out on the table. I like being direct and having others be direct with me. If that creates conflict for some people, that's their problem. My style is to stake out the territory when I have a strong opinion and then see what's left to discuss. One of my strengths is that I don't lose sight of the goal, so if one path doesn't get me there, I search for another that will."

"Are your team members with you in pursuing the goal, or not?"

"Yes and no," John answered. "My people are all technically competent. They understand the goal, but they are not particularly driven to get there. So I get impatient and I push hard. We've made great progress here over the past few years, and I can tell you that it wouldn't have happened without my taking strong positions."

"How are your team meetings?" John confessed to being dissatisfied. "We do get the issues out but it often ends in conflict—especially between me and Wayne, the head of marketing and sales. Then we get deadlocked."

He described his relations with corporate staffers as equally frustrating. "The people in Westchester just don't add value. They don't understand what it's like in the field, but that doesn't stop them from making decisions. We would be much better off if corporate would go back to shuffling papers and just leave us alone. I probably wouldn't be in this hot water if I just played along with them and was very *politic* whenever I went down there, but that's not how I operate. I'm not good at glad-handing or political games. Most of my contact with the corporate people is adversarial, with me arguing against the dumb plans they want to shove down our throats."

The consultant was intrigued with John and his situation. He liked his very direct and unpretentious manner. On the other hand, he had trouble reading John's reactions. His face was often impassive: a stony mask that concealed his thoughts and feelings. Sam could understand how subordinates might feel on edge, not quite sure what John was thinking.

Near the end of the meeting, John declared, "I don't think I can change my personality. What do you think?" Sam said that it seemed more a matter of behavior than personality, and that John's style was easy to misunderstand.

"What do you mean?"

"My hunch," said Sam, "is that you actually invite people to disagree with you and respond positively when they're direct." John nodded. "However, others, especially those who are lower in the hierarchy, are probably afraid to be direct—especially since your expressions are hard to read. Right now, for instance, I cannot tell from your facial expressions and body language how you are responding—whether you are in agreement with what I'm saying, just thinking about it, or actually disagreeing. That can be disconcerting to some people.

"Furthermore, I wonder if your tendency to strongly state a position doesn't turn interaction into a contest, creating resistance. When that happens—when an issue becomes a contest—both sides tend to dig in and advocate for their positions. That's no way to solve problems. And since you have the power, as boss, your people know they cannot win. So they shut down. Maybe that's why you feel the need to push them all the time.

"Another problem may be that you are confusing what is organizationally smart with being 'political'—to use your term. They aren't the same. If you don't want to be controlled by corporate directives, you must negotiate your freedom. They have responsibilities you may be overlooking; they need to know that you aren't going off in directions that will cause problems for other areas of the corporation. A person with your forcefulness and directness should be able to assure them without resorting to politics."

"So, in a nutshell," John asked the consultant, "is my leadership style a fatal condition, or can I do something about it?"

"The good news, from what I can tell at this early stage, is that you don't need a personality change and you don't have to abandon your leadership style entirely. In some situations, how you act is very appropriate. Instead, you need to *expand* your style. Your strengths and leadership style have gotten you where you are, but they are blocking your upward progress. The need to manage in ambiguous, highly complex, and interdependent situations is what higher level management anywhere calls for. You can't be completely in charge, because the Canadian operation is part of a larger system. It isn't your company to manage alone. You must learn to thrive in a situation where you're accountable but not totally autonomous."

"Well, how would I do that?" John asked. "Where would I begin."

"You begin by getting the facts," Sam responded. "I can help you set up a process through which you'll get the information about how others react to you. That feedback is the first step in creating a new way of relating to the people you work with."

Sam described how he would interview John's direct reports and then set up a series of sessions at which they would change how they dealt with John and with each other. Also, Sam would coach John on how best to relate to corporate people in the United States. He estimated that this set of activities—fact gathering and coaching—would take six to nine months. John was intrigued and agreed to move forward.

Both John and the consultant were pleased with their initial meeting. John was impressed with how quickly Sam seemed to understand him and Sam was struck with John's apparent openness to learning. Later he mused, however, "I wonder how flexible he'll really be? Can he accept approaches other than his own?"

It was agreed that Sam would interview some of the corporate staff who interfaced with Canada. Two months later, he would come to Toronto to interview John's direct reports and then meet with the entire team. Meanwhile, John was to explain to his staff his desire to change, the role of the consultant, and their plan for the next nine months.

CORPORATE VIEWS

"He's difficult to work with." That's how people at the company's Westchester headquarters described John Sloan. Everyone Sam interviewed in Westchester had the same opinion: "He wants to do things his way and ignores our suggestions." One person described how John had refused to allow a corporate real estate expert help the Canadian division acquire a new location. Another related how a very senior corporate executive had to order John to take the advice of their specialists in an acquisition. According to some,

John's style even impaired their ability to work smoothly with his subordinates: "They have divided loyalties. We and his people might agree on something, but it's likely that John will step in and veto that agreement once they return to Toronto."

Despite John's combative reputation at the corporate head-quarters, one person attributed part of the problem to Ken Warner, whom he described as too ready to avoid conflict. "He has a hard time saying 'no' directly, so things drag on, and are ambiguous. I can see how that would drive John crazy."

Views of John's Staff

The consultant then flew to Toronto to interview John's im-mediate staff. All four of them praised John's competence and integrity but described him as highly opinionated, dog-matic, and difficult to influence. "He holds onto things like a bulldog and won't let go," one complained. They discussed his "stake in the ground" style, where, when he felt strongly on an issue, he would take a seemingly immovable position and force the group to try to argue him out of it. "We end one meeting thinking that we've convinced him, but he shows up at the next meeting with the same position and new arguments as to why he is right. After awhile, you just give up trying to contribute."

The Monster in the Cave

Another problem identified through these staff interviews was the fear of "awakening the monster in the cave." This re-ferred to the occasions when John became so upset that he verbally attacked people with eyes blazing. He accused any-one who opposed him of being tied to the status quo, and would embarrass them in front of their peers. This led mem-bers to plan before meetings what they would do. If anyone ever took on John, it was Wayne, whose long friendship with

John gave him the confidence to fight and survive. At times he would be supported by Bill. Martha and Darryl had no stomach for these battles and usually went silent, wishing the conflict would end.

Too Far Too Fast

The third area of complaint involved John's apparent impatience. According to his direct reports, John was unrealistic about how quickly his vision could be implemented. "He tries to push us too far too fast," Darryl said. "John has great ideas, but we have to deal with what's feasible. We are responsible for keeping the business running and producing while we work toward his vision. We can't simply stop what we're doing, flip a switch, and give him what he wants." Despite seeing value in many of John's suggestions, they resisted because of the pace.

Wayne confirmed Darryl's complaint with an example, "He wanted to convert a century-old piece-rate system to team production *tomorrow!*"

A related problem arose from John's failure to specify the steps needed to reach his ambitious goals. He saw this as empowerment, but it made the others see him as impractical or hasty. Sometimes they opposed him directly, or simply dragged their feet. All of this led John to make more extravagant demands or do end runs around them and deal with the field directly. The field staff liked this because it gave them direct contact with their division president; on the other hand, they were often confused by the mixed messages they received.

Decision Making

There were also problems with how decisions were made. It wasn't that John was autocratic—he was just the opposite. He insisted that *all* decisions, even minor ones, be made unanimously by the group through discussions that were painfully slow. For example, when the new division headquarters was being built, John and his team spent hours reaching unanimous agreement on such things as paint color, and floor layout. "We wasted days on those petty decisions; but they are just the tip of the iceberg of the problem we have with making decisions around here."

To cope with the problems, John's people avoided bringing tough issues to the table: "The less you bring to our meetings, the more you can manage your own area, and the less silly things fill up the agenda," Bill told the consultant during his interview. "You work your own area by yourself and then meet one-on-one with John. Alone, he is more easily influenced and less likely to be dogmatic."

The Boss's Style

The individual managers of Applico Canada responded to John's leadership style in different ways. Bill was the least bothered with John and the interactions of the management team. His focus was on production; as long as John left him alone, he was happy. He would speak up (usually in support of Wayne), but since he didn't like conflict, he wasn't the lead protagonist in team meetings. Darryl, the youngest, (in his early 30s) had his hands full trying to develop an integrated information system for the division; his goal was to get out of meetings as soon as possible with the least amount of hassle.

Martha, the financial manager, was the most repelled by her boss's style of leadership. After a number of unsatisfying attempts at working with him, she had simply given up. "There's no point in dealing with him once he's made up his mind about something," she confided to Sam. "He's like a pit bull. Once he's on to something, he won't let go." Sam learned from others that Martha tended to be silent when arguments broke out, and would just complain to others afterward. She was a lame duck in any case, soon to finish her rotation assignment and return to corporate finance.

Wayne, who had been in his job longer than any of his peers, seemed to enjoy knocking heads with his boss. ("I sometimes provoke John just for the fun of it.") There was, in fact, an undercurrent of rivalry between the two men, as Wayne's next logical career step would be John's position as president of Applico Canada. This move was impossible, of course, as long as John remained.

Each of the four managers expressed skepticism about the likelihood of change in John's interactions with them. Some even doubted the sincerity of his stated intentions. "Is he doing this just because Ken is putting pressure on him?" one asked. Another questioned the ability of anyone—and John in particular—to change. Sam urged them to give the process a chance, and encouraged them to raise their concerns at their upcoming two-day meeting. Most grudgingly agreed, though Martha was suspicious and noncommittal.

Concerns All Around

That evening, in reviewing his notes, Sam wondered what the next day would bring. Would the long buildup of frustration lead the four managers to turn on John in a destructive manner? He knew that this was unlikely; the greater danger was just the opposite: that they would pull their punches and avoid coming to grips with the problem. Experience had taught him that subordinates are often quite vocal when no action is required, but back down when the opportunity to confront the boss presents itself. After all, if the leader were to change, they might have to change as well. Subordinates will often stay with a dysfunctional situation where they can continue to blame the boss.

John, too, had misgivings. The night before Sam's scheduled two-day meeting, his wife asked him how he was feeling. "You know, after Ken raked me over the coals, I told my managers about it and said I'd be working with a consultant to solve the problem. But I still don't know exactly what I've been doing to cause them to complain about me. It's really frustrating. And there's been plenty of tension ever since I let them know," he continued. "We're all walking on eggshells."

"Frankly, I don't know how this will all work out. I don't recognize the John that they think they see. Am I supposed to act like a penitent, or like a boss who's responsible for getting things done? I know that I have to encourage them to vent their gripes at me, but will they be fair? Will they chicken out and leave me guessing about what they want? I don't know if this will work."

THE TWO-DAY RETREAT

John, Sam, and the four key managers meet early the next morning at a resort hotel two hours outside Toronto. The casual ambience of the hotel, the fall colors of the surrounding woodlands, and aroma of fresh-brewed coffee took some of the edge off everyone's apprehensions.

John started the session by talking about the feedback that he had received from Ken, and about his personal desire to change. "But all that feedback was secondhand," Sam pointed out, "from others through Ken to John. It's important for John to hear from you directly. Feedback like the comments Ken provided isn't grounded in events. It consists of little more than generalizations and is not very useful. What we have to do here is provide John with the specifics of the problems and what is causing them."

Sam's remarks led to a discussion of those aspects of John's behavior that were causing problems. The initial comments were muted and Sam was afraid that his worst fears were being realized. "They know that they're in the room with the guy who signs their paychecks," he told himself. But as the managers saw that John was not defensive and didn't answer their complaints with attacks of his own, they began to open up. They told John how difficult it was when he set up an adversarial position, and how hard it was to read his expressions. Finally, after much hesitation, they told him how they feared arousing his anger and bringing it down on themselves.

The comments of the four managers were very painful for John to hear. Though he had prepared himself for their complaints, their words rocked him as badly as Ken Warner's had earlier. They didn't square with his perception of himself or with what he was attempting to do at Applico Canada. "I'm not an autocrat," he told himself, "but that seems to be how they see me."

As his subordinates reeled off specific examples, however, John began to recognize how his actions and his manner could be interpreted as overbearing and dominating. The topic of "one-stop shopping," came up; it was one of John's pet projects. Under this plan, the customer would have a single contact person for everything: ordering, billing, complaints, and service. John had brought up this idea repeatedly, only to be met by universal opposition from his team. He responded by pushing harder, which produced the conflict and deadlock that all disliked. He had been trying to sell what he thought of as an important idea, but they had seen him as forcing it. One-stop shopping had thus become a symbol of frustration and irritation between John and the team.

"But if I don't push for change," John responded, "who will?" This question led to genuine exploration of the dynamics of their typical interactions. For the first time, everyone recognized that the team and John had been locked into a negative, mutually reinforcing pattern. John's forceful pushing for his seemingly radical ideas made his team members feel overwhelmed; their natural response was to resist, which in turn made John feel that he was the only one who wanted change. So he would push still harder, and on the cycle would continue. Identifying this pattern helped everyone see what they could do to break the cycle.

The group continued to give John feedback about problems they had with his style. He tried to respond nondefensively but these comments were difficult for John. Sensing his discomfort, Sam asked, "How are you feeling about all of this?"

He said quietly, "I see now how I am causing these problems, and it is overwhelming. Am I doing anything right?"

John's admission freed others in the room to remark on how much they respected his ideas and his drive. His acceptance of his role in causing the difficulties allowed his

managers to acknowledge the part they had played in facilitating the behavior of which they complained.

Discussion then shifted to what they could do to improve
the situation. The consultant pointed to two issues: John's
style, and how the management team operated. Central to
the latter was the sort of team they wanted to be. Did they
want to operate as an advisory group to John, or did they
want to share responsibility for running Canada? "There's a
big difference between these roles," Sam warned them, "and
it has to do with commitment. An advisory group requires
little commitment from its members; their loyalty and commitment is to their own subareas. An advisory group behaves like a federation. A team that shares responsibility for
overall organizational success, on the other hand, demands
greater investment from its members: more direct discussion
of differences, more complete exploration of issues, and
greater commitment to joint decisions."

"That's what I've always wanted from this group," John
said. "Perhaps my style has made it impossible." The four
managers all agreed that they wanted to share responsibility with John.

"If a shared responsibility team is what you all want," Sam
remarked, "then I suggest that you make a list of things that
stand in your way. Examples might be John's habit of staking out a position, somebody else's habit of putting his own
area's interests ahead of the organization's, and so forth."
Members spent the rest of the afternoon compiling a joint
list of obstacles and beginning a discussion of how to deal
with them. As the session ended, they decided to set these
aside. "It has helped that we identified them; let's do some
work and deal with these if they arise."

They started the next day by working on vision and values. All acknowledged the importance of the mission, vision,
and value statements, but in the past these had always been
seen as John's statements. Could they now be owned by the
group? Working on these would be a useful test of the team's
ability to work together in a new way. Since John felt
strongly about the existing values statement, it would be

easy for him to become dogmatic. Likewise, it would be easy for his direct reports to slide into talking only to John rather than functioning as a joint decision-making team. As the morning went on, there were times when John and others started to step into these traps, but they caught themselves (and each other) and were able to recover.

Although their task wasn't completed by the time they broke for lunch, considerable progress had been made. After lunch, the team asked the consultant if they might postpone completion of the values statements to a later meeting in order to tackle an important policy issue that required immediate resolution: nepotism in hiring. There had been considerable confusion about this subject, because of the contradictions between the pledge not to discriminate against any potential employee and an earlier policy that restricted hiring of family members, no matter how qualified.

Despite his strong feelings about nepotism, John held his old habits in check. He was able to facilitate discussion by the team members without trying to sell the solution he preferred. He did not conceal his opinions, but worked to bring out the views of others. As a result, the meeting was very different from their usual antagonistic discussions, and John demonstrated that he was already taking earlier feedback to heart.

At the close of this first retreat, people generally felt very good about what had happened. Darryl was excited because "Maybe we can now get on with doing what we are here to do, which is to run the business." Only Martha remained dubious about John's capacity to change. She would, she confided to Sam, "wait and see."

THE NEXT SEVERAL MONTHS

In the weeks and months that followed the retreat, John Sloan worked hard to implement the changes he had agreed to make. He went out of his way to drop by the offices of his managers and keep the lines of communication open. He consciously checked his dogmatic impulses during team meetings and worked at improving a collaborative decision-making style, seeking to become more problem focused. Instead of rushing to sell his views, he actively solicited possible solutions from others.

During this period, John publicly abandoned the one-stop shopping program, a concept near and dear to his heart. He realized that continued opposition meant he should rethink it. (Later he understood that it didn't fit the Canadian operation. "It was a solution in search of a problem," he admitted.) This action was seen as a positive sign that he could be influenced. Those who dealt with him remarked that he had become more self-disclosing about his concerns and less inclined to play his cards close to the vest. These changes did not come easily to John. He was often impatient and frequently felt caught in contradictions: "How can I express my feelings without getting into a 'sell' mode?" he asked Sam McIver during a phone call. "How do I facilitate the team when I have strong opinions about the topic we're working on?" John also struggled with nonverbal signals. He wanted to be himself, but feedback indicated that his stern look was interpreted as disapproving.

Eager to make his changes stick and his efforts pay off, John decided to make a public record of his intentions and his understanding of what his managers were asking him to do. This took the form of a memo directed to each of the team members.

John's managers had their own opinions about what was happening. Darryl summarized his view of the management team in a conversation with Sam:

> *There is some optimism that things will get better after the retreat, but also fear of a relapse into our old ways—both John's and ours. So we are on our best behavior. The problem is that we have become very cautious. No one wants to raise issues that will rock the boat, especially without you there to play referee. Unfortunately, we're holding on to those until our December follow-up meeting.*

Applico (Canada), Inc.

TO: Management Committee

DATE: October 26

FROM: John Sloan

SUBJECT: YOUR FEEDBACK FROM 10/6

I just realized that I hadn't shared with you the notes and impressions I took away from our session on October 6. Let me do that now.

When I asked you for your ideas to help me improve my skills in three key areas, this is what I heard:

On "Enabling" or Empowerment

- I need to recognize your skills as individuals and the team's contribution to achieving the "Vision."
- I need to show you the same respect I show all employees.
- I need to be sure I'm discussing problems and not solutions.

On "Encouraging" or Recognition

- I need to accept the "insatiable appetite" we all have for recognition—including yours.
- I need to seek more ways to celebrate.

On "Modeling" or "Walking the Talk"

- I need to clearly acknowledge problems and then be open to solutions.
  - Mutual respect, especially with diverse opinions.
  - Being clear on my real issues—not hiding behind questions or distractions.

I'm sorry for the delay in feeding this back to you. Please let me know if your notes or memories differ from mine. I appreciate your input.

John

Bumps in the Road

Like his team, John also felt that there was genuine progress in the weeks following the original retreat. As he described events to Sam in early November:

> *We are much more relaxed. I am especially so with
> Wayne and Darryl, somewhat with Bill, though no real
> change with Martha. What is nice is that I am getting
> support. A couple of days after the retreat, Wayne
> came into my office and thanked me. He said, "That
> took a lot of guts and you can count on me to help." And
> he has been a big help already. In our meetings, Wayne
> helps us stay focused. He will say "We're slipping
> back into our old habits, people," and then we correct
> ourselves.*

Yes, the process was going smoothly, but it was destined to
hit a few bumps. Two weeks after John's report to the consultant, he learned that there was a high likelihood of Wayne
moving to a corporate assignment. With the prospect of
Wayne leaving, John thought it best to postpone the upcoming retreat. "No sense in having an important meeting until
all the players are on board." And since he was told by Ken
Warner to keep Wayne's situation confidential until his
transfer was officially confirmed, he could not explain the
delay. Holidays, travel schedules and a delay in getting Gerald, Wayne's replacement, permanently on board slowed
things further. Wayne and Gerald were shuttling back and
forth between Toronto and Westchester so that the meeting
kept getting postponed. This created suspicion that John
was backsliding and forgetting his commitment to change.
Nevertheless, the team managed to collaborate in dealing
with the vacant Human Resources position. John and the
team members interviewed each of the internal candidates
sent up by corporate human resources, then met to make
the decision. Though each of the finalists had important

skills, the full team, including John, could not agree that any was the ideal candidate. "This is too important a position for us to compromise on," they said. Turning down these candidates would postpone the selection for months and possibly antagonize corporate HR. But the team collectively decided to accept these consequences.

On the other hand, other events compounded the problem between John and the team. Canada and the United States had signed the Free Trade Agreement. Corporate, as a cost-saving measure, wanted to integrate all shipping and distribution of the Canadian with the U.S. operations. John (and his team) opposed what they saw as a too hasty move.

"We didn't necessarily reject the idea," John told the consultant later, "but we had two concerns. One was that they may not have examined the fine print of the trade agreement—there still seemed to be plenty of customs problems. Also, we were in the middle of important changes in Canadian plant operations, and we wanted to complete those before the distribution function was integrated." As usual, John's points had merit. But he reverted to his stake-in-the-ground approach with corporate in getting them across. They, in turn, put heat on his team members, who felt caught in the middle.

Another problem that plagued John's relationship with the management team was an unintended consequence of one of his efforts to change. He had been told that his tendency to scowl when concentrating was interpreted as either anger or disapproval. This feedback motivated him to hold back frowns. Because he was awkward and self-conscious at this, John tended to restrain *all* noverbal reactions, which made him even more inscrutable.

John's issues at work spilled over into his home life. Not surprisingly, many of the same behaviors that had caused difficulty with his direct reports had also affected his personal relationships. Couples learn to live with each other's idiosyncrasies, especially when they think that change is not possible. John's wife had made these accommodations. But as John talked about his subordinates' feedback with his wife, she confirmed that she had often felt similar reactions. His behaviors at work were, indeed, mirrored at home. So now he was working those issues on two fronts.

The strain that John was under was apparent to all who knew him. He was visibly tired and seemed to carry daunting burdens. That strain also took a toll on the work the management team tried to perform together. Later, John recalled the deterioration experienced during that period:

> *By early February it was clear that we had moved backward. But I didn't want to admit this to the group; I too was concerned that our whole plan for change would blow up. Also, our second retreat always seemed to be right around the corner; I kept hoping that it would get us back on track.*

So as the cold Canadian winter wore on, the meetings became more formal. Everyone was afraid to confront the boss on these issues for fear that they would regress into their former dysfunctional state. And with Wayne around only occasionally, no one took the lead. Meetings settled into a low-conflict mode where only safe topics were discussed. Everyone was putting the difficult issues off until the next retreat, which was finally scheduled in April—fully six months since the initial one.

The Follow-Up Meeting

Since Gerald, the new director of marketing, permanently joined the group just weeks before the April meeting, one of the goals of this second retreat was to integrate him into the team. Another objective was to review how John and the team had operated in the past seven months, and the third goal was to examine some of John's "hot buttons" that they had mentioned as most likely to "stir the monster from the cave."

The meeting started with expressions of anger at John (and the consultant) for postponing the meeting so long, and for not including them in those decisions. John shot back: "If you felt that strongly about it, why didn't you say something when I announced the postponement? I explained to everyone later *why* I postponed this meeting: It was because of confidential information about Wayne's transfer. Why can't you appreciate the dilemma I was in? What would you have done in my place?"

Bill and Darryl admitted that they hadn't really confronted their boss with their feelings about the sliding meeting date. They had simply taken his unilateral decision as a sign that he had not really changed. This admission relieved some of the tension. Martha explained her behavior by telling John that "I can't give you feedback. I don't know how to read you—I can't tell whether you welcome feedback or not." Bill and Darryl agreed. John responded that he felt trapped, damned as "too dug in" if he said what he felt, and damned for being "impossible to read" if he didn't.

Bill tried to help: "John, there's a difference between expressing feelings early in a process, before they are fixed, and pronouncing conclusions that only reveal the final opinion. It's the former we want. When you go silent, we don't know where you stand—we have to guess. But if you did your thinking out loud, early in the process, then we'd have a chance to influence you before your views were chiseled in stone."

As John pondered that suggestion, Darryl asked for a clarification of what John had been thinking earlier. "Ten minutes ago you smiled at something I said. Were you amused by what I said, or were you laughing it off?"

"I agreed with what you said," John responded, "but I didn't say anything because I thought we needed to move on."

Slowly John began to understand more about how his silences and nonverbal sternness impacted members, and they began to see that they were making interpretations based on fear rather than facts. Darryl asked John, "Would it be okay with you if we asked what you are thinking whenever we're puzzled by your expressions?"

"Of course!" John replied. It was agreed that the members would no longer try to interpret John's expressions, but would ask him directly.

Feeling understood, John talked about the stress he had been experiencing and the trouble he anticipated in negotiating with Westchester about the potential integration of Canadian shipping and distribution with the rest of North America. "We could use our connections with our corporate counterparts to influence the outcome if you would share the problem with us," Bill responded. "Keeping that to yourself means that we can't help."

The balance of the meeting reviewed work on mission, vision, and value statements, which the group had begun at the initial meeting but never completed. Their failure to return to this task over the intervening six months was not caused by disagreement about direction, but by the lack of specific action steps. Since John hadn't articulated his ideas on how to move toward it, the absence of implementation plans made the vision seem unrealistic to members. But this time, John spelled out the intermediate steps he had in mind. Just as important, members agreed that they would push John when they thought he was not revealing his intermediate thinking.

This session seemed to bring events back on track. John saw that his tendency not to share his concerns caused confusion and mistrust. Bill, Martha, and Darryl realized just how conflict avoidant they were, partially due to painful memories of past battles and partially due to their personal difficulties with disagreements.

That evening, after the meeting ended, John and the consultant talked about possible next steps. Sam suggested that John help the group see the value in raising differences. Both agreed that team members needed to understand the difference between disagreement and personal attack. Furthermore, they needed to understand the benefits of open disputes—even those that one loses. Disputes force everyone to clarify their ideas. Conflict, they agreed, could lead to creative alternative solutions that incorporated the best points of each of the original arguments.

The consultant pointed to ways that John could encourage productive conflict. He could support the expression of minority views, encourage the group to examine downside risks in the preferred alternatives, and ask for creative new options when the group got stuck in debating only two alternatives. Finally, he could separate disagreement from personal disapproval.

THE THIRD MEETING

Between April and June, the team worked more effectively than ever before. Members confronted John when he seemed to be holding back feelings, and he responded affirmatively. Relationships with corporate improved.

A third off-site meeting held in June was productive but uneventful. There were neither fireworks nor major breakthroughs. The meeting had a calm atmosphere because John had adopted a less abrasive management style and the team was working together more effectively. John was more open about what he was thinking, and had dropped his habit of taking and doggedly defending set positions. For its part, the team had learned to explore the issues, make the most of everyone's contributions, and self-correct when they found themselves getting off track.

There was still work to do, however. Observing the interactions between John and the team members, the consultant noted how discussion was often directed to John, and how his opinion continued to be sought. Members were more inclined to ask questions than to make clear statements of their views. Though questions were preferable to dogmatic declarations, they represented an indirect approach to discussing issues. Nor had members lost their hesitance to put the really tough issues on the table—especially if they contained the seeds of conflict. Still, the progress from the previous retreat was significant and heartening.

NEW FACES, NEW ISSUES

Martha finished her stint with Applico Canada in July and returned to the corporate finance office in Westchester. Due to her continued suspicion about John Sloan, her departure removed a barrier to better collaboration between the division president and his key managers. Though the selection of her replacement was officially a joint decision between John and corporate finance, John made it a team decision. They selected an inside candidate, Ian, who was both technically competent and a team player. A new director of human resources was selected in the same manner. Because of the importance of that position, John suggested that the decision be unanimous; any single member would have veto power. They agreed and after everybody had individually interviewed the short list of candidates, the team met and selected Kathy. The consensual selection process facilitated the integration of Ian and Kathy as team members.

The group had grown into an effective and cohesive team. The "us versus John" mentality had largely dissipated. Members actually looked forward to their joint meetings, which were now productive and capable of dealing with contentious issues. Personal interactions had become more positive.

John continued to work at being more open and disclosing: expressing his opinions earlier; sharing his concerns and feelings. The team appreciated his efforts and provided feedback about how much he had changed.

One event in particular cemented the team's relationship with John. Darryl came into John's office one day and said, "I just need to tell you that I am having a hard time performing up to standard. I am going through a very difficult divorce."

John sensed that this was more than an apology about performance. Darryl needed to talk about his problem. "Darryl, let's get out of here for awhile. I have to buy some new stereo speakers and I need your help. We can get some lunch while we're at it." John used the time out of the office to give Darryl a chance to talk about the problems in his marriage.

Later, Darryl recalled: "John made it easy for me to talk about how the divorce was affecting my work. After a quick trip to the audio store, we went to a cafe for lunch and ended up talking for at least an hour. And not about business. He was willing to listen to however much I wanted to say about my situation. As a result I felt understood and supported.

"As we walked out of the cafe, who did we run into but my wife! The minute that we stood exchanging pleasantries felt like an hour. It was clear that she knew that John knew, so it was awkward for everyone. I was quite shaken by the event, but John was like a rock (he had been through a divorce himself, so he really understood). At that point, I didn't think of him as my boss but as my friend."

This event changed the tone around the office, with everyone showing their concern and support for Darryl. Previously, personal issues were expected to be "checked at the door." John's intervention on behalf of one of his managers was affectionately noted by the team as another sign of the progress John and others had made.

The incident with Darryl coincided with the period during which the next year's budget and objectives were being developed, and the more positive atmosphere at Applico Canada enhanced the outcome of those difficult tasks. The team felt so good about its ability to deliver, that the performance goals they generated were very ambitious. This was contrary to the corporate budget game that usually led managers to create lowball, more easily achieved targets.

When Ken Warner saw the Canadian division's budget draft, he thought it was too great a stretch. "Think about a little downward revision," he wrote in a memo to John.

THE FOURTH AND FINAL MEETING

For its final meeting, the Applico management team returned to the same resort hotel at which they begun their long process of change. It was now late November, and the grounds around the hotel were already blanketed in snow.

The team began with a review of personal interactions over the past two months. Generally, they gave themselves high marks. Though some problems remained, the members discussed them objectively, with no finger-pointing. Then they turned to reassessing their proposed budget, mindful of Ken Warner's cautions. At Ian's suggestion, they began with a reexamination of underlying assumptions about growth, market projections, and so forth. Each person's assumptions were scrutinized objectively.

Discussion of the budget took up the entire morning and continued into the early afternoon. In the end, a few projections were adjusted downward, but not substantially. The ambitious goals of the draft budget were essentially maintained and accepted by John and his managers in a final budget to be submitted by Ian to Ken Warner.

The balance of the day was dedicated to the behavioral dynamics of the group. Both John and the team members sought feedback about the quality of their contributions and interactions. Sam, the consultant, moderated this discussion. Each person made helpful comments about ways people had changed and identified additional areas for development. There was broad satisfaction all around.

Sam, however, pointed out a tendency to use humor in a nonconstructive way. "Perhaps you don't notice it, but as an outsider I can't help seeing how some of you are covertly 'zinging' each other. My experience is that people use humorous barbs to avoid a more direct complaint they have with another person. Kathy, you zinged Ian a few times during the budget discussion; what do you think about this?"

Kathy flushed with embarrassment. "You caught me. I admit that on the surface, we are supportive of each other and 'shoulder-to-shoulder against the world.' But we aren't very good with conflict and so take these clever shots at each other. Sorry, Ian."

Ian nodded his forgiveness.

"Humor is a good way both to let off steam and to send a message," Sam told the group. "But if you're dissatisfied with someone else, a zinger will not settle the issue. So instead of skewering someone with a sharp remark, be clear and direct about your complaint. That's the only way you'll get it settled."

"Thanks for that sound advice," John told Sam as he prepared to adjourn the meeting for dinner. "For a man without a *real* job you have remarkable human insights." *Zing!*

"I'm glad to know that the last laugh is on me," said Sam. "I'll add it to your bill."

After dinner, Applico Canada's difference with corporate over plans to integrate all North American distribution operations bubbled to the surface. This was a sore subject for Bill, who accused John of being the source of the problem. Darryl, who rarely confronted Bill, jumped in. "Bill, you're always on John's case. Why don't you lighten up. It's like you can't let go of the past. Even though we've made progress, you keep dredging up old stuff."

Bill was taken aback and, on reflection, admitted that he was still responding to the "old John." "Okay," he said, "I'm ready to bury the hatchet." This was an important milestone for the team, symbolizing a move to another level of collaboration, and a willingness to admit that John had really changed.

The subject of integrating distribution headed the next morning's agenda. John's dogged opposition had put the Canadian division and the parent company at loggerheads. The suggestion was made that one way to move beyond their present impasse would be to set up a task force to research this issue. "We've always assumed that corporate failed to recognized the complications integration would cause for us in Canada," said Gerald. "It's time to verify that assumption. Let's see if those complications really exist, and if they do, try to measure their logistical and customer service effects. And let's involve corporate staff in this issue. Let's show them that we can collaborate." The team selected Gerald, Bill, and Kathy as Canadian representatives on a task force set up to study the problem of distribution integration. John supported this approach.

The group ended the day by returning to John and his relationship with people at corporate headquarters. Even though he had been working on being more collaborative, he

November 23

Mr. Ken Warner
President, Applico International
Westchester, New York

Dear Ken:

We have now completed the fourth and closing team-building session with John Sloan and his management group. This report summarizes the result.

The group is in a very good place in terms of its internal relationships and commitment to an agreed direction. They are ready to take off as a cohesive team focused on the major issues. They have worked through past problems with John's style and have reached agreement about how he is now operating. They have agreed on objectives and procedures for the team and put the norms of openness and directness into practice. The two new managers have been integrated to the point that they feel like full contributing members of the group.

Some potential rocky spots remain. Members still need to test out their agreements on some difficult business issues (although they worked through a couple of core problems in good order). Furthermore, they will need to avoid backsliding. Nevertheless, I am optimistic about the future performance of this group.

Several factors have contributed to the improved interactions of this group and augur well for the future. The first is the change in membership. The new members carry no old feelings about John's previous style, and they are much more committed to making the new team relationships work. Second, Bill has made peace with John and is ready to look toward the future. Finally, John has made impressive changes. Over the past fourteen months he has been exposed to some very jarring feedback. He has both accepted that bitter medicine and made the necessary changes. His leadership style has changed significantly and for the better.

John and his group have asked that I consider a follow-up diagnosis in about nine months. I will make myself available for that purpose, though I doubt that it will be necessary.

Ken, you have a very good team there and should expect great things from them. If you wish to discuss this further, give me a call.

Sincerely,

Sam McIver

had a reputation and a trail of damaged relationships to overcome. The group discussed what John needed to do (and not do) to improve those relationships. He listened and said he would try but would need ongoing feedback if further problems developed.

As this meeting ended, Sam McIver felt that the team was now able to manage itself, self-correcting when necessary. He said that he would be sending his final report to corporate, but be available if needed, which he thought unlikely. They had come a long way. The team agreed.

OUTCOMES

The management team went on to work effectively together. Its members lived up to their commitments, and its leader continued to learn and manage in new ways. As members saw it:

"We have become less functionally focused and feel responsible for the whole business."

"Our meetings are fun, and the team keeps improving."

"We bring the problems we encounter in our functional areas to the team instead of attacking them on our own."

Two years later, after continuing to do an excellent job in Canada, John Sloan was invited to Westchester to take on an important new corporate position. He had been president of the Canadian division for six years—twice as long as his two predecessors—and was ready for a new challenge. Wayne, the former market and sales director, was appointed by Ken Warner as the new head of Applico Canada.

John's initial plan was to work to the end, say good-bye, and leave without fanfare. But his management team had other ideas, which included a series of farewell events at division plants and regional offices. John was uncomfortable with this but agreed after the team stressed the importance of letting others say good-bye. These farewells turned into gala events, with elaborate themes and preparations, since employees in the field and in Toronto had developed a great deal of respect and affection for their departing comrade.

LEADER–MEMBER
AMBIVALENCE

The remarkable transformation of John Sloan and his team, described in Chapter 4, illustrates the benefits of successful post-heroic leadership. Teams are able to arrive at more creative, high-quality decisions; there is greater commitment to implementation; and everything takes less time. These outcomes are the result of numerous changes in working processes:

- Individual team members and the group as a whole can influence the unit's most critical issues and each other to a greater extent.
- Members have more clout with the leader.
- The leader no longer has to hold back strong opinions or hide power since the members will push back if they disagree.
- Disagreements are open and task related, not covert battles for dominance.
- All have an opportunity and an obligation to contribute.
- People hold one another accountable for performance.
- All team members pull together.
- Information is shared, not hidden.

- Problems and positions are visible.
- People can ask for help when necessary since neither leader nor members are expected to have all the answers.
- Meetings create energy.

The positive outcomes observed at Applico are similar to those at Pharmco, which we introduced in Chapter 1. In both cases, teams developed through post-heroic leadership were able to handle problems that few managers would have thought possible. They demonstrated that sharing management responsibilities can benefit the organization, the team, the individual members, and the leader. Why, then, doesn't every leader adopt this superior way of managing—and why don't the people who report to them insist that they do?

The reason is that most leaders and their subordinates are ambivalent about working in the post-heroic world. They are attracted to the payoffs but are uncertain about the changes that go with it. Both share general concerns about this new approach:

- Will I lose control (and risk poor performance)?
- Will being more open make me too vulnerable?
- Will openness lead to more conflict?
- Will I be required to openly disagree with and confront authority?

CONTROL

For the leader, managing post-heroically requires a relaxation of personal control in return for greater team member motivation and higher quality solutions. But sharing control neither diminishes nor destroys it; in fact, control gains strength through acceptance of the vision for the unit and increased peer pressure from a strong team. Instead of being dependent on a single leader, control is reinforced by many.

Traditional leaders remain ambivalent, however, because of fears related to control.

Decisions May Not Be the Leader's First Choice

Operating by consensus, the leader no longer retains exclusive veto power; this changes the criterion for an acceptable decision from "We will take my first choice" to "Is this a decision that I can live with and support?" Each person on the team uses this criterion, so that anyone, including the leader, can veto a decision that he or she can't support.

Leaders surrender exclusive veto power when they adopt shared responsibility, but this loss is offset because decisions made by a competent group of individuals using appropriate procedures will generally be superior to decisions made by a single person. This is particularly true for complex problems.[1]

Occasionally, the titular leader is the most experienced and knowledgeable person on a particular matter and should just make the decision. Usually, however, the traditional leader's insistence on control of decisions is less a matter of expertise and more a matter of personal comfort. Giving in to the group's views is more often an issue of personal uneasiness than a danger of mediocre decisions.

Reduced Control of Meeting Interactions

Meetings held by post-heroic leaders are less predictable and potentially more volatile. Leaders are less preoccupied with doing the planning and politicking that assure the outcomes they seek. Nor do they keep contentious issues off the agenda.

Traditional leaders fear a loss of control in this new approach. Many are accustomed to meticulous meeting planning and spend a great deal of time thinking through everyone's likely responses, lobbying individual members before meetings, and planning how to get the right outcomes.

In the post-heroic world, this is time wasted and a deterrent to superior collective decision making.

Greater Independence for Direct Reports

To the traditional leader, the idea of greater independence for direct reports is the equivalent of loose cannons on the deck—there is no telling what damage they'll do. Control from the top is the time-honored antidote to this danger and most leaders are loath to relinquish it.

Under shared responsibility leadership, direct reports are not straitjacketed by narrow roles, rigid rules, and overcontrolling supervision. They do not have to check everything in advance. There are also fewer boundaries between roles. Because direct reports are encouraged to work things out among themselves, they cross functional boundaries, improvise, and engage in mutual influence on many cross-unit issues.

Paradoxically, greater independence for direct reports actually increases the total amount of control. As the leader loosens his or her grip, the more effective control imposed by vision, values, agreed-to strategy, and peer pressure takes its place freeing the leader from petty supervisory chores.

New Forms of Accountability

Leaders have always been held accountable for results. What gives traditional leaders pause is the notion of *shared* responsibility. They worry that sharing responsibility divides it, and is actually double-speak for "Don't blame me for this fiasco, it was a group decision!" It is never acceptable, however, for the leader to blame members, even when they have shared in the final decision; the leader remains accountable. Responsibility is about who takes part and who feels ownership, while accountability is about who must answer for the outcome. That will always remain with the leader.

Indeed, accountability is a major source of ambivalence for those who make the transition from traditional to post-heroic leadership. If the leader is accountable to higher-ups, doesn't the leader have to give full approval to every decision? Such preoccupation with control is short-sighted. Since both heroic and post-heroic leaders will be held accountable by superiors, isn't it safer when direct reports feel the same concern and investment in the outcomes of decisions? When they hold each other accountable for contributing their best? When they fully share all relevant information? When they use sound decision-making processes? Sharing responsibility in this way cannot prevent all failures, but it increases the probability of success. Relying on direct reports as partners may increase uncertainty and ambiguity, but is worth it when it leads to better results.

Shared responsibility is neither delegation ("You all make this decision and I will accept anything you do") nor abdication ("I don't care what you decide and won't influence it"); instead, it is a mutual influence process. The leader can have a strong voice in the important decisions without being the only voice that matters. He or she can still set limits within which members can operate. For their part, members must take responsibility for pushing back at predetermined boundaries that seem unnecessarily restrictive or vague.

Mutuality initially takes time for everyone to get used to, especially when the leader is accustomed to making all the important decisions and subordinates are accustomed to delegating upward. But the superior decisions and greater commitment to implementation that result should smooth the way to change.

Despite romantic touting of empowerment as the freeing of employee energy, team members have their own concerns about loss of control. Post-heroic leadership increases their influence, but it can also decrease their control. Under the traditional system, peers engage in an unspoken collusion: "Stay out of my area and I'll stay out of yours." This collusion is not possible when team members are expected to take the larger perspective to raise questions and concerns, even to make suggestions to each other with the understanding that these are not orders.

Heroic subordinates also exert control over what they choose to communicate or withhold. They decide whether to tell their boss about customer rumblings, slipping schedules, organizational and performance problems, or new business opportunities. In fact, some subordinates are masters at protecting their autonomy by controlling information flow.

For example, the leader asks "How do you think the marketing division will respond to the idea of moving to direct mail for this campaign?" The team member knows that the leader is enamored of the idea and wants marketing to cooperate. But he also knows that the VP of marketing, his friend Kate, believes that direct mail is a waste of money for this kind of product and will do anything she can to kill it. Instead of saying that—and threatening his relationship with her—he responds obliquely, softens the message, and delegates the problem back up to the boss: "I'm not sure, but you know how Kate is about wanting to be the one who decides about marketing strategy. I doubt whether she'd go for direct marketing. How much of your personal capital do you want to spend fighting it?"

In cases like this, the team member relinquishes potential upward influence for the benefit of holding onto personal control, irrespective of what would be right for the project. He can back away from arguing the limitations of direct marketing if the leader isn't willing to fight the battle or can express more doubts about Kate's willingness to bend if the discussion continues. The leader comes away feeling that the subordinate has been loyal and perhaps even helpful. And if the whole thing blows up, the subordinate can say, "Gee, I told you that Kate likes to make these decisions and wouldn't think much of direct marketing." This kind of protective camouflage is so common in heroic organizations that the leader may never single out the member as any less honest or trustworthy than others. The open communications demanded by shared responsibility leadership undermine this information control.

VULNERABILITY

By some standards, John Sloan was a fearless leader, especially when he disagreed with corporate higher-ups. He wasn't afraid to fight for his beliefs or to oppose those he thought were pushing his division in the wrong direction. Yet until he began to receive feedback about his need to change, he was afraid to appear uncertain or dependent. His reticence in sharing his inner thoughts with colleagues suggests a fear of appearing confused or of lacking all the answers. Like other heroic leaders, he was tough and persistent when challenged, but he had difficulty when unsure how to answer or how to get his way.

Heroic leaders feel vulnerable when they depend on others. They fear that their subordinates will question their authority and their value: "If the boss doesn't know, then he's no smarter than the rest of us." "If the boss cannot figure it out, why do we need him?"

To his credit, John Sloan overcame the need to appear all knowing, something that many traditional leaders fail to do. A truly strong person—a self-confident person—can admit to faults, doubts, idiosyncratic foibles, and areas of ignorance. Heroic leaders attempt to conceal these flaws, believing that they will only command respect if they are always right, always confident, and always "in charge."

Post-heroic leaders must be more disclosing about problems, concerns, doubts, and hunches to reduce distance and opaqueness in their decision-making processes. They can't hide behind their roles, but must admit when they are in doubt, are confused, or have made a mistake. Greater openness has many benefits:

- Members spend less time trying to interpret what the boss is really thinking.

- Misunderstandings are reduced in instances when members' inferences are wrong.
- Members have more opportunities to contribute.

Openness by the leader serves as a signal for others to reciprocate. When leaders are forthcoming, it decreases the natural self-protection that arises from the tension between needing to collaborate with colleagues who are also competitors and thereby potentially dangerous.

"But," the anxious leader thinks, "what if other people use my openness to attack me? Will I be viewed as weak or indecisive if I admit my doubts ? Will I lose respect and my ability to influence those who see my inadequacies?"

Decades of working with executives and executive teams have convinced us that these fears are unfounded. The leader who asks for help receives it. Those who admit their humanness get the support they need. This assumes that the leader is basically competent even if humanly flawed; if genuinely incompetent, no leadership system protects for long. When members have stored-up feelings, as was the case at Applico, the feedback can start out feeling punitive to the leader; readiness to improve, however, ultimately pulls supportiveness from others. But testimonials probably do little good if you believe, "My case is different; *my* subordinates won't respond with compassion." This fear stokes the fires of ambivalence.

Team members likewise feel vulnerable. They too are reluctant to reveal their uncertainties, doubts, and concerns. Will they be negatively evaluated, attacked, or discounted if they admit to not having the answer? The heroic mind-set brings them leader-like concerns, while they try to act as though they have everything covered.

The desire to appear confident, on top of all issues, and fully knowledgeable is mutually reinforcing. When team members hide their uncertainties from the leader and one another, they encourage others to conceal their own vulnerability. It is like a grotesque game of "chicken," seeing who can keep from turning the wheel of the speeding, organizational car before crashing head on. This makes it difficult for people to work effectively together. When team members spend so much energy in hiding problems and trying to look good, less power is available to do excellent work.

To hold each other accountable and share the burdens of the leader, group members must be willing to acknowledge shortcomings and shortfalls. Teams can only cooperate fully when everyone's guard is down.

GREATER OPENNESS CAN LEAD TO INCREASED CONFLICT

If one set of dangers threatens personal vulnerability, another arouses the fear of uncontrolled conflict. If the post-heroic leader loosens the reins of control in meetings, won't dissension run rampant?

Many leaders view themselves as the lid that keeps a cauldron of discord from boiling over. Traditional control mechanisms give them the means to turn down the heat. They can redirect debate to safer subjects or cut it off entirely, make a unilateral decision, rebuke anyone who has become visibly emotional, take arguments off-line with individuals, or use their personal authority to quiet rabble-rousers. Leading in a new way that puts all the toughest issues on the table and asks people to wrestle with them guarantees more disagreements and arguments. When leaders first attempt this, they find themselves in the middle of highly contentious meetings. Their impulse is to grab back control.

But suppressing conflict is not the mark of tough-minded leadership. What looks like toughness in heroic leaders is often nothing more than conflict avoidance. The new leadership requires a willingness to raise uncomfortable issues (even with one's boss), and to let discussion develop, even when it generates a great deal of heat. Doing this is all the more difficult for team members, who cannot use position power to shut down undesired conflict when it erupts.

It requires personal strength to insist that team members and colleagues face the hardest issues, to be demanding and still supportive, to give honest feedback to someone who is well-liked but underperforming. It is surprising how many so-called tough managers evade these situations; those who face up to such challenges earn real respect.

Greater openness has the potential to make the leader the center of conflict—John Sloan became the focus of heated controversy. Certainly other leaders must feel that the post-heroic environment would make them fair game for criticism as well. Few managers are eager to let upward criticism come at them without filters, as John Sloan did, and no one likes to be vulnerable to negative feedback.

Openness, vulnerability, and conflict are the continuing conditions of leading in the new way. Shared responsibility is only possible when leaders and team members can wrestle with the toughest issues. Individuals who are invulnerable to influence cannot be members of an effective team. And in a changing world, team members will not, and generally should not, always agree. Their differing vantage points, expertise, and experiences will lead them to different views, which are key to excellent decisions. The post-heroic environment is not characterized by extended periods of calm punctuated by an occasional brief conflict. Instead, disagreement over difficult issues is commonplace. But if everyone buys into the larger vision of the organization, and gains skill at mutual influence, these arguments will be constructive and issue-centered.

DISAGREEING WITH THE BOSS

Since virtually every leader is also a subordinate to some other leader, everyone worries about opposing their bosses on important issues. "How effectively can I advocate for something if the person who opposes me is the person who writes my performance review and determines my salary?" In the world of heroic leadership, the maxim "Don't cross the boss" is the number one rule. In post-heroic leadership, *not* crossing the boss is the number one failure since it means holding back vital information and letting the boss make foolish mistakes. Partners do not do that to each other.

Just as the heroic approach allows the leader to hide his or her vulnerabilities, it relieves subordinates of responsibility and added work. As long as subordinates see the boss as all-powerful, they can coast along in their own narrow domains. Though they may complain about their lack of influence on bosses and peers, there is a security in their powerlessness. They can complain about the boss's decisions without fighting for alternatives or being held accountable for results ("Well, I told her it was a bad idea").

There is a huge gulf between cautious, watered-down disagreeing with the boss—perhaps after having one try at being relatively direct—and doing the hard work of finding and fighting for a superior alternative. If responsibility is to be truly shared, members cannot weakly dissent and walk away. Instead, they must advocate for what they think is right, even when what is right for the unit takes precedence over personal comfort or pleasing the boss.

Example at Electrobuild

Lee, the HR manager of "Electrobuild" was meeting with Herb, the CEO, to discuss ways to reduce excessive turnover among women who were midlevel engineers and managers. Herb attributed these departures to the pull of family on these particular women. "I don't think it's that simple," Lee argued. "Some aspects of our company make it an inhospitable place for many women."

Lee wanted to explain the elements of the company culture that caused the turnover, but Herb turned to his telephone, indicating that he didn't want to discuss the issue further. Lee realized that he was fighting an uphill battle, and like any subordinate, he was tempted to back off. Herb didn't like being pushed on touchy subjects. But Lee felt strongly that this was a critical matter with far-reaching consequences that Herb simply wasn't seeing. So, taking a deep breath, he tried again.

"I can see that you're not interested, Herb, but you haven't heard my point yet. The same culture that is encouraging some terrific women to leave is no less uncomfortable for some outstanding men." Herb stopped to listen. "Our tendency to pit one employee against another turns a lot of people off. They're choosing not to play the game, Herb. And some of the best ones are leaving to work for our competitors."

Herb turned away from his telephone and leaned forward. "Tell me more."

Most subordinates understand too well the concept of the *career-limiting move.* In heroically based organizations, they recognize their vulnerability and operate under the "better safe than sorry" principle. Unlike Lee, the HR director, they do not test the willingness of their bosses to hear bad news. And experience teaches them not to trust managers who claim to want to hear their ideas.

But subordinates too often use the fear of retaliation as an excuse for not testing whether pushback is possible. They interpret innocuous behavior or incidents as signs that the boss can't be pushed. Even when a manager is sincere in adopting a new style, ambivalent subordinates can always find something to support the belief that their boss is only mouthing slogans and really hasn't changed. Remember how John Sloan's reasonable decision to postpone a scheduled off-site meeting was seen as proof of his reverting to old behavior?

Leaders are not the only ones whom team members must learn to challenge in the post-heroic environment. They must also learn to challenge each other. This means that certain comfortable habits, such as the old compact of "you stay out of my area and I'll stay out of yours," must be set aside. Furthermore, as the leader becomes more open about problems and concerns, team members must respond in kind. As the leader welcomes feedback from members, they should be open about performance issues with each other. All these factors can create a sense of personal vulnerability and ambivalence about moving toward shared responsibility.

Finally, while team members may welcome greater vulnerability on the part of their managers, they may be unsure how open they want to be with their subordinates. This can be nerveracking if the members have become comfortable with the idea of being slightly immune to honest feedback from below. Heroic organizations provide cover for managers: They can dodge the consequences of a negative outcome by passing the blame upward.

AN INTERACTIVE SYSTEM

The ambivalence of leaders and members to sharing responsibility for managing the unit can play back and forth in a self-defeating dance that keeps ending up where it started. When both leader and team members are ambivalent about managing post-heroically, the resistance of one party activates the concerns of the other. They keep the vicious circle turning. Fears about losing control cause the leader to tighten his or her grip, proving to team members that the leader isn't genuinely interested in change. When team members react by holding back, they confirm the leader's conviction that it would be premature to let go. When leaders are uncomfortable about their own vulnerability, they deliberately mask their uncertainty, supporting the belief of subordinates that openness is somehow dangerous. If team members disguise their own vulnerability to play it safe, the leader suspects they are concealing something, and responds with caution to what they say. If the leader is conflict avoidant, team members hold back controversial views, fearing retribution. Their reluctance to work at resolving genuine disagreements convinces the leader that they are not ready to share full responsibility. And so the circle turns.

A pivotal meeting at Biotekk between Ben, the director of training and development, and Patrick, the CEO, shows how the interactive pattern between a leader and a team member can reinforce mutual ambivalence.

Example at Biotekk

Patrick bought into the notion of managing post-heroically, which would be a major change from the heroic style of his predecessor. But Patrick had doubts. He worried that this large organization might not be able to internalize a major shift in management approaches.

Patrick had initiated the change process at the level of his executive team, but the new management approach had not cascaded to the ranks below. To remedy the situation, he asked Ben to design a training program for that purpose.

Ben had mixed feelings about his assignment. He was personally receptive to the new form of leadership but thought that the individualistic culture of the company would find shared responsibility demanding. He also questioned whether the commitment at the top was sufficient. Employees already joked about Biotekk executives being charter members of the "Fad-of-the-Month Club." Would this new cure-all be another passing fancy? He also knew that there would be resistance and that he would have to expend some of his credit to gain acceptance. He didn't want to squander his time and credibility championing a program that would be left high and dry by Patrick and other senior executives.

Ben laid out his plans for the training program to Patrick. After going over the details, Patrick leaned back with a worried look and asked, "Ben, this looks good, but do you think that this is too much too soon? Do you think our managers are ready for a change of this magnitude?"

Ben's heart sank, but he mumbled that he thought it would work. Leaving the meeting, Ben stepped into the office of Debra, a colleague in whom he frequently confided.

"Deb, I'm worried about the new leadership program. I'm not convinced that Patrick and the executive team are really committed to it. It's going to take us months to develop this program, train the trainers, and get people through the sessions. But will Patrick and his people back us up if we meet serious resistance? And what will happen the first time a manager explodes when his subordinates tell him what they think about his management style? Will Patrick come around to pick up the pieces?"

Although Ben continued to work on the program, his heart wasn't in it, and he created a watered-down version to be "sure that we don't make managers too uncomfortable." As a result, the first two pilots were not well received, the program died a silent death, and the executives concluded, "Our managers aren't ready for this." Biotekk's middle managers chalked it up to "another fad that came and went." Patrick blamed Ben for not creating a strong program, and Ben told his colleagues that Patrick and his team weren't ready for real change.

Patrick and Ben reinforced each other's ambivalence, reducing Ben's willingness to invest in a valuable training program. His avoidance of risk reduced the program's effectiveness, confirming to his boss that the organization wasn't ready for a new leadership style. Failure to address the ambivalence the participants brought to the program's development resulted in wasted effort and resources, and lost opportunity.

REDUCING LEADER AMBIVALENCE

It should be clear by now that it is not sufficient for the leader to become less controlling and assume that team members will automatically fill the vacuum of leadership and control. More is needed. The linked behavior of leaders and subordinates makes it necessary to change the system of mutually reinforcing interactions. While members must be certain that the leader is committed to change, the leader must be assured that team members will take up the mantle of shared responsibility, surface the critical issues, and be alert to backsliding.

The leader must usually make the first move in the process of change. But will the others follow? They will if four conditions prevail:

1. *The leadership approach is situationally appropriate.* Post-heroic leadership is not a universal model. There are circumstances in which a more controlling, heroic form will achieve equal or greater performance with less effort. Shared responsibility is only appropriate when:

   • Work tasks are highly interdependent.
   • External change is rapid.
   • Members have expertise the leader lacks.
   • The goals of most of the team members are compatible with those of the leader.

   If change is slow enough that the leader is able to keep up with technology, new processes, and customer needs, and if subordinates are neither competent nor committed to similar goals, then heroic leadership can work well. If direct reports work relatively independently of each other, the leader may be able to provide the necessary coordination and control without having to micromanage.

2. *Team members can meet the challenge.* Members must be willing and able to acquire the skills necessary for sharing responsibility. If most of a group is relatively dependent and passive, unwilling to deal with conflict or take the larger perspective, shared responsibility is misplaced. But before too quickly concluding that members aren't up to the task, consider the possibility that their dependence and passivity may reflect their reaction to the current system. Have they just adapted

to heroic leadership? Is their show-me style true opposition or only a fear of being duped by the latest fad? Some will be ambivalent about the new leadership; others cannot or will not take on the new challenge. To proceed, most members must be capable of contributing to team activities. If there are serious doubts about particular members, the leader must decide whether to include them in a shared-responsibility team, or remove them before proceeding.

3. *The leader can resolve ambivalence.* Executives can do this by testing their ideas with peers at the same or other companies. Since most organizations have been reexamining their leadership practices in the past several years, it is now possible to find leaders who have dramatically changed their own practices, who know the joys and terrors of giving up control, becoming more vulnerable, and fostering healthy conflict. Personal testimony from a peer can be reassuring.

4. *The leader has support from above.* Not every potential post-heroic leader is as fortunate as John Sloan, whose boss was both supportive and willing to provide resources. That kind of support is not always necessary. Nor is the boss's traditional style of leadership an automatic impediment to change. Very few leaders, no matter how heroic their styles, will stop a subordinate from any managerial practices that produce superior results.

   It is less difficult to negotiate freedom to manage as you wish than ambivalent managers assume. You request autonomy for your style ("I need to manage in the ways that allow me to perform best") in return for agreed performance goals ("And then I can deliver the following . . ."). To do this you have to understand the boss's concerns and speak to them; your team's performance must be linked to the organization's basic goals (for more on this topic, see Chapter 8 and Appendix A, "Power Talk: A Hands-On Guide to Supportive Confrontation").

BEING POST-HEROIC IN A HEROIC ORGANIZATION

The last of the preceding conditions creates difficulties for managers who aim to adopt post-heroic leadership within a larger organization that continues to follow traditional leadership forms. How is that possible? Normally, change is seen as starting at the top and percolating down through the different levels of the organization. But, post-heroic leadership can start anywhere.

Example at First Data

Bob Radin was general manager of the mutual fund processing division of First Data, a financial services conglomerate. Since the division's inception six years earlier, Bob had been managing in countercultural ways, sharing responsibility with his team, using their detail orientation to complement his selling skills, doing all the people-oriented things that few other senior managers in the company bothered with or respected. Few in senior management of this numbers-driven company understood or supported Bob's style.

"I drive some of them crazy," he told us, "especially my boss, who lives and dies by the numbers."

Although the compounded growth rate of Bob's division exceeded 20 percent, his boss complained that Bob could have done better if he were more of a driver and less concerned about his employees and their morale. Bob's response was straightforward: He was interested in long-term growth and sustained relationships with customers. He was not interested in driving up one year's numbers at the expense of service deterioration. When pressed, he reminded his boss of what the CEO told him years earlier, that consistent growth from year to year was most important, and that it made no sense to borrow from next year's business by artificially pumping up a good year's performance.

When his boss got on his case about his soft style, Bob pointed to his track record, saying, "I am who I am; I'm not going to change what I believe or how I manage, but I will keep delivering growth and profits." Inevitably, the boss would mutter about how much better Bob could have done, then back off.

Bob was gratified by recent developments in the company. The senior management group engaged a team of expensive consultants who pushed the "value-added service profit chain" concept. Bob found this amusing, describing it as a fancy name for what he had always done. Even more gratifying, customers interviewed by the consultants gave their highest satisfaction ratings to Bob's unit, which was now being held up as a model to the other division heads. Bob told people that a manager's relationship with subordinates and their relationship with customers is closely linked. "Treat your people right," he said, "and they will treat the customers right."

Bob had discovered that strong financial and customer satisfaction results were his best defense for a leadership style that appeared too soft. Not only did he protect himself by delivering, but he had a clear business rationale for why his style worked.

The Leap of Faith

The leader who wants to build shared responsibility must resolve his or her ambivalence to the point of withstanding the temptation to fall back on old ways of leading and managing at critical moments. The ambivalence, to some degree, will probably always be there. But faith in the new approach must have the greater weight.

Do not underestimate the importance of committing to the new leadership without total proof in advance. Faith is, indeed, a precondition for important change in general. Motorola president Chris Galvin revealed to members of the Total Quality Forum his personal discovery that introducing new practices into any organization demands a commitment from the leader that often involves a leap of faith. Since any new idea is by definition unproved, the leader must somehow become convinced that it is worth the risk. Without the leader's deep commitment, the organization will never go through the pain and learning required for implementation.

Faith can come from a sudden insight, from contact with a persuasive advocate, or from an experience that causes one to see the world in a different way. Any of these may trigger a conversion through which the leader sets aside earlier beliefs and assumes new ones, suddenly seeing a pattern in previously unconnected views. We have witnessed these conversions in corporate executives who attend our leadership seminars. There, honest feedback from subordinates, peers, a boss, or strangers often flips some internal switch; the executive sees the potential benefits of post-heroic leadership and vows to try it.

But leaders must sustain their faith long enough for the initial attempts at post-heroic leadership to produce measurable results. During that time, ambivalence and resistance urge a return to the status quo. Once there has been measurable progress, however, it is easier to persevere through setbacks and team member skepticism.

RESOLVING MEMBER AMBIVALENCE

Leader commitment goes a long way toward overcoming the ambivalence that team members have about switching to the new leadership. In the interaction between Patrick, CEO of Biotekk, and Ben, head of training, Patrick's lack of commitment intensified his subordinate's ambivalence. Had Patrick said "I am behind this program all the way and in order to make it successful will do whatever is necessary to overcome my reservations about the readiness of others, and make sure they can handle this." Ben likely would have exchanged ambivalence for confidence.

We have observed leaders who were attracted to post-heroic leadership, but whose own doubts, like Patrick's, inevitably undermined the change they sought. In one high-tech company, the leader kept flirting with shared responsibility but backing away from the difficult strategic situations the members needed to address. Whenever they appeared uncomfortable about an impending decision, the leader would "take their views under advisement" and then make the decision alone. The executive committee finally told him, "If you want to do this, you'll have to go all the way. Otherwise, we will gladly go back to the old ways and let you make the tough decisions."

Determination to go forward does not prevent the leader from admitting to doubts or concerns. Subordinates would be surprised if their leaders didn't feel some doubts. The key is to simultaneously express commitment even while acknowledging that there is much to learn in making the post-heroic style work.

Ambivalence may persist even in the face of actual change; it took the members of John Sloan's team a long time to believe that he truly intended to change his leadership style. The best way to deal with lingering and deeply seated member ambivalence is to surface all concerns and deal with them openly and directly.

Example of Fortune 500 Executive Team

Executives of a Fortune 500 company had initiated several efforts to become a team, but their enthusiastic starts had always sputtered to a halt. The CEO was still determined to make it work. As a final attempt, he scheduled a four-day off-site meeting to break through the inertia.

The meeting started with a discussion of the team's activities. The consensus was that this team was not working well. Suddenly Tom, a key manager, broke in:

"What you have said is all true, but we have been there before. We all vowed that we'd change the way we operate, but there hasn't been any follow-through, and so nothing has changed. Why should I expect anything different this time?

"Frankly, I'm tired of this process. Every time we try this, it gets bloody, and one of us ends up leaving the company. Trying to change the way we work just hurts people. Why should we go through it again?"

After a stunned silence, other members of the executive team began to express similar feelings. They weren't enthusiastic about their way of functioning and could see the potential gain from changing, but they were also worried about the potential pain. The CEO acknowledged other, less demanding ways to improve group performance that stopped short of full shared responsibility. "Just improving meeting skills—clarifying agendas, specifying who would be responsible for following up on decisions made, and the like," he said, "would be helpful. But while producing a better functioning group, these procedural changes alone would not produce a real team. Which do you want?"

In subsequent discussion, the executives explored the pros and cons of becoming a team. They also examined some of the reasons why past efforts had been bloody and unproductive. The CEO made it clear that he didn't think they should settle for less than genuine collaboration; anything less would eventually fail.

As a result of being able to surface and openly discuss their feelings of ambivalence, the executives committed to doing the work needed to become a shared responsibility team. And this time they succeeded.

Commanding Change

Paradoxically, the leader cannot always share the responsibility for deciding to move toward shared responsibility, but in many cases, must command it. This is often the only way to overcome the skepticism and ambivalence of subordinates, who need proof that the new management approach is serious. A decision to impose democracy is neither inconsistent nor hypocritical. The leader is entitled to decide which style of management will work best for the organization over the long run, and insist that others adopt it. There is still ample room for engaging the full collaboration of team members in how to implement the new style.

It would be inconsistent with our view of leadership, however, if we argued that only a leader can initiate and help work through ambivalence. Here are some ways team members can contribute without waiting for the command to change:

- *Ask the leader questions.* Are you really committed to this? Are you satisfied with the way we now operate? Are you ready for open conflict?

- *Own your ambivalence.* Admitting your vulnerability will make it easier for the leader and others to acknowledge theirs.

- *Demonstrate understanding and sympathy for the leader's ambivalence.* Acknowledge that it is hard to plunge ahead without more experience, but that going backward would also create problems for everyone.

- *Inquire about inconsistent behavior.* Team members can help by identifying leader and organizational behaviors that are inconsistent with the advocated leadership style.

- *Show the consequences of blocking conflict.* Point out how premature closure of discussion prevented the best decision from being made in particular instances.

- *Demonstrate your own enthusiasm.* When you feel positive, say so. Sometimes others with positive feelings will hold back thinking they are alone; it helps to have someone take the risk of saying that the new way is attractive and worth doing.

- *Push resistant colleagues.* Team members can support change by challenging those who drag their feet, hold back, or try to sabotage the movement to post-heroic leadership. The leader shouldn't the only one to work for the new system.

- *Suggest data collection.* When all else fails, suggest that the team might learn to be more effective if it did a survey or activity that would provide data about work processes. That can provide the basis for an open discussion of how all parties could improve performance, and allow deeper exploration.

CONCLUSION

The payoffs of post-heroic leadership are high, but so too are the transaction costs. And those costs are inevitably incurred before the participants can tally the benefits. Thus, leaders and members must do what they can to reduce ambivalence, keep focused on the benefits, and actively engage in the practice of the new leadership.

Where should one begin? There is no single best way to become a post-heroic leader with shared-responsibility members. The aspiring post-heroic leader can tackle team norms and procedures, core strategic questions, a vision statement, interpersonal difficulties, or almost any aspect of leader-member operations. A good guideline is to begin the change process wherever people are most dissatisfied with the status quo. Wherever the effort starts, the other areas can be addressed as needed. When something is blocking good work, it should be moved to the forefront. Furthermore, most of these issues are never settled for all time. They are worked in iterative fashion, in a deepening spiral. The next chapter, for example, begins a closer examination of the challenges of building a shared responsibility team, but that is a matter of convenience, not rigid sequencing. Teams, vision and mutual influence work together.

THE THREE ELEMENTS OF POST-HEROIC LEADERSHIP

In Part One, the heroic and post-heroic leadership systems were introduced, along with an overview of the attractions and terrors of shared leadership. Part Two explains in depth the three elements needed to implement a new system of leadership: a shared-responsibility team, tangible vision, and mutual influence. Each reinforces the others, making it possible to create a team in which all members feel ownership for outcomes. Shared responsibility for managing and making most important decisions builds the commitment that enables high performance; tangible vision pulls team members together; and mutual influence skills make it possible to get the best from everyone. All three are needed to create a system of shared responsibility leadership and to prevent backsliding.

6

Building a Shared-Responsibility Team

Imagine a team whose members are each committed to the same vision and are fully collaborative. Everyone contributes his or her unique expertise, and everyone fights for what he or she believes to be best for the unit. These fights are spirited but not personal; they are motivated by differences over the best way to reach the common goal. Comradeship makes it possible for any member to ask for and receive help. Team members hold each other accountable for performance and confront those who are not carrying their weight.

The leader holds nothing back from team members, who will neither automatically give in nor resist because it comes from the boss. Instead, they embrace what makes sense and push back against what does not. There is no one-upsmanship, only total commitment to unit goals.

In view of the advantages of team decision making and team-based implementation, how many powered-up teams exist? How many bring people together to solve crucial problems, openly raise differences, or become deeply committed to each other's success? How often do executive teams achieve the free-flowing creativity that allows them to "jam" like musicians and invent the future together? The fact is that despite the clear benefits of teams, and despite the deluge of books and articles about them, most organizations do not use them. There are many "groups" but few effective teams, giving rise to this complaint from a senior marketing executive:

> *When I think of a team, I think of interaction, give-and-take, and shared purpose. Here, we're a collection of strong players but hardly a "team." We rarely meet as a team—rarely see each other, in fact. We don't particularly share the same views. I wouldn't say we actually work at cross-purposes, but a lot of self-centered behavior occurs. Where's the "team" in all this?[1]*

Listen to a member of a Hewlett-Packard customer service reengineering team contrast the old group battles with genuine teamwork:

> *Normal meetings are about assault and battery. You go in to stake out a position, defend it, and make sure you don't give up any ground. Here we're just accountable for business results . . .*
>
> *Here, we all ask questions and we all have to answer them. There's less individual risk and more team risk. . . . no individual is going to have the best idea, that's not how it works—the best ideas come from the collective intelligence of the team.[2]*

Another HP team member exclaimed:

> *I don't even relate to the notion of "working hard" anymore. I used to work like a slave, and when I dragged myself home all I wanted to do was drink. Now I don't feel that distinction between work and personal life. I couldn't tell you whether I work hard. What I know is that I don't suffer anymore.[3]*

Groups versus Teams

Most face-to-face collections of people in organizations operate as groups, even though many are (mis)labeled as teams.[4] Group members represent the areas for which they are held accountable. Groups may make decisions but are less likely than genuine teams to engage in the active problem solving that characterizes fully collaborative work. The emphasis in groups is to run efficient meetings with the aid of strong leadership that focuses discussion.

Teams are very different from groups. Though individual accountability remains, teams create a collective product. In meetings, teams mark their success by the quality of their decisions, not by the number of agenda items checked. Leadership is more generally shared among the members. Shared-responsibility teams can make the toughest decisions together. They face up to difficult strategic problems, redesign work processes or the organization, determine team member assignments, and when necessary, confront the leader and each other on troublesome behavior. This is unlike most management groups, even at the executive level, which rarely raise questions about a leader's methods or a peer's performance. The unstated objective in too many groups is to lobby for one's own area, and hope that the top executive will make a final decision favorable to it.

There is a place for groups, as Jon Katzenbach and Douglas Smith have written:

> *Working groups are both prevalent and effective in large organizations, where individual accountability is most important. The best working groups come together to share information, perspectives, and insights; to make decisions that help each person do his or her job better; and to reinforce individual performance standards. But the focus is always on individual goals and accountabilities.*[5]

Groups, however, do not create performance that is greater than the sum of their members' individual achievements.

They fail to add complementary perspectives and skills to the tough, complex decisions that address changing and difficult competitive environments. They may do good work, but they rarely soar.

High-performance teams are the basic vehicle for moving to post-heroic leadership. If members are to share the responsibility for the management functions of the overall team, they have to grapple with and resolve the core problems, and not just advise the leader. This requires that they embrace the larger good and not doggedly represent their own areas at all costs. In a top management team, each executive shares with the CEO concerns about companywide issues along with the perspectives of their respective functions or business areas; middle-level team members likewise share the leader's unitwide concerns.

Sharing in management demands that members challenge and influence each other. When members take on typical leadership responsibilities such as coordination and control, the leader can allow more discretion and autonomy. Mature teams can directly and constructively raise the difficult interpersonal issues.

Finally, teams are the best site for individual and collective learning. Becoming a learning organization can only happen when team members join together in diagnosing what is going well and what can be improved. Groups, with their separate fiefdoms, favor mutual protection or sniping at a distance, rather than the tough self-examination that is the basis of individual and collective learning. When a team has built trust and a sense of common purpose, everyone is freer to learn from experience and from one another.

BUILDING A TEAM

In the early 1990s, the executive team at Krupp faced difficult conditions: the company was stagnating; there was a global downturn in demand for its products; profitability had fallen into the cellar; and it faced a hostile takeover threat. Nevertheless, the company learned to operate in the new collaborative mode:

> *But the Krupp executive committee is something more than a collection of strong individual managers. The group has also worked hard to balance individual strengths with a highly integrated perspective on the long-term needs of the business. . . .*
>
> *In the old Krupp, senior managers played classic functional roles, and different points of view were never fully reconciled. The company's various parts did not reinforce one another. The current group of five executives brings all the pieces of the business together among themselves, arguing out the points and pressing one another to see if they have enough knowledge to act. They are continuously re-thinking the company's course.*[6]

To gain effectiveness, the executive team at Krupp focused on four areas we deem critical: Change leader and member role expectations; learn to deal effectively with the organization's strategic issues; deal with those issues through consensual problem solving; and complete the several stages of group development that end in full collaboration.

CHANGING ROLE EXPECTATIONS

One reason real teams are rare is the lingering presence of the heroic mind-set. That mind-set fosters expectations about the roles of leaders and team members that preclude change. The leader must be explicit about his or her intentions to operate in a different way, and about his or her expectation that team members will also change their behavior. In the absence of this clear message, members will question the leader's depth of commitment and wonder whether it is safe to state their opinions forcefully or push back against the leader's views.

The relationship of members to leaders must also change. Members must stop thinking and acting as deferential subordinates who offer only opinions; they must begin behaving as committed junior partners. Members must also change the ways they deal with one another; they must become partners in the success of the overall team, holding each other accountable for more than subunit performance.

Based on their previous experiences and assumptions, most team members believe that the team is "the boss's team," set up to provide advice and counsel at the boss's pleasure. This attitude runs deep and is supported by the beliefs of the wider culture. Thus, most members reflexively accept the top person as the one who decides the tough issues. For a team to function effectively, it must exorcise this embedded attitude. Team members must understand the difference between being a group in which members are supposed to give advice and counsel, and being a team where the members and leader share ownership of the decisions. This is the first step in getting members to share responsibility.

Changing expectations require that people free themselves from past experiences. An executive in a major oil company recalled to us how he learned to stay in the subordinate role:

> As a young manager, I attended a meeting that was going off-track. Members were taking potshots at each other's projects and deviating from the meeting's agenda. I decided to take responsibility for getting the meeting back on track. I thought that it was my duty as a team member to do everything in my power to improve the quality of the meeting. I found out otherwise! I was immediately characterized as insubordinate. Who did I think I was? Why was I acting like the section supervisor? I was ostracized and punished for months.

It takes only a few experiences like this to reinforce the idea that subordinates should remember who is the boss and, like obedient children, speak only when spoken to. The aspiring post-heroic leader, then, must establish new norms. Bob Saldich did this when he was CEO of Raychem. He formed a new Division Managers Council and told its members that they were "to collectively be the COO and act together with that mind-set." According to one participant, this announcement was greeted with shocked silence. After he left the room, the first comment was, "But we can't really define our role until the executive team first defines its role." Even when they had the green light to act, these high-level executives held back. Followership is difficult to give up, so compliance with the new dual role does not come automatically. Clarity about the leader's expectations helps.

When Raymond Gilmartin took over as Chairman and CEO of Merck, company executives wanted only to promote the interests of their own areas. He quickly insisted on a different orientation. As *Business Week* reported:

> *Without criticizing his predecessor, the much-admired physician-CEO P. Roy Vagelos, Gilmartin has quietly dismantled the turf-conscious, defection-ridden culture Vagelos left behind. . . . Gilmartin pushes staffers to air problems and debate without regard for hierarchy—and without getting personal. "Where you want the contest is not among people but among ideas," he says. "It's very important for people to be able to challenge, to be very open."*[7]

DEALING WITH THE BIG ISSUES

One way for the leader to demonstrate real commitment to the new style of managing is to involve team members in resolving strategic issues through joint decision making. This indicates that more than "advice and counsel" is expected from them.

Team members cannot be moved to share responsibility for overall team success if they are not dealing with key decisions. No amount of preaching about collective ownership is as effective as replacing the minor tactical problems that fill most agendas with the big issues that determine the team's success or failure. Why would members invest in the team, and wear that second hat, if they are not dealing with matters of central importance?

Katzenbach and Smith argue that truly important tasks are rare so there can only be a few teams in any organization. This is only true if "important tasks" are thought of as big, once-in-a-blue-moon projects, and not the central responsibilities that managers traditionally reserve for themselves: decisions about purpose and direction, products and market strategy, job assignments, budget allocations, staffing, and promotion.

We have asked hundreds of managers to list the core problems of the next 12 to 18 months that must be addressed by the teams to which they belong. Typical answers include:

- "What's the life expectancy of our major product lines; is what's in the pipeline sufficient?"
- "Should we build or buy the new product? Should we joint venture?"
- "Can we afford to cannibalize our leading product? Can we afford not to?"
- "Should we move into a new country or region? If we do, how will we manage it?"
- "If we expand overseas, should it be just for sales, or include product development and manufacturing?"
- "How can we retain our key employees?"
- "We are not developing the kind of managers we will need; what should we do?"
- "We have overcapacity in one of our plants; what should we do about it?"
- "Our cost structure is out of line with our competitors."

When we ask, "And what is on the agenda of your regular staff meetings," we are greeted with nervous laughter, then apologetic answers:

- "Nothing of importance."
- "It's show-and-tell time, with each area reporting on its successes and trying to hide its problems."

- "We review the latest financials, update forecasts, and sweat bullets over being exposed. When real problems emerge, the boss says he will take them up off-line."

Every company has enough core issues involving policy, direction, people, and resource allocation to keep any team busy indefinitely. The world is changing too fast and competition is too aggressive to think that the critical work will ever be completed. When the tasks involved in sharing the team's management are added in, the list of what is important grows longer. Jointly dealing with issues that used to be considered the manager's prerogative, such as selection, job assignments, setting budgets, coordinating and controlling, can coalesce members into functioning as a true team.

Having said this, does this mean that teams operating at middle and lower levels will have no opportunities to handle major issues? We think not. Critical policy and managerial issues exist at all levels of the organization. The senior executive team has no monopoly on strategic issues; individuals and teams at any level in the organization can and should think strategically. Departments should examine their core functions, their positioning in the organization, who uses their services, and how those functions link with the larger organizational direction. They need to monitor the added value and alignment of key activities and programs with the organization's strategic intent.

External crises can also be used to galvanize into a shared responsibility team. A state of emergency or an impending disaster has a way of "concentrating the mind," as Samuel Johnson once said about hanging. Krupp faced a host of crises, and the willingness of its team to address the way it functioned was mainly due to the pressure of wrestling with those crucial external problems.

Crises help make the implementation of post-heroic leadership possible because the centrality of critical tasks becomes apparent to everyone. Also, the leader's commitment to change is more readily apparent and believable during a crisis. It is one thing to have the leader say, "I'm going to

---

How Much Is Too Much for a Developing Team to Handle?

There is a dilemma in giving a developing team big issues to wrestle with. A group that is not prepared to tackle them will quickly dissolve into unproductive forms of conflict. On the other hand, sticking with safe topics slows down a group's growth. The leader must somehow find a way to stretch the group without tearing it apart. We recommend the "Bradford and Cohen 15 Percent Rule" as a way out of this dilemma.

The 15 Percent Rule is this: To develop the team, the leader should stay about 15 percent ahead of the team's readiness (and perhaps the leader's comfort) to deal consensually with core issues. Each time be somewhat more open than is the norm; discuss more contentious, critical issues than usual. Keep raising the ante. Being way out front may be a larger step than leader or members can handle; doing less slows down the team development process.

---

change because I'm excited about this leadership book I just read," and quite another to be staring big problems in the face and hearing the leader say, "Our usual methods of managing are no longer working; we need to pull together and solve this if we are to survive."

The difficulty with relying on crisis as the force for changing leadership style is that the perceived need to act as a team may dissipate once the crisis passes. People tend to revert to old habits when the pressure is off. To avoid this, leaders and subordinates should build their new relationship around issues that are central to the organization's future and that will continue to challenge them over long periods.

PROBLEM SOLVING THOUGH CONSENSUS

Even when a team tackles strategic issues, it must choose how to make these decisions. Broadly speaking, there

Table 6–1. Decision-Making Options

Autonomous	Decision is made by leader alone.
Delegated	Decision, within specified parameters, is made by individual or group.
Consultation	Decision is made by leader after advice from team member(s). (Decision is leader's first choice.)
Joint	Decision is made by members and leader together through true consensus. (Decision not made until leader and members can actively support it even if not first choice.)

These choices are adapted from V. Vroom and P. Yetton, *Leadership and Decision-Making* (Pittsburgh, PA: University Press, 1973).

are four alternative ways of making decisions, as shown in Table 6–1.

The difference between consultation and joint decisions by consensus is that consultation leaves the ultimate decision with the leader, who has sole veto power, and reinforces the traditional assumptions that responsibility belongs with the leader. A sympathetic consultative leader who listens well may get good information and even spirited opinions from team members. However, the difference between the leader having the last say and joint decision making is profound. It is comparable to the difference between advising a friend to spend a great deal of money on a super vacation "because you really deserve a fling," and paying for half of the cost of the trip out of your own pocket. The depth of thought, level of risk, and personal investment in the outcome are significantly greater. Feeling your own toes stepped on is quite unlike seeing someone else's foot being tromped on, no matter how empathetic you may be. When the leader makes all important decisions, the members easily become interested observers and not committed partners, even when the leader makes decisions with which they agree.

Despite the superiority of attaining consensus for certain critical decisions, each of the four decision-making styles is appropriate at one time or another. Which style to use depends on:

- Who has the expertise (the leader, one member, the members collectively).
- The readiness of the team or individual to adopt the unit's goals.
- The time available for discussion.
- The commitment needed to carry out the decision.

In the right circumstances, a post-heroic leader can, and should, make some decisions autonomously, without discussion. If the leader has all the necessary information or expertise, the issue is not critical, and the solution can be carried out without full commitment of team members, then deciding alone is appropriate, not autocratic. In genuine

---

Table 6–2. When to Use Each Decision-Making Style

Autonomous
- You have sufficient expertise
- You have private information that can't be shared
- Time emergency
- You have made up your mind and won't be moved
- Problem is trivial

Delegative
- There is one clear expert
- Problem not that important
- Would be a developmental task
- You/team can live with the solution

Consultative
- It is within one person's area to implement
- Problem is of intermediate importance
- Want to avoid major errors
- Team is not (yet) working well

Joint
- Problem is important and complex
- No one expert; members together have the expertise
- High quality solution is desired

---

emergencies, there may be no choice but to act. However, when issues are complex and no one person is the expert, decisions by consensus are usually of higher quality if members are in basic agreement about the central strategic direction and are willing to take the larger perspective. If they operate only from the perspective of their individual functions, then consensus will be difficult. In this case, the decision will be made either by inappropriate compromises or by pushing the problem back to the leader.

The inability of teams to make decisions through consensus produces an interesting Catch-22. The leader thinks, "These people can't make decisions, so I'll only allow them to deal only with minor issues, or ask simply for their advice and counsel." When this happens, team members are permanently locked into the parochial orientation that fulfills the leader's expectation. With no opportunity to make important decisions through consensus, they never demonstrate their ability to do so. Then the leader never wants to share responsibility.

Even those who sincerely desire to move to post-heroic leadership get stuck on the concept of consensus decisions. "What if the team insists on doing something that seems wrongheaded to me?" they ask. "Should I go along?" Our answer is straightforward:

No leader should accept an obviously incorrect team decision on an important issue.

But how often is a team of intelligent managers obviously wrong? What if the criteria for a consensual decision appear to be met and still the outcome doesn't quite feel right to the leader? To answer this one, review the five criteria for a consensual decision. In general, a decision should be made jointly when:

1. The problem is complex.
2. No one person, including the leader, is clearly more expert than the collective expertise of the group.
3. Members have the relevant information.

4. The team is working well together, uses sound decision-making processes, and is aligned with overall goals.

5. The members are capable both of representing their own areas and considering the overall unit needs.

If the problem is truly complex but the other conditions are not in place, consider correcting the conditions. But if all five conditions fit and the decision still doesn't feel right, here are ways of determining whether the team is adhering to the preceding criteria and, if so, whether to override a consensus decision:

Do I really know more?

Ask yourself, "Am I really smarter and better informed than the collective team members?" The odds of this are not great. But if you think so, then ask, "Since each person has a preferred way of working, is what I want more a matter of personal style than objective quality?" Nevertheless, there are times when the leader knows more but cannot easily explain why.

In his research on artificial intelligence, Nobel Prize winner Herbert Simon concluded that a person needed about 50,000 discrete experiences ("chunks") to be an expert.[8] In any particular instance, the leader may actually have the 50,000 chunks, but they are so embedded in the daily experiences of 25 years of organizational life that it is difficult to be precise about why that answer is more likely to be right. The leader might have better ability to see a pattern in chaotic data, and thus have justifiable conviction about the outcome that others do not share. It could be difficult to convince them when "proof" is impossible.

Does the decision rely too heavily on rational or quantitative arguments?

This can be a problem with newly minted MBAs, who often believe, "If you can't measure it, it doesn't exist." Sometimes, however, the leader (or a member) has an intuitive understanding that does not readily compute or fit with the rigorous analytical methods that many rely on for decision making. This is particularly important when key decisions about the future are made. Even the most thorough market and technical analysis is incapable of providing a total answer about the future. In these cases, an experienced person may have insights that transcend quantifiable data. Colleagues who work from hard data and who manage by fact are not inclined to put much weight on these insights. But as senior partners in a top consulting firm known for its thorough, analytical work, and for trying to overwhelm clients with facts, confessed to us: "Sure, we need to crunch the numbers and pay close attention to the data, but when push comes to shove and we have to make recommendations to the client, we rely on what feels right."

Is the team completely committed to the unit's vision?

Members may appear to buy into the vision, but on a critical issue may have very different stakes and values. For example, it is one thing to agree in the abstract "that the company needs to become more global," but apparent commitment can evaporate when the time comes to place existing business units under a new global VP.

Is the team less fully developed than it appeared to be?

The team may appear to have grown, but members are still colluding to avoid touchy issues. Do business conditions, for example, call for a new distribution system that would displace a well-liked colleague? The team may turn itself inside out to avoid making such a tough choice, even though everyone knows it is imperative.

Are members captive to outdated assumptions?

Team members may be blind to radical changes in circumstances. Experience can create perceptual filters that block the ability to recognize new conditions. The team might be working well together, but within an obsolete set of assumptions. Eileen Shapiro has written convincingly about executive teams that can't see the handwriting on the wall, even when it is in large capital letters. They get into trouble, she says, using Will Rogers's colorful expression, "When what they think they know ain't so."[9]

Options for the Leader

When the team is going astray, the leader may have to step in and say, "Sorry, but we need to do it my way, even if you disagree." Doing this runs the risk of unraveling whatever progress has been made through the stages of group development. Overriding a team decision in the early stages of development, before trust has developed, risks the possibility that members will say, "When push comes to shove, the boss doesn't really mean it." Grabbing back the reins too often will confirm this belief and cause regression to the old heroic state.

But overriding team decisions is not the leader's only option when those decisions don't make sense. This could be the opportunity to deal directly with the difficulties in a way that further develops the team's commitment to a new way of operating. If the leader sees the team's questionable decision as a product of self-protection, he or she can bring this to members' attention. If the erroneous decision appears to be a function of inexperience, it may be possible to create opportunities for team members to obtain that experience. For example, if the environment is changing, it would help for members to meet with key customers who are dissatisfied or with prospective customers who have new, unrealized demands.

Another option is to consider whether some vital aspect of the post-heroic model is missing. This is especially important when disagreement about a decision stems from the failure of the leader and team members to share the same vision of what the organization seeks to accomplish. In this case, the disputed topic should be put on the shelf while leader and team members build alignment with a common vision.

Yet another option is for the leader to raise every concern about the decision and challenge the team to speak to each. This puts the burden on the team to come up with answers to the anticipated problems that make the leader reluctant. It asks the team to solve the problems rather than drawing the leader into inventing heroic solutions or more objections, and acknowledges that there may be unanticipated paths to a satisfactory resolution. Many leaders have discovered that the challenge to the team results in them developing a solution that is creative and wildly successful, because more options are considered and the team is more committed to its implementation.

Finally, the distinction between heroic and post-heroic leadership is *not* the abolishment of autonomous decisions; it is the responsibility that the entire team feels for the management of the unit. An occasional autonomous decision contrary to the wishes of the group won't automatically shift that responsibility back—especially if the leader has a track record of consensual decision making on crucial items. When there is trust, the group will "give one to the leader."

The rare occasions, such as the bet-the-company decision, when the leader can't avoid taking back major responsibility should not become an excuse for leaders to revert to the old way of managing. Although the desire to build shared responsibility must be balanced against the need for timely, bold action, when the team is developed, aligned around appropriate goals, and willing to take on each other and the leader, the leader seldom knows best. The option for rejecting member convictions is always there, but must be used sparingly and with great care.

DEVELOPING THROUGH STAGES TOWARD FULL COLLABORATION

The challenges of moving a management group from its current state of separate fiefdoms to sharing responsibility for the core issues can seem overwhelming. Is it possible to get the members to communicate openly, to hold each other accountable, to consider all the relevant data before plunging into decisions, and to work through interpersonal differences and individual agendas? Even top management teams often suffer from inadequate or difficult individuals, collective skill deficiencies, groupthink, and the fragmentation that comes from executives pursuing their own agendas.[10]

One of the most useful ways to begin the journey to shared leadership is to think of group development as proceeding through stages.[11] Research indicates that task groups develop through five fairly predictable stages: (1) membership, (2) sub-grouping, (3) conflict, (4) individual differentiation, and (5) collaboration (or shared responsibility)[12] (see Table 6–3).

The stages are sequential and skipping any one usually causes problems. Each stage adds a crucial dimension to effective team interaction and creates the platform for the next stage. Passage through these stages should not be rushed since any central issues not fully resolved will cause problems later. Thus, the job of both the leader and member is to help the group work the issues at each stage.

No model ever replicates reality perfectly, and this one is no exception. In practice, groups move backward as well as forward, and can get stuck, especially around the conflict stage. So it is not inevitable that groups naturally will progress to Stage 5—in fact, relatively few do so unless there is conscious and concerned effort by the leader and members.

In the following sections, we briefly examine each of the five stages, describing the core themes and the typical behaviors of members. This sequence generally is applicable to any interdependent work group—a newly formed management team, a temporary task force, or an established group trying to convert to the post-heroic leadership system. (The task force, however, may compress the time in the stages, either moving rapidly through them or dissolving at the Subgrouping stage because members fail to commit to the goals.)

Teams can complete real work in all stages. This is not a matter of "development now for productivity later." At any stage, a team must accomplish whatever the unit requires. In early stages, however, the leader must pay extra attention to group process, (the *way* the group works), and more actively manage it than in later stages. Over time, members will assume a greater share of the responsibility for monitoring and improving the group's processes. The leader's overall focus

Table 6–3. The Stages of Group Development

	Membership	Subgrouping	Conflict	Differentiation	Collaboration
Group Issues	Finding one's place	Finding allies	Fighting over direction	Doing one's job	Sharing responsibility for team success
Atmosphere and Relationships	Cautious, feelings suppressed, low conflict	Apparent closeness within subgroups, cross-group sniping	Hostility across subgroups	Workmanlike, satisfied, mostly open, honest differences	Supportive, demanding, open, direct, expressive, fights over issues
Goal Understanding and Acceptance	Low, not clear to all	Some misperceptions but increasing clarity	In dispute	Most agree	Commitment to tangible vision
Listening and Information Sharing	Intense but high distortion and low disclosure	Similarities within subgroups less than perceived	Poor	Reasonably good	Excellent, rapid, direct
Decision Making	Dominated by active members	Fragmented deadlocks, to boss by default	Dominated by loudest, most powerful	By individual expertise, often by boss after consultation	By consensus when all resources needed, individual when one clear expert
Reaction to Leadership	Tested by members, tentative	Resisted, often covertly	Power struggles, jockeying for position	General support, individual variations in influence	Highly supportive but free to disagree vigorously
Attention to Group Process (way the group works)	Ignored	Noticed but discussed only in subgroups outside meetings	Used as weapon against opponents	Sometimes displaces tasks, or is accepted uncritically	Discussed as needed to aid work, anyone initiates

Note. Adapted from Steven L. Obert, "The Development of Organizational Task Groups," (Ph.D. dissertation, Case-Western Reserve University, 1979).

on team development should be on helping the team make decisions that move it through the earlier stages.

Teams are built to accomplish complex and demanding work. The primary purpose is not to make people feel good or to like each other. Thus, the best way to move team members to real collaboration and shared responsibility is through day-to-day work. Social activities, outdoor adventures, and off-site feel-good sessions may temporarily increase goodwill, but rarely create lasting collaboration.

To understand the dynamics behind the five stages, it is important to keep in mind the issues that groups face and members experience. Each team has to:

- Establish norms of behavior.
- Determine how power and influence are to be exercised.
- Decide what can be talked about directly.
- Agree on how disagreements are to be handled.
- Determine the roles and responsibilities of the leader and members.

Being in a group also raises individual issues of acceptance, power, authenticity, and accomplishment: Am I accepted? How do I get influence? How am I supposed to act? and, Will my goals be met?"[13] These are concerns that the five stages must address.

Stage 1. Membership

The first stage deals with joining up. Members are concerned about the price of membership and ask themselves:

- To what extent do I want to be a (full) member of this group?
- What are the requirements for being a member? Can I meet them?
- How committed do I want to be under those conditions?
- Will I have a meaningful role, be respected, be listened to?

- Do I want to be part of a team that shares responsibility, or do I prefer the traditional way?

Whether the group is newly formed or one making the transition to post-heroism, all members struggle with these questions. People feel each other out and try to figure out what the game will be. Early meetings are cautious; members float trial balloons about their interests or suggest possible goals to test their influence. A fair amount of joking covers personal anxiety.

Unless the leader intervenes, individual concerns about membership make it difficult for a team to accomplish any serious work during this stage. Only safe subjects are discussed; only safe opinions are ventured on conflict-laden topics. A bold individual may try to preempt the views of others on important subjects, but since members are more concerned with their influence than with the quality of their decisions, such initiatives are usually blocked. Conversation tends to be guarded and decision making labored as people assess each other and try to position themselves in a favorable light.

The leader and members can move a group quickly through this initial stage, aiding natural progress. They can make space for members to talk about their histories and skills, their objectives, or their concerns about the group. Members "join up" at different times and with different levels of commitment, but relatively quickly the group will move to the second stage.

Stage 2. Subgrouping

Members of new teams, or of teams with new charters, are concerned about being isolated or left out of the action. Therefore, the central question for individual members in Stage 2 is, "Who are my allies?" Seeking allies is a natural way to reduce isolation. It is similar to the cocktail party phenomenon: When people enter a party where there are many strangers, the first thing they do is scan the room until they identify a familiar face; they'll then move toward that person, even if he or she is not a particular favorite. If no friends or acquaintances are visible, the individual tries to spot someone who looks *simpatico,* using whatever evidence is available—usually dress and other nonverbal signals such as posture and facial expression.

Thus, people quickly form subgroups with those who seem similar in beliefs and goals. Relieved of the fear of isolation, members offer verbal support for the positions of their new allies and signal their disapproval of nonmembers of the subgroup through nonverbal means: exchanged glances expressing "us-against them" solidarity, eye-rolling, shaking of heads in disagreement.

Although the Subgrouping stage is marked by more direct expression of views than the previous stage, conflict remains veiled. Because so much of what members actually think and feel is expressed only outside the group's meetings, or appears on hidden agendas, discussions are like wading through molasses; meetings proceed in slow motion (with members wishing that they could fast forward the videotape). The universal jokes about meetings and groups ("we keep minutes but waste hours") underscore the lack of directness that makes group work torturous. These feelings cross many cultures: Even the rational French have a wonderful word for endless meetings, *reunionitte,* a sarcastic diminutive of the word for meeting, *reunion.*

This veiled way of operating creates tension for members, who want to shape the decisions that the team is now beginning to address, but don't feel sufficiently secure to be direct. Overt conflict would be too threatening, but total passivity would allow others to prevail. So opposition goes underground and expresses itself in blocking or passive noncompliance.

This stage has value in that the peer support of subgroup allies results in more issues being put on the table, even if the degree of directness and openness is less than desirable. Peer support is a necessary precondition for the next stage. Few people want to be in the position of total isolation in a group, and fewer still will express strong views or provoke conflict without some assurance that others will provide support.

If the leader is trying to move to the post-heroic leadership system, subgroups may form between those wanting full partnership and those who are skeptical about it or about the leader really behaving as promised. So the subgroups can be formed around preferred operating styles as well as around strategy, policies, or other business issues. Unfortunately, many groups never progress beyond the subgrouping stage. They can't handle conflict directly, so become frozen into unproductive time-wasting.

Stage 3. Conflict

This stage of group development is the great divide. As the team deals with increasingly important business and procedural issues, members naturally want to shape the outcome. Reasonable people can and usually do differ—often passionately—as to the best strategic direction, the optimal resource allocation, or other future-defining issues. Resolution is essential to move forward. Members must deal with several critical questions: "Whose views will prevail?" "Will this escalate out of control?" "Will any of us be hurt if we fight?" and "Will I remain a respected member if I lose an argument about the future?"

Differences are not only inevitable but highly desirable. Without it, teams develop excessive conformity or "groupthink," and fall prey to distortions of reality. Leaders rightly worry when they hear no dissenting voices. As the CEO of a global financial services firm put it:

> *There's a lack of genuine debate. Sometimes there's a half-hearted "devil's advocate" gesture, but they really don't confront each other or me on the big issues. We're too comfortable, too self-congratulatory. It's become obvious to me in the past few months. I have to find a way to shake things up.*[14]

Differences must be thoroughly argued and resolved if quality decisions are the goal.[15] Still, many people are inclined to avoid or suppress differences and the conflict that goes with them. For some groups (and managers), the thought of impending conflict is so frightening that it is quickly suppressed and the group stalls at Stage 2.7. The fear is that the very existence of the group may be threatened by conflict: "Will we break apart if different sides go head to head?" Individuals worry whether they will lose face or standing if they lose a fight. They also worry about the effect of conflict on relationships: "If the two of us disagree, will that permanently damage how we interact?"

The underlying concern is that task disagreement will degenerate into a personal attack. Team members now have more data about the interpersonal styles of the others, and more feelings about them. Does Terry have to dominate discussions? Will Juanita ever say what she is thinking? Can Fred stop making jokes at Jean's expense? Can we really expand our customer base given Bart's tendency to disparage non-technical buyers? It can seem impossible to raise these interpersonal issues without being personally attacking, but it is hard to get work done when the style of others is so closely intertwined with their ability to be effective and the interdependence among members.

In other situations, the battle is joined but successful resolution is never achieved—an experience both painful and nonproductive. As a result, disagreements go underground but continue in the form of unproductive sniping. Groups that fall into this trap never develop as successful shared responsibility teams. In other cases, contending factions sink to open warfare in which winning becomes more important than the quality of the solution. This has the advantage of putting the issues out on the table, but results in compromises at best, not creative solutions.

Groups are only able to move beyond Stage 3 when their members learn how to deal with differences. Few groups make this transition, which explains why so many meetings are unproductive. Complaints such as "We never seem to close on a decision, and even when we do, the agreement unravels and we have to go through it again next time," or, "Meetings are assault and battery" are tell-tale signs of a group that can't face its differences squarely and get them resolved.

Moving through conflict is so central that Chapter 11 is devoted to showing what leaders and members can do to move the group to the next stage.

Stage 4. Individual Differentiation

Something remarkable happens once a team has successfully worked through a major dispute and come to agreement. The atmosphere changes—and for the better. Discussions are reasonable and sniping ends. Suddenly, everyone has found an acceptable place on the team. No one needs to hide behind a subgroup any longer; instead, all can act as individuals, (the reason for calling this stage "individual differentiation"). Subgrouping may still occur, but membership is now fluid and changes as people reconfigure alliances around specific issues. Members are trusted to do their jobs; those who fail to deliver hear about it. Meetings are no longer time-wasters, but occasions for getting work done. Members look forward to meetings and the time they spend with their colleagues. This new atmosphere follows the resolution of differences about the underlying tasks of the team and its interpersonal relationships. Even more important, team members have acquired ideas for how to talk through disputed issues; this gives them confidence that they can solve future problems.

In struggling through to this stage, the team usually has to deal with interpersonal baggage accumulated in earlier periods and discuss ways for individuals to live and let live. For the most part, members have satisfied their needs for acceptance, influence, and goal attainment. They feel free to be themselves. The group learns that it can deal productively with disputes, so that people and relationships will survive. The team is able now to examine the way it operates; this usually leads to agreements about more productive methods of dealing with conflict.

Organizational life would be vastly improved if all teams could reach this stage. However, the great potential for teamwork remains over the horizon. Having resolved a major conflict does not guarantee that new ones will never arise, and until a team gains confidence in its ability to work through any conflict, it can shy away from the big issues that fully developed teams can face.

At its worst, differentiation just allows everyone to pursue his or her subarea without conflict, but also without collaboration. As a frustrated CEO put it:

> *In our zeal to give autonomy, we've created a bunch of fiefdoms. Everyone's pursuing their own objectives. Right now, there's very little natural, informal communication or collaboration among these folks. We're facing some new marketplace shifts which affect the whole company, and unless we can get our act together, we will be passed by.*[16]

At its best, differentiation allows each person to feel responsibility for an area, and to trust that others will do their parts. But no one feels obligated to do more than hold others accountable for their commitments; going out of the way to help or to tackle cross-area problems isn't required. Stage 4 teams don't create synergy across members, where together they can invent solutions for marketplace shifts, unexpected new competition, more rapid product innovation and development, and so on. Whereas individuals are now free to be themselves, they do not benefit from collaboration, the goal of Stage 5.

Collaboration is achieved by making sure that the most problematic issues are fully addressed, the potential for interdependence among team members is understood and leveraged, and the development of every member is seen as the responsibility of all.

Stage 5. Collaboration

The central characteristic of this stage is fully shared responsibility, full commitment to the overall unit's goals and to the success of its members. Members share management of the unit with the leader, making the decisions on critical issues by consensus. No subject is out of bounds, including the leader's performance. The toughest issues are tackled in a timely way, with all members contributing both their functional expertise and general problem-solving skills. Members care for one another's welfare, but also hold each other accountable for results. In Stage 4 the group is only as strong as its weakest member; in Stage 5 it is stronger than its strongest member, because members adjust to and compensate for each other's styles and weaknesses, and give powerful support rather than accept benign co-existence.

In this stage, the team has the fluidity of a championship basketball team. Though each member has a primary role, improvisation occurs as needed, with instant shifts back and forth between offense and defense. Any member can flow into any activity to help the team win. Job descriptions do not limit a person's ability to contribute. John Sloan, general manager of Applico, Canada, labored mightily with his team to reach this stage; once they did, one member proudly observed:

> *We are now less functionally focused. We not only speak to others' areas but feel responsible for the whole business. A stranger who walked into one of our meetings wouldn't know who had which job because everyone is involved with the whole business.*

LEADING THROUGH THE STAGES

The stages just described provide a framework that can help a leader and members determine where a team is and how to move it along. The sequential process makes the job easier: One need only think about the next stage and what is required to get the team there.

When a group is in the Membership stage, anything that will help team members to understand each other's goals, aspirations, and concerns is useful for advancing it into the Subgrouping stage. Once it is in Subgrouping, the leader can help members spell out their differences, making them comfortable with the idea that conflict is inevitable, natural, and welcome.

In the conflict stage the leader can help the group focus on the real issues, avoid win-lose arguments or sub-optimizing decisions by exploring creative solutions, and openly address interpersonal disputes without letting them deteriorate into personal attacks.

Once a group has passed through conflict and into the Differentiation stage, the leader can move it forward by placing the organization's most important and challenging issues on the agenda, and expect the team to take responsibility for their resolution. Here, one of the advantages of post-heroic thinking becomes evident: What a traditional leader would view as a nasty problem—something too hot to handle—can be treated as an opportunity for growth. Once a team is into the Collaborative stage, the leader can be confident that team members will tear difficult problems apart, not each other.

Chapters 9 through 12 of this book revisit the Pharmco case to show how one company successfully worked through each of the five developmental stages.

In the iterative process of dealing with the most important issues by consensus, two key concerns are whether members will take the larger perspective and be able to resolve disagreements. The best safeguard is the development of a vision of the unit's highest aspirations. Once that vision is created and embedded in the way everyone thinks and behaves, the unit will rarely get off course.

7

CREATING COMMITMENT TO
A TANGIBLE VISION

In the early 1980s, when we did the original research for
Managing for Excellence, few people were talking about vision in organizations, and we groped for words to describe
it, eventually settling on the awkward term "overarching
goals."[1] Only a dozen years later, almost everyone has
grown cynical about vision and is sick of hearing about it.[2]
Telling a group of managers that they are about to embark
on a vision-building retreat is a sure way to induce eye-
rolling and wisecracks about "the vision thing."

Despite the power of vision to transform commitment and
performance, it has meant little more than empty slogans
for most managers. They have wasted valuable time formulating vision statements that were never embedded in practice. In other cases, visions were clear to people at the top
but meaningless phraseology to the people below. Or statements were too often about relationships and not about the
work that defined the organization.

Nevertheless, we have come to praise vision, not to bury it.
As much as it is scorned, it is critical to success today. A recent worldwide survey of 2,664 upper-level line managers
indicated that they ranked "actualizing a tangible vision"
as their highest need for effective leadership."[3] They also

reported that they were not very skilled at doing it, which may account for some of the skepticism.

Another problem is that academics and consultants have developed a profusion of related concepts and words to guide organizations as they choose direction. These experts have created their own definitions and have gilded them with subtle nuances. This lack of standard terminology has created a certain amount of confusion. In the present discussion, we apply the following meanings to these key terms:

- *Mission.* Objective description of the organization's business, purpose, or function.
- *Tangible vision.* A vivid, exciting description of the core purpose/mission; may include core values and beliefs. Can be applied to any unit within an organization.
- *Strategic intent.* A bold, strategic goal beyond the organization's immediate capabilities, but attainable in the middle future.

THE NEED FOR VISION

Vision is important to all leaders, but especially important for post-heroic leadership. Shared responsibility confronts leaders and direct reports with difficult challenges:

- Dealing with critical issues will be contentious. On what basis will we agree?
- Why should I give up the security of just dealing with my own area? What's the benefit?
- Sharing responsibility for managing requires that we influence each other. What will keep it from turning personal?
- My leader says he wants me to take initiative, but I'll be put into the penalty box if he doesn't agree with what I've done. How do I know what decisions to make?

- I will have to give up hands-on-control. How can I be sure that others will make the right decisions? How will team members coordinate with each other?

If subordinates are to act as partners with the leader, if they are to think and act without constant supervision, if they are to give more than is required, if their contributions are to have a context, then they all must be in close alignment about what the organization aims to accomplish. Members and leaders must be on the same wavelength. This is the purpose of organizational vision.

Robert Haas, CEO of Levi Strauss, reinforces the ways in which vision supports the post-heroic organization:

> *In a more volatile and dynamic business environment, the controls have to be conceptual. They can't be human anymore: Bob Haas telling people what to do. It's the ideas of a business that are controlling, not some manager with authority. Values [and a vision] provide a common language for aligning a company's leadership and its people.*[4]

Formulated well and used right, vision can be a driver of superior performance. Talking with Stanford MBA students, Carol Bartz, president and CEO of Autodesk explained:

> *I hate the word vision. But frankly I have come to appreciate the fact that you have to have a process that allows people to articulate a vision for the company. Now, what I get mad about is people spending months and quarters crafting the precise nine words that hang together. That's not what is important. What's important is having some sentences that allow everyone in the company to say: "Oh, I understand that, and therefore I know the direction this company is going."*

When properly implemented, vision is far more than a slogan; it is a means to inspire, coordinate, and align people.

When embedded in everyone's consciousness, vision provides a frame of reference for important decisions by team members that can be used for dealing with the unexpected and unanticipated. Vision makes it possible for individuals to transcend their narrow concerns and share in the management of the entire unit. It gives them the capacity to act in ways that are consistent with the organization's aspirations. It helps align individuals with other team members, with the unit, and with the larger organization.

Henry Ford did more than turn out cars; he had a vision for what his company could accomplish:

> *I will build a motor car for the great multitude . . . it will be so low in price that no man making a good salary will be unable to own one—and enjoy with his family the blessing of hours of pleasure in God's great open spaces . . . [In time] the horse will have disappeared from our highways, [and] the automobile will be taken for granted.*[5]

Ford's statement is more than the *mission* of his company—building motor cars—and more than its *strategy*—offering them at an affordable price. He wanted to excite people with the motor car's potential to transform society and make it possible for families to roam the great open spaces together. His vision is potentially inspiring, partly because it talks to human needs (whether or not people were previously aware of them) and partly because his evident passion for transforming leisure is captivating.

Because vision is so important, it isn't just the responsibility of top management, but of every manager throughout the organization. The larger vision must be retranslated at each level and connected closely to the specific work of that unit. Even when an organization has a well-formulated and accepted overall vision, each unit must determine its special, unique contributions, and have a way of describing the unit's work to give it as much significance as the whole organization's purpose. This chapter will focus on formulating and embedding vision in the middle of organizations.

One day, Bob Weissman, CEO of Dun & Bradstreet, was walking through the collections department and noticed a wall banner stating: "We Make Sales." Weissman did a double take, thinking that it was an unusual vision for a collections department. The department manager explained it to him this way:

> *If customers don't pay, it is for one of two reasons: They're angry at us because we somehow messed up, or their business is having troubles. If it is our mistake, and we fix the problem, they pay. If they're in trouble and we find a way to help them, they pay, and are grateful to boot. Either way, we bring in the equivalent of new sales, because it's money we wouldn't otherwise have. They might even order more. Besides, if you worked in this area, wouldn't you rather think of yourself as making sales than as hounding deadbeats for payments?*

This department leader saw beyond the routine to a grander vision that would make a difference to the people on his team and to those they serve. He didn't have fancy language, but gave new meaning to existing work and expanded their activities into new areas. Visions that are tangible, close to home, and compatible with the vision of the larger organization make a big difference in how people perform.

THE TANGIBLE VISION

An organizational vision is a verbal image that frames the organization's purpose and direction—what it stands for and where it is going—in an inspiring way. It is not a statement of "what we do," but of "what we could become." Yet it needs to be specific enough to be used as the basis for making decisions. The term *tangible vision* helps bring vision down to earth as a practical aid to decision making from the top of the organization to the bottom.

A tangible vision that has an impact on people is more than a lofty statement of intent enthusiastically delivered. In practice, it describes who is to be served, with what kinds of products, and often, modifies or expands the unit's practices.

There is a paradox in the tangible vision: It is as elusive as it is tangible. It identifies the direction to follow, but pinpoints no final destination. It is like the compass used by a voyager traveling west. A westward bearing will always be available from the compass, but the journey is potentially endless. There is no place called "West"; it is simply a direction, always beyond the horizon.

For organizational units, the tangible vision is like the journey west. They should pursue the vision without any expectation of reaching it, at least not for a long time. If it can be reached in the short term, it is not a vision but an intermediate task. Organizations that confuse tasks with vision, and then reach them, suddenly find themselves without a purpose.[6]

Formulating the Vision

Formulating the vision is a process of massaging the ideas and coming to understand their implications, not of seeking to "discover" a buried statement fully composed and ready to use.

For any given unit, there can be several possible visions that will work and still be compatible with the overall organization's vision. For example, think of the human resources department at a publishing company. It could see itself as "making work life easy for creative people," or as "providing the people and policies that assure an outstanding workforce." It could be a department devoted to helping streamline work processes to enable timely and low-cost publications. Any of these might fit and make the work meaningful.

Compare those options with the philosophy of the human resources (HR) department at IDG, a publisher of magazines on the computer industry and other information-based services. IDG is fast and entrepreneurial, with a decentralized structure in which each magazine's editor runs his or her own company. The rapid growth and entrepreneurial style have created a freewheeling culture. They don't easily sit still for HR rules or broad values statements. As a result, Martha Stephens, VP of HR, leads a department that has arrived at a quite different vision. She explained to us that her department aspires to "put ourselves out of business"—or at least out of the traditional HR business.

In running their own units, IDG managers are responsible for making and living with their own HR decisions. The HR group contracts with the manager to provide only those traditional HR activities desired—hiring, firing, setting pay, training, legal compliance, and so on—or the HR group can simply provide counsel to managers as an external consultant, with absolutely no control over whether or not the manager takes the advice. There is no forced conformity with the central HR group. The strategy to accomplish this fee-for-service involves doing only what the individual publishers and their magazines are willing to pay for. They negotiate yearly contracts with each unit to provide only the services they request.

The fee-for-services relationship forces IDG's HR people to be very close to their customers, to be efficient in delivering services, and to create services perceived as worth their costs. This has made the IDG HR group market-focused to the extent that it is now planning to turn itself into a profit center servicing both IDG and outside customers.

Two Forms of Tangible Vision

There can be two forms of tangible vision, *task-based* and *organization-based*.[7] Task-based vision refers to the work of the unit, the types of products, services, or technology that it wants to deliver better than others. Organization-based vision is about how the unit will operate, especially in relation to its employees and customers. What kinds of values will the unit aspire to? The "Aspiration Statement" that Robert Haas and his executive team development for Levi Strauss is more focused on the culture and how organizational members are to treat each other than it is on the role of blue jeans and leisure wear in society. Similarly, Hewlett-Packard pushes the "HP Way"; though this vision contains a commitment to high-end quality products, its emphasis is on relationships and conservative financial policies. The model of the post-heroic leader is itself a vision, in this case a vision of how to manage, and how leaders and followers should carry out their work.

Both forms of vision are important for post-heroic leadership. Task-based vision is central, since it is tied to everyday work and cannot be ignored. Organization-based vision is required to indicate how those directing the work want to treat one another, what practices will be aspired to in order to have everyone feel valued.

A unit that is driven solely by organization-based vision runs the risk of being so process-focused that its products or services may not be economically viable. Allan Kennedy, coauthor of a pioneering book on organizational culture,[8] became so enamored of the power of culture that he tried to build a management consulting firm dedicated to becoming a progressive, people-centered, and caring organism. After that firm failed, he acknowledged that he had been preoccupied with employee happiness at the expense of attaining sufficient business. Similarly, some managers are so preoccupied with the latest in leadership practices that the basic tasks of their units receive little managerial attention. They forget that the end of leadership is to get the organization's work done.

Although post-heroic leadership is an elaborate vision of how work should be conducted and people treated, as with any vision, it does not lend itself to wholesale adoption. It has to be adapted to specific situations, with mutual understanding of what the components mean in that setting.

WHY TANGIBLE VISION IN THE MIDDLE IS RARE

Vision in the middle is as rare as it is powerful. Why? What keeps leaders at all levels from embracing vision and making it work for them and their teams? Is vision a good idea but almost impossible to implement? There are six main barriers to implementation, all resolvable:

1. *Organizations still conform to the traditional conception of "middle management."* One of the traditional differences between leaders and managers was that only leaders were supposed to have vision—ideas about basic direction—while managers were supposed to be implementers of that vision.[9] Hierarchical organizations were not designed to have people in the middle take the initiative and think outside the box in bold new ways. Their role was to send orders down and pass information up. With rapidly changing conditions, however, everyone must be proactive, not just a passive transmitter. They must become *middle leaders,* and get past the conditioning of middle managers that encourages traditional behavior.

2. *Expressions of passion or emotion are discouraged.* Most managers have been taught to be rational and objective. Vision, however, inspires passion, which is scorned as soft-headed. They are thus naturally reticent about engaging a vision or revealing their passions.[10] Better to stick to agreed-on, attainable goals and not think about the larger meaning of the work. Others have been too often burned by buying into visions that their superiors have dangled beyond their reach. As one veteran executive we worked with lamented:

I have worked in a variety of supposedly well-managed companies such as IBM and Memorex. They all claimed they were doing great things. But they never lived up to their pronouncements . . . . I guess I would like to belong to one organization that does it right.

3. *Middle leaders lack influencing skills.* For middle leaders to rally people to a unit vision, they must be able to influence others. These influencing skills are often absent or undeveloped. Since team members are usually committed to the priorities of their own areas, any manager who tries to draw them into a consensus on a tangible vision for the entire unit invites conflict that many would rather avoid. If the vision is also going to spell out the values and norms by which the team will live, then members are supposed to confront one another about failures to uphold the desired behavior. In the absence of an explicit vision, this policing function is the job of a higher leader, and many would prefer to leave it that way and avoid the conflict that goes with it.

Another source of discomfort could arise if upper management does not agree with the unit vision, or inadvertently behaves in ways that undermine it (or the declared organizational vision). The obligation to push back can seem dangerous.

4. *Vision is believed to require charisma, a scarce commodity.* Vision is often associated with charismatic heroes: Martin Luther King Jr., George Patton, Winston Churchill, and others. Few managers picture themselves in that league. But creating and embedding a vision has little to do with personality.[11] Charisma doesn't sell poor ideas for long; it is the power of good ideas and their appeal to team members, once understood and committed to, that makes tangible vision an effective element of organizational life.

Almost every manager has something like a vision for his or her unit. Simply ask "What would you do if you could run this department just as you would like?" Most managers will light up and start to talk about how things could be. When you ask why things are not that way, they blame others:

"I'm too overworked to get it off the ground."

"My boss would stand in the way."

"Our employees wouldn't go along."

Nevertheless, their enthusiasm for a better way is just below the surface.

5. *It's risky to commit to anything in times of rapid change.* When conditions are in flux, managers prefer being agile and adaptable to betting on any particular direction. While fast footwork is certainly important, it makes it even more important for team members to have a sense of basic direction, an affirmation that there is more to work than survival.

What is needed to convert vision from a rarity on the business landscape to a common feature is a process that can formulate and refine an embryonic vision, and work on it with the team, so that it gets clearer, more appealing, and shared by all. That isn't easy. People sense that commitment to a vision focuses behavior and provides direction, but also precludes other directions. What if the direction isn't the one you prefer, or even worse, is one you abhor?

6. *Who will control the visionary?* One of the authors worked in an organization that had been led by a relatively weak leader without an enacted vision. When he announced his retirement, members were thrilled by the possibility of a strong, visionary successor. As the search progressed, however, they realized that the former leader's lack of vision had given them a great deal of personal autonomy. They began to worry about what would happen if the new leader was strong and visionary, but "wrong," in terms of their own interests.

A leader who has developed a powerful vision can be out of touch with the market, overly enamored of being right, hooked on the ego trip of being out in front, or right but too far ahead of the time.[12] There are numerous examples of entrepreneurs like Steve Jobs (Apple Computer) and Edwin Land (Polaroid) who succeeded once by going against the conventional wisdom, but who failed at a new generation of products or in another company because they had overlearned the value of their own stubborn determination, or fallen in love with their own (limited) ideas.

These factors produce the ambivalence that encourages participants in vision-setting exercises to argue endlessly over wording. They keep the flip charts turning, drawing puffy clouds filled with vision language doomed to remain at the level of abstraction.

There is a silver lining in these many barriers to vision: Since so few have mastered the ability to implement a vision, the opportunity to do so and have a major impact is substantial. You can be among the first on your organizational block to take advantage of the potential power in using vision well.

FORMULATING THE VISION

Vision in the middle may be rare, but is less difficult to create than managers have come to believe. Recognition of the barriers and planning for them makes them easier to overcome. Even when there is no articulated or accepted vision for the entire organization, it is still possible to create a tangible vision for any unit in the middle. It just has to be broadly consistent with the implicit direction of the organization, which is usually inferable from top management statements, annual reports, and organizational practices.

To formulate a tangible vision that can actually make a difference, leaders must:

1. Obtain high involvement of team members from the beginning.
2. Connect the vision to the team's tasks.
3. Seek compatibility with the wider organization's vision, even if that vision is not explicit.
4. Link the vision to the hopes and dreams of most individual team members.

INCLUDE THE TEAM

Must team members be partners in the vision-setting process? It is not absolutely necessary, since some creative entrepreneurial leaders have personally crafted compelling visions and then enrolled talented people to pursue them. (If you are one of those geniuses, more power to you. Too few leaders are so fortunately endowed.)

Solo vision formulation saves time and avoids the problems created by dissenting individuals. In most cases, however, involvement by the team leads to a richer, more potent vision, since members have differing perspectives about customer needs and ways to serve them. In addition, members are the experts on what they would find exciting, motivating, and meaningful. Team involvement in formulation also prepares the way for participant commitment to embed vision in practice.

In most cases, the leader should initiate *and* the team should be involved. The leader has to make it clear that the work of determining the vision is important, and that it will be brought to resolution and implementation. Insisting on movement is not the same as dictating the vision, and can keep the team moving forward as it wrestles with formulation. The leader's commitment prevents members from avoiding personal involvement by treating the discussion as mere word smithing. Any hint that the leader is not really committed to using tangible vision may unleash all kinds of foot-dragging tactics. For sheer agony, little in organizational life beats protracted theoretical discussions about whether the team knows enough to have a vision, whether vision is dangerous ("after all, Hitler and James Jones were visionaries"), which industrial leaders had erroneous visions that got their companies into trouble, and so on. It isn't that these topics can't be discussed, but they are more often raised to stall progress than to increase understanding.

Because the formulation process has been spelled out in our earlier book, *Managing for Excellence,* and more recently through the work of Peter Senge and others,[13] we will discuss it only briefly here. Several approaches to collaborative vision formulation have been successfully used. Sometimes, the leader and a few members launch the process after thinking about possible visions. Alternatively, entire teams have gone through exercises designed to help envision the team's future.[14]

A sensible way to develop a vision is to begin with diagnosis of what the team does to make a difference to its external and internal customers. Identifying what is unique, challenging, value-added, and transforming about the unit's work can support initial thinking about a task-oriented vision.

Another approach begins with introspection about what team members find personally exciting and challenging, then works outward. The reason that tangible vision can be motivating, after all, is because it taps the aspirations of most of the members. Finally, a close look at the organization can jump-start the formulation process, as the team identifies the way it wants to operate and the culture it prefers. John Sloan and his team at the Canadian division of Applico used a variation of an exercise called "The Ten Commandments."[15] In this approach, team members are asked to agree on the current unspoken rules for getting along in the organization. They then work toward consensus on new commandments that would be better suited to helping the team achieve its goals.

It probably doesn't much matter for formulation which method is used as long as the atmosphere encourages open exploration rather than self-protection or disengagement. The key ingredients of successful vision formulation are:

- The planning session should be off-site in a retreat setting to enable creative, uninterrupted thinking not usually possible in the office. A creative process is different from the usual rational/analytic problem-solving mode and needs the proper shift of space and time. People also need time to get comfortable talking about their intimate feelings, the hopes and dreams that are the personal side of vision's power.

- Background analytical work, such as competitive analysis, market trends, projected technological trends, customer segmentation, and the like, can be useful. It can help locate the product or service territory that might be central to the task-oriented vision. But vision must ultimately capture the heart, appeal to the emotions of people in the unit; this requires more than analysis. Team members need to identify what would be exciting and challenging for them, and how they want to be dealt with, so that when the process is done, they can enthusiastically commit to the shared vision.

- Everyone should participate. Except in the rare case when the team is totally fragmented or the leader is a visionary genius, the leader's views should not dominate, especially in early stages of exploration. Members must get past the desire to play it safe by saying nothing, or by saying nothing with which the leader might disagree. The formulation process only advances in the free flow of suggestions.

- As ideas flow, a common view of the broad domain of the vision will slowly emerge, independent of the eventual language decided on. Slow down the rush to capture it in a phrase or slogan; in operation, the vision will be a complex set of interacting assumptions and beliefs that go beyond the vision statement. Do the exploratory work first, and let the specific language follow.

Example of One Company's Experience

The utilities business had been one of the most stable and predictable of all industries. That changed during the 1980s. Increased costs (partly from expensive nuclear plant construction and operations) coupled with soaring interest rates, resulted in the need to hold down demand through conservation. At the same time, the threat of new competition through deregulation forced electric utilities around the country to rethink their slow-moving, bureaucratic ways. They had to come up with new services such as home audits, new products such as insulating blankets for water heaters, new alliances with companies that provided insulation, and new consulting services for contractors.

Faced with threatening changes, the Electric Division Sales and Marketing Department executive team of "TransPower Gas & Electric" (TPG&E) met to examine these changes and agree on the shift in focus from consumption to conservation and service. They decided that they were "selling the complete package and not just energy units." They also determined that the biggest obstacle to addressing these changes was the departmental culture, which mirrored the company's culture.

The departmental culture was shaped by bureaucratic rules: three signatures needed to hire the lowest level clerk; approvals by senior managers for minuscule expenditures; de facto lifetime employment; promotions based on length of service; and general avoidance of conflict.

The culture taught people to smother new ideas with responses like, "We tried that before and it didn't work," or "We have always done it this way."

The marketing and sales executives held a two-day offsite meeting to determine the kind of organization they would need to compete successfully. To develop a profile of the current culture, they were paired up and asked to answer this question: "Suppose you have a friend who is about to join the company and wants to know how things are really done around here, how to act and follow the informal rules. What would you say?"

Based on their responses, the "Ten Commandments" of the current environment were identified; these included "document everything to protect yourself from blame," "do it by the book even if that doesn't work," and "keep your head down; it's the nail sticking up that gets pounded down."

As they were read off, the innovation-killing Commandments produced bursts of laughter. However, members of
the management team gradually recognized that each of
them had had to break the rules to get to where they were.
Each had personally taken risks and done things differently. Following the rules kept people out of trouble, but it
helped neither the individuals nor the company.

Through brainstorming and winnowing, new commandments to support innovation were developed—desired behaviors such as "simplify, simplify, simplify" and
"do what's right, not just what you've been told." When
they checked whether the commandments meant the same
thing to all present, however, they discovered many disagreements. What did "the customer comes first" mean in
practice? Write off disputed bills with a smile? Pay over-
time to provide convenient hours? Did "be direct and honest" really mean that it was permissible to confront one's
boss in public? It took heated debate to reach agreement
on the meaning of the new commandments, and still more
heat to agree on their operational applications.

As the work progressed, the visioning team understood
that it had to seek input from below; simply announcing
the rules would have no effect. Others would have to grapple with the specific implications or the commandments
would be meaningless.

Testing the Vision

Vision is only meaningful if there is *clarity* (about the meaning), *consensus* (as to the implications), and *commitment* (to
use the tangible vision).[16] Any statement of vision is worthless without these components, and it is necessary to test
the extent to which each is satisfied. There also must be a
test of the trade-offs among parts of the vision. For example, does "customer focus" take precedence over "low-cost

producer," or "fastest at developing new products" conflict with "top quality?"

The visioning activity must alternate between the general and the specific, testing broad statements against specific events, possible actions, and subunit activities. Four ways for team members to test the emerging vision is against past, present, and future aspects of organizational life:

- Look at key past decisions and ask team members what they would have done differently if they were using the vision as a guide. Is it sufficiently tangible? For example, how would a recent downsizing decision have looked if the team had been committed to the proposed statement about "full and open communication?"
- Ask each member to indicate how his or her area would be changed today in light of the proposed vision.
- Look at upcoming critical decisions, and ask how these would be affected. For example, if the department wants to be "the people who provide actionable and timely information to managers in the company," what would it no longer do, or what actions would members avoid?
- Since vision takes the core purpose and reconfigures it, the team discusses the alignment of present practices and potentially new products and services.

This testing process increases the clarity of the vision's meaning. Vision without clear implications for decision making is just puffery and a waste of time.

Language Matters

If a vision is clear, varied statements can represent it; if it is not clear, not even the craftsmanship of a Shakespeare could make it memorable. The language of some formulations can rouse people to extraordinary efforts, while dull, plodding, repetitious, and pretentious locutions (like this one) make the same people yawn. When Martin Luther King Jr. gave his "I have a dream" speech, millions were moved to tears, and some to changed attitudes and behavior. But even there, it was shared experiences, values, and meanings that gave power to his speech, not the language alone.

Remember, too, that the English language is ambiguous and its meaning cannot be taken for granted. A visioning team must test to see how common language is being used.

Example at Babson College

Babson College recently decided to focus its business programs on educating managers to be "entrepreneurial leaders." Those two simple words, however, had different meanings for different people. The school's faculty, staff, trustees, advisory board members, and others could not be certain what they were committed to. Did the term entrepreneurial leaders narrowly describe people who created start-up businesses? No. Did it mean that a person had to be a formally designated leader to use what the school was teaching? No.

Discussion led to a modifying phrase—"from any position in organizations of different sizes"—being appended to the original term. This clarification failed to settle the issue. Did the new teaching focus apply equally to undergraduates, full-time MBAs, part-time MBAs, and executives? Yes. Did it mean that the liberal arts portion of an undergraduate's education was considered to be irrelevant? No; it was enthusiastically agreed that the skills and attitudes imparted by general education were critical for entrepreneurial leaders.

The final Babson statement evolved to incorporate the complex, multiple implications of the entrepreneurial leader concept. As important as the language in this case, however, was the shared understanding gained by the many individuals who participated in the discussion of those two simple words.

INTERNALIZATION

Getting the vision out of the heads of its formulators and into the thinking and behavior of people is the most critical but often overlooked step of the visioning process. The management team that has labored mightily to formulate the vision too often sees this step as one of communication. The group leader plans a few stirring speeches. Then the posters go up, the wallet cards are distributed, and the leader and his or her inner circle breathe a sigh of relief: "We now have a vision and we've told people what it is. They can now go forth inspired!"

Communicating the vision does not finish the job; the vision must be internalized by members of the organization. It must be understood and embedded in peoples' psyches such that using it for decision making and guidance becomes almost second nature.

Internalization is a task that takes time to accomplish. And it is never-ending in the sense that there are always new employees to educate about the vision and its implications, and the vision requires modification as the environment and company's experience changes.

Some kind of cascade activity is needed, in which people lower in the organization translate the vision to their areas, thinking about what it might mean for them and the way they operate. No matter how vivid a company's overall vision is, the managers who are responsible for divisions, units, departments, and teams below still can derive great benefit from the development of tangible vision for their own area.

Example: TPG&E Revisited

The top management team's struggles to agree on the meaning and implications of the vision taught them that it would be valuable to obtain full agreement of others about the vision's meaning. They also knew that managers on the front lines had more experience of day-to-day implementation problems, so the team sought input from below.

Two weeks later, they convened an all-day meeting of 100-plus managers representing the next three lower levels of the organization. The morning was designed to gain clarity about the current culture and its consequences, and increase understandings about the proposed new culture. The division general manager read through the list of the Ten Commandments of the current fossilized culture, again evoking widespread laughter. The general manager then described the kind of organization the executive team wanted to create, as prescribed by the new commandments.

Managers were assigned to nine mixed work groups, with every department of the division represented in each. Each group also included a member of the division's executive team.

Team members wanted to know more about the desired ten commandments and the meaning of each. They began to offer their own examples of implicit current commandments and consequences. The session closed with the executive in each team asking how the desired commandment list could be expanded or re-worded.

The work groups, minus the executive members, were then asked to identify current policies and activities that supported the desired vision, and those that undermined it. While they labored on this assignment, the top team reconvened to revise its vision statement using feedback from earlier discussion.

Later that morning, each work group recorded its answers to the assignment and reported them to the reassembled audience. There was substantial agreement across the nine groups, but also some important differences. The executive team reported its rewording of the commandments, demonstrating that earlier input had been heard and incorporated.

The remainder of the day would identify critical barriers to implementation of the newly revised mission and provide a mechanism to have them addressed soon after the meeting. During lunch, a subgroup of the executive team consolidated the answers of the various work groups into a list of 20 items, which was reported to all participants as they reconvened in the early afternoon. A quick round of voting reduced this list into a half-dozen highly dysfunctional habits that stood between the current division and the organization it hoped to become. These ranged from "unnecessary bureaucratic rules," such as the multiple approvals required for hiring data entry clerks, to "lack of training opportunities for the skills required by a flexible, nimble organization."

New teams were formed around each of the half-dozen priority items and these brainstormed for solutions. Again, a member of the executive team joined each group to listen and contribute. By late afternoon, all reconvened in the main meeting room, where each group reported its suggestions. These were assigned to existing departments, a responsible individual, or a new task force.

The division general manager adjourned the meeting with his thanks and the announcement that a senior middle manager would be named "Chief Honcho" of the project, with responsibility for seeing that progress was made in tackling any and all barriers that separated the division and its vision.

Less than three months later—lightning speed for this division—the same assembly of managers reconvened to review progress. To the surprise of many, the organization was already far more nimble and responsive; it had removed the multiple layers of sign-offs needed for mundane activities, raised spending and decision-making authority, and begun to consider restructuring.

In TPG&E's approach to vision internalization, the primary task of the management team was to develop an early version of the vision for feedback from below. This identified the factors that supported or undermined the vision, and created an agenda for change. In this way, all organizational members had responsibility for realizing the evolved vision. Contrast their approach with the typical process where top management makes pronouncements, and those below wait passively to see what develops. The TPG&E approach expands responsibility, which reinforces post-heroic leadership.

The vision lives when all participants have tested their own behavior against it, checked whether their understanding of the implications is reasonable, and have had a chance to shape the meaning for the organization and themselves.

SUSTAINING THE EMBEDDED VISION

After the initial steps of moving beyond communication of the vision to the real work that makes a difference to the organization, everyone in the original cascading process can move forward by developing a compatible tangible vision for their own unit if one does not already exist, then conducting a similar "reaction and suggestion" meeting with his or her organization, to examine the impact of the vision. They too must identify the actions they should take or avoid to align with the vision, then follow up periodically to see how the adjustments are going.

Use It as a Decision-Making Guide

Many organizations post vision statements but leaders never mention these statements again, even when making decisions that could have been informed by the vision. Real commitment comes from actions reflecting the vision. The top management team at Biotekk had the company vision statement prominently displayed on the wall of its meeting room, but no reference was made to that vision during 18 months of biweekly meetings. That silence merely confirmed the skepticism of those team members who doubted the practical value of the vision statement.

The antidote to this silence is to put the vision to use on a regular basis as the key criterion for decisions about what markets to enter, products and services to develop, advertising and marketing programs, and organizational style. When hiring a new person, members should ask, "Which candidate will best help us achieve particular aspects of our vision?" Similarly, the vision can be used as a standard for designing training programs, evaluating service performance, and making investment decisions. Throughout Levi Strauss, for example, people talk about actions "not being aspirational," or "in line with our aspirations." Each use of the vision in conjunction with operating activities or decisions drives it more deeply into the consciousness of employees.

The Symbolic Act

For true internalization to happen, executive actions count far more than exact language and inspirational talks. If their actions are inconsistent with the proclaimed vision, the cynics will prevail. Does a reserved parking lot for managers match the notion of "no boundaries among levels?" Does the downsizing buyout package match the rhetoric of employees as the most important asset? Does the division president flying alone to Japan on the company jet (at a charge-back of $150,000 versus $12,000 by first-class commercial flight) match the vision's low-cost producer aspiration? Does closing the oldest plant in a small community to move production offshore, match the stated concern for the communities in which the company does business? Top management actions have a symbolic significance that far outweighs official and informal declarations. Thus, one way to reinforce the vision is to do something bold—a *symbolic act*.

An AT&T executive told us not long ago about a symbolic act made by Frank Stanton, then head of that company's network operations. For years, Stanton had tried to move customer service performance to the top of his team's priority list, but without success. His team members argued that the network was operative over 90 percent of the time, the best rate in the industry. Ninety-plus percent didn't satisfy Stanton; he knew that he had to do something dramatic to demonstrate to the team that there was a problem and that they had to address the vision of outstanding customer service.

Eventually, Stanton thought up an exercise to prove his point. At an executive meeting held at a hotel, he brought the team into a room where there was a stage hidden by a curtain. His fellow executives were puzzled. "I have a simple assignment for you," Stanton told them. Drawing the curtain, he revealed a bank of AT&T switchboard operators. "Each of you will take two service calls from customers as they come in," he told his perplexed colleagues. "Your task is simple: Solve each customer's problem within 24 hours, but do not reveal your status in the company to anyone in AT&T, since that will bias the response you get." As the execs moved reluctantly toward the operators to take their calls, Stanton continued: "We'll meet back here in 24 hours to hear how you did."

The next day, a chastened group of executives sheepishly admitted to serious problems with customer service. Each executive's attempt to solve just two service problems in 24 hours had generally met with failure. Response times were painfully slow, and it had been difficult to find out who could provide help.

The AT&T managers discovered a painful truth through Frank Stanton's symbolic action: AT&T might have the best record on downtime, but when customer networks were down, those customers didn't care about who had the least downtime; their operations were disrupted and they wanted the network restored now! Customer service was not an empty phrase in the vision—it was a real issue that had to be addressed.

Walk the Talk

Symbolism can cut in the opposite direction. According to the late Herb Caen, columnist for The *San Francisco Chronicle,* when Fireman's Fund was in deep financial trouble, its CEO called together all the managers and made an impassioned speech about the need to continue slashing expenses and driving down costs. When he finished, he raced to the company helicopter for a ride to a golf tournament at Pebble Beach. We do not know the reason for this CEO's choice of transportation, which might have been perfectly rational, but we can imagine how this story undercut the credibility of his commitment to cost reductions. What may have been the most convenient mode of transportation to facilitate attendance at an event with genuine value to the company became a symbol of executive insincerity.

The Power of Brute Attention

Peters and Waterman coined the term *brute attention* to emphasize the need for repeated references to any change goals.[17] Brute attention applies equally to the job of internalizing vision. Contemporary managers and personnel have so much information and so many appeals directed toward them that repetition is necessary, otherwise the message may fail to register. The vision can be repeated in many forms and forums: meetings, memos, one-to-one conversations, and personal evaluation. To repeat: *Important messages may be lost if not hammered home many times.* (Do we need to say it again?)

Public repetition also builds commitment in the person making the statements. If the leader says it often enough, he or she can't help but think of other ways to follow up and drive the vision home. And, with luck, the repetition will also be heard and taken seriously by those to whom it is addressed. Each use keeps it fresh and current.

Periodic Adjustments

Navigators who traverse broad regions of the earth's surface or seas rely heavily on their compasses. In foul weather, when the sun and stars cannot be seen, the compass needle always points to magnetic north. From that reference point, other bearings can be determined. But magnetic north is not always true north. Depending on one's location, magnetic north and true north may deviate by a dozen or more degrees. So, adjustments must be made during a long journey.

Visions also need periodic adjustments in language or application. Some organizations can rely on their stated visions for a long period. But changing conditions often demand adjustment and recalibration. The application of a tangible vision is more likely to change than the vision itself. In this sense it is rather like the U.S. Constitution, which remains constant, subject to infrequent amendments, but is constantly being interpreted as the issues of the day change. Short-term goals and plans are most subject to modification, though guided by mission, strategic intent, and strategic plans. In a rapidly changing world, no "long-term strategy" is likely to remain potent for long; indeed, some like Tom Peters argue that the best strategy in a world of fast-paced change is to remain flexible and agile—to be without a strategy and ceaselessly experiment.[18]

Until the 1980s, "concern for people" was an essential element in the visions of IBM, AT&T, Hewlett-Packard, Digital Equipment Corporation, and Sears. This led to no-layoff policies and acceptance of mediocre performers. Changes in the competitive environment, however, made these policies and the vision that supported them unsustainable. Adjustments were required. Eventually, the no-layoff policies fell by the wayside as these companies found other ways to exercise their concern, such as preparing people for employability and making generous severance and employment counseling arrangements.

CONCLUSION

A vision that is broadly accepted and understood within the organization gives leaders the confidence in subordinates they need to loosen their grip. If they know that team members share the same vision—if they are guided by the same unerring compass—leaders are more inclined to share decision-making power with them. This approach helps ensure that those with the most knowledge on issues collaborate in the management process. But as discussed in Chapter 8, teams work best when everyone, leader and members alike, are skilled in influencing each other.

8

ENHANCING POWER THROUGH MUTUAL INFLUENCE

Post-heroic leadership is about powering up—increasing the total power of each individual, every unit, and the entire organization. That is a hard goal to disagree with, but individual managers are often more interested in increasing their own power, believing that they have too little. The concept of shared leadership makes them nervous, because it suggests that they will have to give away some portion of that meager supply of power. Yet we offer power enhancement, not power dilution.

Most managers think about power too narrowly. To them, power is the control that comes from formal authority associated with position: the power to give orders to subordinates and know that their orders will be followed. This power is, in fact, in increasingly short supply. In today's environment, that kind of license is not likely to expand since it presumes a static world in which leaders know all problems in advance and their expertise perfectly matches their organizational position. Even less available is the power of coercion. Managers who long to force compliance are now handcuffed by employee rights and attitude, cultural disapproval, and organizational complexity. The old command-and-control style no longer works.

There are still situations in which power determined by formal authority is appropriate. Certain rules must be set and enforced for legal and precautionary reasons; boundaries must be established and maintained. It is still necessary to invest certain people with the power to authorize spending over prescribed amounts, to sign documents in the name of the company, to formally hire or fire, and so on. Even post-heroic leaders must occasionally make autonomous decisions based on their positions in the organization, and certain delicate issues need one person in charge.

While this kind of power must be maintained, its extension into many other aspects of organizations is inappropriate. Power determined by management level cannot work where knowledge is widely dispersed, where changes in technologies, markets, and competition are rapid, and where employees are highly educated. Employees at all levels need the power to act; otherwise, the organization will be too sluggish to compete. Responsive organizations need the cooperation of peers and higher-ups who cannot be given orders or forced to be helpful.

When they view power as a scarce resource, managers are not inclined to share what they have. They behave like Molière's hilarious but sad character in *The Miser,* who lovingly crooned "my money" again and again, even though its use could have helped his daughter find happiness with her true love. His desire to preserve his treasure kept him from discovering that it could be an investment with a huge return. Many leaders feel the same way about power. Even when they know that they should share it, they prefer to hoard it.

INFLUENCE AS A FORM OF POWER

To be successful, post-heroic leaders must rely on another form of power: influence. Influence is the ability to get others, below, above and laterally, to respond in desired ways without coercion. Influence may be less glamorous than unadulterated control over others, but it can power up an organization if properly applied.

Along with shared responsibility and a tangible vision, influence is at the heart of post-heroic leadership. The shared-responsibility team is the setting for collective problem solving and decision making; the tangible vision aligns individuals with the unit's larger purpose. But neither of these components will work effectively if the leader and team members lack the skill to influence each other and be influenced in return. Leaders must have the influencing skills to induce members to work as junior partners instead of as deferential subordinates. Team members must be able to disagree without being antagonistic. They must know how to hold others accountable even though they lack the authority to command compliance. They must be able to gain the cooperation of others and turn the leader from paths of error.

Effective influence is about both clarity in stating what is meant and openness to receive the messages of others. Problems arise not only from members being less direct than is necessary, but also from their unduly resisting influence attempts. The organization also loses if leaders hold back for fear of overwhelming members.

Leaders are also peers and junior partners to their colleagues and bosses; they must be able to influence them. This is no small challenge given that those colleagues and bosses may not have bought into the new style of leadership. They may be less inclined to be open to influence, less welcoming of disagreement with their ideas, and less amenable to being held accountable from below. These problems make influence more difficult, but not impossible.

MUTUAL INFLUENCE

To master these challenges, leaders and team members alike must understand that influence must be mutual, and not a one-way street. Mutuality means that each party can influence the other, no matter who is in the higher hierarchical position.

Mutual influence is not the same as equal influence, since those with more knowledge and formal accountability ought, on balance, to have greater influence. Traditionally, this has meant that the leader has more influence than anyone else on every issue in his or her unit. In a rapidly changing world, however, that is no longer possible. Expertise shifts from person to person, depending on the issue. Only rarely does one person have all the information, and all the history and wisdom to make solo decisions about every complex problem. It no longer makes sense to keep all formal decision-making power with the same person.

MUTUAL INFLUENCE CREATES MORE TOTAL POWER

From the leader's perspective, mutual influence is a matter of self-interest. It not only increases the open flow of information, but also increases his or her effective power by enlarging the total amount of influence in the unit, and by decreasing resistance from people who want to retain the ability to be heard. This counterintuitive conclusion—that enhancing the power of those one hopes to influence is the key to greater influence—rests on important psychological truths. Most adults, most of the time, do not like to feel dependent and resist it or withdraw from the relationship.[1] Thus, when a leader whom they cannot influence makes subordinates feel dependent, they seek ways to redress the balance by any available means:

- Withdrawing and disengaging.
- Covert resistance, such as playing dumb.
- "Cover your backside" tactics.
- Making careless "mistakes."
- Disparaging the leader to others.
- Doing all those things that confirm the boss's Theory X belief that subordinates have no initiative and must be watched closely.

The same people who resist dependence, however, are willing to be *inter-dependent;* they accept being influenced by others who are also willing to be influenced in turn by them. This more nearly equal relationship, with reciprocal dependence, is less threatening and therefore less likely to produce resistance. Mutual influence allows each party to affect the other, creating more total influence than would be the case if virtually all the influence resided in one of the two. In a continuing relationship, the proportion of each person's influence on the other may remain relatively constant even while the total influence in the relationship expands. Thus a leader may retain greater total influence while encouraging reciprocal influence:

Increasing the influence of others increases one's own influence.

Paradoxical as it may seem, moving from command-and-control thinking to mutual influence does not diminish or divide power, but expands it, as in inflating a balloon. To understand this paradox, you must recognize that influence is not a static commodity; there is not "only so much to go around." It is more useful to think of influence as you would think of capital in the economy: It expands as it is used and invested. Likewise, it is possible to expend influence widely and increase an organization's total power. As influence grows, there is less concern about how it gets divided, since it feels as if there is more than enough for everyone.

Two conditions are needed to expand the amount of influence. The first is an openness to creative problem solving aimed at win-win solutions. Instead of focusing on traditional win-lose thinking ("I aim to find fault with your ideas so that mine will prevail"), everyone focuses on creative problem solving ("I want to understand your ideas so that its best parts can be incorporated into a superior solution"). That avoids compromises, where no one is right, and seeks alternatives that yield more for everyone.

The second condition for expanding influence is an expansion of influence areas (i.e., finding more ways different parties can influence each other). New, undeveloped relationships are often constrained; neither person has many opportunities to influence the "stranger." But as knowledge and trust develop, both parties allow themselves to be influenced in more areas. As a leader and direct report get to know each other, it becomes safer to discuss goals, aspirations, and concerns, and to put ideas on the table. The leader receives important information and is able to show the direct report the connection between the subordinate's interests and the required behavior. The leader gains a better feel for appropriate assignments, effective coaching (whether to prod or support), and acquires a better sense of the person's career goals, and so on. In turn, the team member learns how to push back on the leader, what topics are especially sensitive, and how to accommodate to the leader's preferences without compromising his or her own agenda.

It is commonly believed that trust is required for influence. While established trust can make most interactions easier, it is not the critical factor. More important is having well-developed influence skills. With skill, constructive dialogue is possible even between people where trust is low. In turn, dialogue allows successful exchanges, which build trust. It is not necessary, therefore, to refrain from influence attempts until high trust is established.

INFLUENCING MANAGERIAL STYLE

It is difficult for any manager to argue against the idea of being influenced by team members who have superior expertise on a given issue. When a decision needs to be made, who wouldn't want to have all relevant information? Powerful traditions reinforce the concept of informed decision making. Still, many managers are loath to accept the idea that members should also influence the manager on matters of style: his or her way of inquiring, listening, responding, gathering data, running meetings, and so on. This would seem off limits, an intrusion on managerial prerogatives. Traditional thinking tells them that subordinates should accept the manager's style as a given, and adapt to it. One manager who attended our influence workshop had this in mind when he burst out:

> *I always had to totally adapt my style to my boss's ways, and he never adapted to mine. If he wanted short memos, I wrote short memos. If he wanted me to show up Saturday mornings whether or not there was pressing work, just to appear loyal, I was there. If he never set meeting agendas in advance, and wasted our time, I sat there and tried to be interested. Now you're telling me that when I am the boss, I have to let my team influence my style? It's not fair!*

Our response to this manager was: "It may not seem fair, but which would you rather be: right or effective? It might achieve justice to finally cash in on all the years of paying dues, but does it make for better work? Did all that obedience produce excellence?" In the realm of leadership style, it is in the leader's interest to work out mutually satisfying work relationships with team members, to get them to act more like partners, and to foster conditions that get the most from everyone. The leader does not have to abandon his or her style and preferences, but neither do team members. Mutual accommodation allows all parties to be both satisfied and highly productive.

MUTUAL INFLUENCE IS IN EVERYONE'S BEST INTEREST

Building mutual influence among everyone on the team produces benefits for both the post-heroic leader and the team:

- *More honest communication.* If members know that it is safe to disagree—that messengers won't be shot—they will be more willing to express their views, without censoring them to fit the leader's preconceptions.

- *Higher quality decisions.* Greater openness leads to better data, allowing more informed, creative decisions. Where heroic leaders see disagreement as a barrier to progress, post-heroic leaders see it as an indicator of which uncertainties and assumptions must be examined.

- *Greater commitment.* Members know that they can't win every battle. But freedom to argue one's views and be taken seriously increases support for final outcomes. The discussion process also facilitates the ability of team members to explain the decision rationale to *their* direct reports.

- *Increased responsibility.* Mutual influence is not just a license to raise problems and delegate them up to the leader. If something is wrong, the member has the obligation to bring it to the surface and seek joint resolution.

- *Frees the leader to be strong.* When members can be counted on to say what they think, the leader is free to be forceful without fear of overwhelming members. Working with handcuffs on may have pleased Houdini, but it frustrates strong leaders. As Shel Davis, then a manager at Digital Equipment Corporation, put it, "In order for my subordinates to feel powerful, I don't want to be less powerful. I want each of us to be as powerful as we can be."

  Leaders who bully their subordinates into silence win the battle but lose the war. Heroic leaders win these contests because they are not conducted on a level playing field, and everyone knows it. The losers are justifiably resentful and strike back by reducing their interest and commitment.

- *Increases member-to-member influence.* All members, not just the leader, have the ability to confront those who are not delivering.

- *Helps members' effectiveness outside unit.* To be effective, members need to gain cooperation across unit boundaries. Once they know how to influence without authority, they can do this more effectively.

Some fear that influence in the hands of team members will be a prescription for "business prevention," where dissident or difficult people can slow the pace of urgent work to a crawl. Anyone who has seen the Congress of the United States in action *(inaction)* would say, "Please don't make us like that!" This is an unfounded fear, however, if leader and team are in the post-heroic mode and aligned through a tangible vision. Rosabeth Kanter's research has demonstrated that those who feel powerless are most petty and rules-minded;[2] whereas potential resisters who know they can be influential usually feel less need to exert their influence in deliberately negative ways. Best of all, troublesome individuals are not just the post-heroic leader's problem; team members can and will get them into line.

WHY MUTUAL INFLUENCE IS SO RARE

Few of today's leaders will say that what they want is "my way or the highway." The benefits of mutual influence are simply too obvious. Still, subordinates routinely complain that their views are ignored. So why do so many subordinates see their leaders as difficult to influence?

Mutual influence is rare because of two barriers described in earlier chapters: the old heroic assumptions that continue to run deep in the minds of leaders and their subordinates; and the ambivalence that both feel about a more open relationship. Managers have a residual fear about being challenged on everything from particular decisions to leadership style. Will constant conflict erupt? Will they lose control and respect? Direct reports have no guarantee that the boss really meant it when requesting feedback on how to manage better, or push-back after discouraging an idea. Will the relationship—or the lower-ranking person's career—be jeopardized? Despite the benefits of mutual influence, old habits and ambivalence stand in the way of realization. Poor communications, in both the telling and the hearing, are sometimes at the heart of the problem.

Mixed Messages

Some leaders are guilty of sending mixed messages. The leader who thinks that push-back is probably a good idea but worries that encouraging it might unleash forces best left contained, can subtly convey ambivalence without meaning to. Instead of saying "Stop protecting me from your criticism. I can take it. We'll make better decisions if you tell me straight," the ambivalent leader says, "Let's have it straight; I'm tough enough to take anything you have to say . . . and I know you'll be kind." That last throwaway phrase, usually said humorously, is just enough to pluck any reservations members have about how different the boss really wants things to be. If members were already convinced that openness and mutuality were the only way to go, they might ignore the slight hesitation, but more often, their skepticism makes them supertuned listeners to even the faintest negative signals.

Team members are not without fault in sending mixed signals. Ambivalence often leads them to encode their questions and comments, just in case the leader takes offense. As a result, members can walk away from interactions saying, "I really told the boss that time," without having communicated a fraction of what they were thinking.

It is as if members carry a secret code ring; by transmitting in code deniability is maintained. "Have you had a chance to talk to Nick yet," actually means, "You are making a big mistake; Nick will hate this and sabotage the whole deal if he doesn't get a chance to shape it." If the boss fails to decode the message, the team member can claim that he said to talk to Nick. He has technically "told the truth" but in a softened, discounted way that would only be clear to someone using the decoder ring.

Misinterpreting Signals

Communication is always complicated, but when authority and hierarchy are involved, opportunities for misinterpretations abound. Everyone has experienced being in a subordinate position, if only by having parents, teachers, coaches, and bosses. These accumulated experiences filter what members hear from their current leaders and the images they project.

Filtering causes people to hear casual suggestions as orders, and to interpret minor signs as proof of what experience has taught people to expect.

Examples at Chubb and Xerox

One senior executive at Chubb told us he had the expensive misfortune to visit a fancy condo development in Daytona, Florida financed by his division. While walking the site with the local manager, he remarked, "This place is really beautiful; you've done a fantastic job . . . It's too bad that there weren't more palm trees between the building and the ocean; they would have framed the view even better." During his next visit, he was stunned to see $100,000 worth of palm trees planted by the eager local manager, who had heard the "order" to spiff up the view.

Likewise, Bill Glavin has described to us a Xerox Corporation meeting at which a decision on pricing for a new line of equipment was to be made. In his senior management role, Glavin casually asked the staff if they knew what a certain market segment had been paying for comparable equipment. Twelve days later, an eager staff member arrived with a cart carrying a massive study that answered the question—exactly 11 days after the pricing decision had been irrevocably made.

Meetings that involve several levels of the organization are almost always loaded situations in which every little comment is interpreted as a signal of what the leader(s) truly want. One of the authors, for example, observed a manager at a task force meeting in a Fortune 50 company declare, "We can't propose this solution, because Morgan [the leader who commissioned the task force] won't like it. And we all know that at [this company] you cannot tell your boss the truth." When pressed as to why he believed that to be true, he shot back: "Teddy Reilly—remember him?" Nods all around. "He stood up at a quarterly management meeting and told the truth, and he was gone the next week."

As it turned out, Ted Reilly had belligerently declared that inventory was lower than what the general manager was reporting, and therefore insufficient. The general manager had responded, "I think you're wrong, because other companies get by with even lower inventories, but we'll take another look." Ted Reilly had been fired soon after, but for repeatedly missed production targets, making lame excuses, and other troubles going back a very long time. His challenging of the inventory figures had merely been a symptom of his desperation, not the cause of his firing. Still, 10 years later, the incident remained vivid to some of the people who had been there, and these individuals overgeneralized the likelihood of retaliation for telling the truth to include all leaders at the company.

How to Break through to Mutual Influence

Breaking the cycle of miscommunication and fear to create mutual influence is the responsibility of both the leader and members. Because the leader possesses more authority, it is usually easier for the leader to initiate change. The leader is assumed to have the right to determine just how much initiative and overt disagreement will be welcomed. Thus, he or she can set the tone for interactions. But members can also alter influence relationships, and we will examine options from that position too.

What the Leader Can Do

Here are some ideas for what the leader can do to establish the new rules of engagement, the new world of mutuality of influence. Make the new contract explicit, clarifying that directness and honesty are now expected even when that means disagreement with the leader. Without the specification of what is desired, old expectations about not pushing one's boss too hard will be the default choice of most team members. Just announcing the expectations is not enough; too many people will be prone to hear that as if it were the alleged declaration of Samuel Goldwyn, bellowing, "I want you to tell me the truth even if it costs you your job!"

Table 8–1 lists examples of what the leader might say to reinforce the climate of team members speaking more directly.

Actively Support the New Contract with New Behavior

Some managers still actively discourage influence from below. They act defensively, are quick to criticize, view all criticisms as personal attacks, and put down anyone who pushes back. Other leaders are convinced of the desirability of mutual influence, but don't know how to encourage it. They say that they want team members to be full partners but don't take the initiative or have the requisite skills to break through the old concerns.

Using the Bradford-Cohen Leadership Style Questionnaire[3] we have collected data from more than 1000 managers in a variety of industries. Consistently, three of the questions with the poorest results are:

Compared to what you prefer, to what extent does your manager:

a. Encourage disagreements with his/her ideas and proposals?

b. Encourage feedback from subordinates on his/her performance?

c. Talk openly about any difficulties the two of you have in working together?

These are difficult matters for subordinates to raise at first, but most would like the opportunity, and the leader can build a climate where these issues can be discussed.

Table 8–1. Leader Actions That Support Mutual Influence

Leader Action	Sample Statement
Tell members to challenge you when they believe you are wrong, not seeing important data, or not taking an important issue seriously.	"I can't know everything, so I'm depending on you to speak up when you see something we're doing wrong."
Clarify mixed messages.	"When I disagree with your idea, I don't want you to immediately back down. Get more data and develop your arguments. As is practiced at Genentech, each of you is entitled to four 'no's' from me when you want my approval for something you believe in."
Solicit opinions on issues that matter to people.	"Have I heard all of your reservations?"
Invite people to disagree with your views.	"You've heard my views. Tell me what doesn't makes sense to you."
Pick up on tonal and non-verbal cues.	"You are looking hesitant. Do you have concerns?"
Check your understanding.	"I'm having trouble following your argument. Can you explain it another way?"
Ask about your own behavior.	"How am I doing as a leader? Am I inhibiting disagreements? What am I doing to make it hard to argue back? What would help?"
Encourage members to influence each other.	"Are you satisfied with your colleague's position? Don't back off if you aren't."

It is important not only to create a new contract—a set of expectations about mutuality—but to support it with new behavior. Rewarding a subordinate for challenging one of your ideas, whether or not you agree with that view, is just one example of what you, as a leader, can do. If someone reports disappointing news, give that person as much credit for stepping forward as the bearer of tidings of comfort and joy. If a team member advances a plan that competes with the one you favor, give that member every opportunity to make a case for it.

As you support mutuality with new behavior, eliminate the old behavior. Don't respond to every challenge with disapproval. Don't shoot the bearers of bad news. Don't stack the decks against those whose ideas you do not favor.

Acknowledge That You Are Being Influenced

Many leaders, especially men, hate to acknowledge that they have been influenced by a subordinate. As one senior executive joked, "I love to learn, I just don't want anyone to know about it." For many, that takes the form of arguing hard, never appearing to give in, but then incorporating the other's views in the next discussion. A simple, "Thanks, I hadn't seen that and can now change my position on this issue," can do wonders for encouraging future influence attempts from others.

Always remember that your subordinates will be watching for signs of your sincerity. Subordinates have a keen sense of their leader's sincerity and, as discussed, listen for clues and signals. As a leader, be alert to the tests about mutuality and respond immediately, or soon after, with reinforcement of your expectations and desires. Take opportunities to encourage straight talk to you, and among team members.

Example

When Allan Cohen became Academic Vice President at Babson, one of his team members was Tom Moore, Dean of the Graduate School. Tom was an outstanding dean, effective at inducing independent faculty members to work together on curriculum reform, and at working with staff to provide excellent service to MBA students. Allan had a cordial relationship with Tom, though they had not worked closely together.

Allan soon discovered that Tom's experiences led him to initial suspicion of anyone above him in the hierarchy, and they had several exchanges in which Tom made it clear that he interpreted Allan's actions—and in one case, Allan's forgetting to pass on information that Tom considered critical—as possible confirmation that Allan was just another untrustworthy boss. Allan kept talking with Tom about his intentions and desire to work mutually. Soon after, at a meeting of the Deans and Chairs team that Allan led, a minor misunderstanding led to an angry exchange between them. The room fell silent, and all eyes turned to Allan. The traditions of this team had not encouraged open challenges; important disagreements were addressed off-line, or not at all.

"Maybe you're right, Tom," Allan said. "We need to look at more data. How do you suggest we do it?" Tom's proposal for a mini task force was accepted, and discussion continued, still cautiously, but freer than it had been. After the meeting, Tom and Allan reviewed what had happened. Allan returned to his office, wondering how to reassure the others that what had happened was both all-right and desirable. He composed the E-mail message on pages 199–200 to the team.

Ironically, while Allan was sending his electronic message, Tom was mailing a memo in which he apologized for losing his temper. When they talked the next day, both laughed about the crossed messages, and from then on, they were able to work together as partners. Tom was a more experienced academic administrator, and taught Allan a great deal. Together, they planned the processes for radical curriculum reform and other significant changes.

Not incidentally, the discussions at the Deans and Chairs meetings improved dramatically, with other members more directly asserting their ideas and not just pretending to comply.

TO: Deans and Chairs

FROM: Allan Cohen

SUBJECT: LEARNING FROM YESTERDAY'S MEETING

In the spirit of TQM and continuous improvement, I'm reporting on a postmeeting discussion between Tom Moore and me, and trying to stimulate suggestions for improving our process. First, let me be clear that I view the high energy and strong feelings expressed at the meeting as far better than holding back and making nice. We're tackling tough issues, some of which have been simmering for years. Strong feelings are not surprising, and I'm sure there will be more. As long as we keep trying to get at the issues, I can tolerate, and even relish, plenty of heat.

Tom and I talked about what got us woofing at each other, and I think it's instructive to examine what happened. Part of Tom's irritation was because he didn't think I was listening to his point about enrollments being a better number than enrollees. To me, that was so obviously correct that (in my head) I had agreed, and assumed that we would use it for future planning. Of course, he had no way of knowing that. He also was reacting, I presume, to my several references to "Bill [the president] said we must limit the number of course sections." Tom heard this as "If Bill said it, we must comply." I certainly was not assuming we had to comply. In fact we are obligated to see what we can reasonably do. When results don't make sense, we must recognize the fact and make adjustments. Bill doesn't pretend to know that any given number of sections is the right one, and wouldn't, I'm sure, insist that his arbitrary guess be carved in stone.

It was naive of me to assume that all of you saw this as I did. I will try to be clearer in the future about my assumptions.

That connects to another of Tom's points. One of the tenets from TQM is that assignments ("requirements") be made clear by the person requesting the work, and that those receiving the request for work ask questions about just what is required, how detailed the response needs to be, how fixed the parameters are, when it is needed, etc. In general, at Babson we are rather sloppy about this, and I certainly was in this case. It seemed clear to me (again in my head) that this activity was aimed at controlling long-term demand for faculty members and

(continued)

Learning from Yesterday's Meeting *(continued)*

was just the first step in tackling the issues of course size, teaching loads, and so forth. Clearly, few others in the group were aware of all that, and I blush to admit that I didn't make myself clear.

When Tom started raising questions about what we were really trying to accomplish, I got irritated because earlier he had offered to reduce the number of course offerings by 15. So I assumed that he was clear and ready to roll. In hindsight, I see that the questions he was asking were totally appropriate, only better asked at the beginning of the process rather than at the stage we were in. Somehow, our traditions don't seem to encourage the clarification of what is desired when a request is made; in fact, over the year, I have noticed a strong propensity to keep quiet, then walk away cursing the stupidity of the requester, sniping from a distance, seeking confirmation from peers and others of the requester's stupidity (or your favorite pejorative), and then doing only the minimum necessary to get the requester off one's back. This leads to a lot of running around and redoing of the assignment ("scrap and rework" in TQM jargon). Surely we can do better.

For my part, I'll try much harder to make what I want clearer and ask that you refuse to accept any assignment until you are comfortable with its purpose, level of detail, timing, etc. I think that would help us become a part of the management of Babson. You can help by telling me what we need to be doing, and to push hard on me and each other if you get no response.

I like the feistiness that has erupted. I'm still excited about what we are building at Babson, and more committed than ever to making the strategic plan a reality.

Allan

MAKING IT MUTUAL:
WHAT MEMBERS CAN DO

Mutual influence, by definition, is a two-way street. It is not just about what the leader wants. We turn now to the reciprocal behavior of team members, who put the "mutual" into mutual influence.

Powered-up organizations depend on leaders who encourage upward influence, but those below shouldn't wait for the green light from the boss. Mutual influence is an interactive process in which either party can make the first move, even when the other seems to discourage it. Yet we have consistently observed two kinds of problematic behaviors that limit mutual influence. First many subordinates act less powerfully than they could, and second, members do not see how they can increase their leader's receptivity to being influenced.

There are a variety of ways that managers give away their power. The most common way is to go silent when they disagree with their leader or a colleague. Silence is perceived as a low risk option, though it often sets up strange interpretations or discomfort in the person who is causing a non-verbal response. Almost as limiting is phrasing disagreements in question form. This might be a safe way to express negative reactions, but it has low impact. For one thing, it produces a self-fulfilling prophecy. If the leader hears the question but not the disagreement behind it, and responds accordingly, the member will conclude that the leader has strong views and isn't easily movable, so holds back. This assures little leader movement. A third way that members lose power is by prematurely jumping to conclusions about the leader's readiness to be influenced.

Test Your Assumptions

Avoid leaping to conclusions about the leader's intentions. Instead, test the leader's willingness to be influenced.

Example at a Chip Fabricating Plant

"Marty Grand" was production scheduler for a chip fabricating plant and a member of its management team. His boss, "Luke Damico," was a nice person, but not very good at running team meetings. Discussions wandered; they seldom reached firm conclusions; and they did not address some of the serious problems affecting the chip failure rate. Luke was no tyrant, but whenever the discussions got close to the heart of issues, and emotions started to rise, Luke would step in and smooth things over, signaling that he did not like conflict.

Marty decided that he had to do something; the lack of decision making or even serious collective problem solving was hurting the plant's performance. So, at the end of a particularly ineffective meeting, Marty spoke up. "Luke, am I the only one frustrated by this meeting? Are you satisfied with the way we are working?"

Marty's teammates held their breath. Luke looked surprised but relieved. "Not really," he replied. We seem to have a hard time making decisions, and most of you aren't saying what's on your minds. I feel like I'm out there by myself, trying to drag you all into taking some initiative about our problems."

Somewhat taken aback by Luke's willingness to address the team's working methods as well as by his apparent belief that the problem was lack of member commitment, several others chimed in with their frustrations.

Marty added his surprise at Luke's response: "We need to talk about what is expected of each of us. I wasn't sure whether you wanted these meetings to be this way or not, Luke, but it sounds like you aren't so hot about them either. I'm willing to speak up more, but to tell you the truth, I thought you didn't want us to make waves. Just today you changed the subject several times when we were getting into critical but touchy territory."

"I did?" Luke asked. "When did I do that? I certainly didn't mean to. In fact, I've wondered why none of you ever grab onto the issues."

By opening the possibility of discussing the team's methods and Luke's leadership style, Marty contributed to the team and to the boss. In effect, Marty was exercising influence where it had once appeared unwelcome. Despite the possibilities for influence, many team members jump to conclusions and hold back their opinions out of fear that to dissent is to be seen as "not a team player," and not on the leader's side. No one wants to be seen as an obstruction. Being perceived negatively is not inevitable; in most cases there are ways to be honest that are perceived positively.

Being on the Leader's Side

Most disagreements between leaders and members are not over ultimate goals but the means to accomplish them. For example, the leader may want to achieve market penetration—a meritorious goal—by launching a new product before it is fully tested. Market penetration is not a disputable issue, as a goal. It is possible, however, to disagree about the timing of the launch, pointing out what happened to Intel when they shipped a high-priced chip before finding out about an embarrassing bug.

Seldom are leaders either totally resistant to influence or totally accepting of all comments; how an issue is raised makes a great deal of difference in the willingness to be influenced. Few leaders mean to suppress dissent, though like Luke Damico they may do it inadvertently. The member has valuable information in this regard: the impact of the leader's behavior. Another way to "be on the boss's side" is to provide the information about the unintentional effects of the leader's behavior. Again, how this is raised matters.

The leader is likely to be personally invested in goals, but receptive to suggestions for achieving them. As long as there is reasonable agreement about the unit's goals, then attempts to influence the leader should be about how best to realize them. When you can be explicit about supporting the larger objectives, you are saying, "I want to help in achieving those goals but I don't think this action will do that."

This approach works for more than disagreements about task issues. The leader's style itself may be seen as a "means" to reaching a goal. When this is the case, team members, without being antagonistic, can show the leader where his or her actions impede progress toward desired goals. In *Managing for Excellence,* we introduced the concept of "supportive confrontation," which is similar to the ideas in this section. Supportive confrontation also calls for getting close to another by linking to that person's aspirations and showing how particular behavior prevents reaching the aspirations.[4]

As in the example of Marty and Luke, pointing out discrepancies between intentions and results can open up new possibilities, making it legitimate to discuss specific behavior. Questions like "What were you hoping for from this meeting?" or "Did you want to get all the data on the table?" can help identify the leader's actual goals. If the relationship is positive, you can make statements like "I see how committed you are to increasing market share; it isn't as likely to happen, however, if the sales force feels attacked. I think you'll get better response from them if we acknowledge how competitive the environment has become." You know the effect of the leader's actions and have a responsibility to help make him or her as effective as possible, just as the leader has the responsibility to help members be effective.

Example of Effective Upward Influence

"Sean O'Sullivan" is a highly effective executive who usually encourages his team to participate in decisions. Every so often, however, some issue will hook him, and no objections or counterevidence offered by his team members will influence him on that issue.

Recently, Sean turned sour on the company's proposed team system. He didn't want to hear any more about it because, as he said, "I just know it wouldn't work." After some vigorous discussion, he exclaimed, "Okay, I've heard enough. We are not going ahead with this, and that's it!" There was a long silence, and team members looked down, pretending to shuffle through their papers, while they thought about how to avoid crossing Sean on this obviously sensitive issue.

Then Mark Ajanian, a senior executive who knew Sean well, said quietly, "Sean, I don't understand why you are so stuck on this. We haven't had an opportunity to discuss the team system proposal in any detail. You usually pride yourself about being logical and data-driven; but on this one, you seem to be dug in and cutting off discussion. What are we missing?"

Sean responded with no apparent enthusiasm, "Hmmm, let me think about it. I'll tell you at our operations meeting tomorrow."

The next morning, Sean came in with new ideas about how to implement part of the proposed team system. He had realized that the options posed were not sufficiently creative and had come up with new alternatives. As soon as Sean mentioned his idea for piloting 2 variations of team and leader composition, Mark agreed and built on it, and a better decision was made. Other team members were surprised by Mark's ability to work with Sean after the previous day's episode; they had been convinced that Mark was in deep trouble for challenging Sean.

Mark enjoyed influence with his boss because he had shown respect for Sean's position as leader. He had treated the disagreement about teams as due to a possible lack of information provided to Sean, had appealed to his pride in being logical, and had questioned whether his position on teams was true to his usual standard.

Though many people believe that *any* disagreement with their manager is a potentially career-limiting move, that danger may be more assumed than real. All leaders want to be effective and are receptive in some degree to influence attempts aimed at keeping them on target. If your attempts to influence are linked to the leader's interests and you are on his or her side, you can push very hard without fear. What is dangerous is the personal attack, the impugning of the leader's motives, or any attempt to undermine basic goals. Blasting the boss and using influence to shape decisions or alter the leader's behavior are two different things. (For more on how to talk more directly while staying on the other's side, see Appendix A, "Power Talk: A Hands-On Guide to Supportive Confrontation" at the end of the book.)

Get (and Give) Support

Lone voices are rarely heeded. It is difficult for one person to influence a group or to counter a group's collective views. But there is evidence that the support of just one other person can bolster the member with an unpopular view.[5] If another team member says "That's a good point—we ought to take it seriously," or, "Brian is not just speaking for himself. I see it that way too, and suspect that others do," the lone eagle who spoke first will be much more willing to stick with the point. Otherwise, the temptation to soften the point or back off entirely may be too great to withstand.

Members fail to support one another because they are afraid of being caught in the undertow of leader reaction or are morbidly curious about what will happen to the adventurer who has foolishly rushed in where angels fear to tread. "Let's you and him fight," is an organizational sport of long standing. We have witnessed several incidents in which team members pledged to support a colleague ("If you bring it up, we'll back you") only to lose heart when the battle was joined. The slightest hint of support for the member who has spoken out can alter the equation in favor of greater dialogue.

The Payoff for Taking Risks

Leaders and team members should seek an environment in which relationships are solid and two-way influence is the norm. In this environment, the leader does not have to worry about sitting around a table with people who wait mutely, offering no ideas and challenging none of his assumptions. Nor do members need to fear the leader's strength. In this environment, managerial life is freer, more fun, and more likely to get the best from everyone.

How to Influence the Leader

Here are a few ways to gain influence with the leader:

- Accept the leader's goals even when you disagree with specifics.
- Demonstrate a concern for the success of the overall unit.
- Do your own work well—meet your own objectives.
- Show loyalty to the team; support their objectives.
- Contribute something of unique value: Accounting techniques, budget status, market information, engineering updates.
- Be a source of customer knowledge: Who is ready to purchase; who is dissatisfied with service; the location of the price resistance; potential defectors.
- Be a source of organizational information: Who is a rising star, who is in the doghouse, where and when reorganizations are pending.
- Serve as the boss's own counselor: Be the one who can tell the boss how his or her behavior is undermining his or her organizational aims, creating hard feelings or resistance, or diminishing motivation.

Once you have determined what your manager most values, you will know what you can give in return for what you need. No matter what end you seek, link your request or argument to what is important to the leader.

If this sounds like wishful thinking, take heart. No matter how stubborn, autocratic, or resistant you believe your manager to be, he or she also has a stake in getting the best from you and your peers, and you can tie your influence attempts to that stake. Remember that the context in which power is important is mutual influence; as a team member you want influence to help your leader manage well, and as a leader, you want to be sure that the people with whom you work are as potent as they can be because that helps them help you. The purpose of power enhancement is not self-aggrandizement.

CONCLUSION

All the ideas about influence upward apply equally to colleagues and members of the team(s) you manage. Peers are influenced by exchanges, as are direct reports. The teams of which you are a member can only operate by consensus on important issues when everyone has the skill and willingness to influence each other and be influenced. Even when you can give orders, it is seldom a good idea to do so, since you want to reinforce the idea of partnership and encourage your direct reports to take up their part of the post-heroic system.

Shared responsibility leadership requires many changes in follower attitudes and behavior; the challenge is to influence them to want to change. You will need to provide something each finds valuable in return for their cooperation, so the same model of influence applies in all directions.[6]

The interconnections among the post-heroic mind-set—tangible vision, the shared responsibility team, and mutual influence—are now complete. Part Three of this book uses the methods and results from one extended case history, Pharmco, to go deeper into how you can put these elements to work in your organization.

PART THREE

ESTABLISHING A SHARED-RESPONSIBILITY SYSTEM

Part One of this book compared the basic mind-sets of heroic and post-heroic leadership. When members and leaders hold similar heroic views about leading and following, they create a mutually reinforcing, change-resistant system. To release the full power within organizations, an entirely new mind-set of shared responsibility must be adopted. Part Two explored the three key elements of post-heroic leadership—a shared-responsibility team, tangible vision, and mutual influence. Part Three uses an extended case study to illustrate how an organization can bring those elements together and, by so doing, establish a system of shared responsibility.

The first chapter of this book introduced Pharmco, a company facing a host of strategic, team, and interpersonal problems. We revisit that company in Chapters 9 through 12 and show how its management team overcame problems of leadership, internal competition, investment choices, and reorganization, transforming itself within a short time from a dysfunctional team to a highly productive organization. The insights of this case are extended to other organizational settings.

9

LAUNCHING CHANGE

Creating a shared responsibility system is a major organizational change. Like other change efforts, it is necessary to plan carefully, involve the right players, articulate a clear vision of the desired outcomes, work from dissatisfaction to assure sufficient motivation, specify the path to get there, prepare the rest of the organization for the changes, and expect the unexpected. Although a shared leadership system may begin within a particular management team, the system above and below that team must also change if change is to last.

Preparing the organization for change requires addressing and altering all those who have powerful assumptions about leadership. Not everyone need accept the post-heroic system, but should know the change objectives. Changing expectations is a way of preparing the soil for planting new practices, new ways of working together.

PHARMCO: A BRIEF HISTORY

Pharmco had been started by Gene Roberts, a chemist who developed a new line of pesticides just when DDT was being phased out. The company was known for both the quality of its agricultural products and its skill at staying one step ahead of its competitors. The ability of crop-damaging pests to develop immunities to pesticides requires a continuing stream of new products, and Pharmco did that very well. Roberts also pushed the company toward animal vaccines, and about seven years earlier he had negotiated the acquisition of a small company working on biogenetically engineered seed products. Two years after that transaction, Pharmco acquired a division being spun off by another company; that division developed and manufactured diagnostic equipment for testing animals. Although he seldom pushed the idea, Roberts had in mind the concept of "surrounding the farmer with Pharmco products."

Pharmco's primary sales strength was in the U.S. plains states, where Roberts had started. Over the years, however, the company had developed sales operations in the southern and western states as well as in Canada, and Latin America. Although the market potential of Asia had been discussed, no tangible steps toward expansion there had been taken.

An irrepressible entrepreneur, Gene Roberts loved getting his fingers into every part of the business he had created—from developing labels for new products to schmoozing with customers. He worked intuitively, trusting "gut feel" more than fancy management techniques. His instincts had, in fact, served him well over the years, and he often anticipated trends before others. His rough, good-old-boy style was much appreciated by the company's dealers and distributors, but it was less appreciated by some people inside Pharmco. Aware that his style could seem autocratic and threatening, Roberts deliberately chose a second-in-command with greater patience and stronger interpersonal skills, COO Bob Mitchell.

Besides Mitchell, several others reported directly to Gene Roberts: the VPs of finance, research, corporate communications, and legal and government relations. The VP of finance had a dotted-line (informal) reporting relationship to Bob. Bob Mitchell's direct reports were the VPs of the line divisions, international and human resources, and he ran

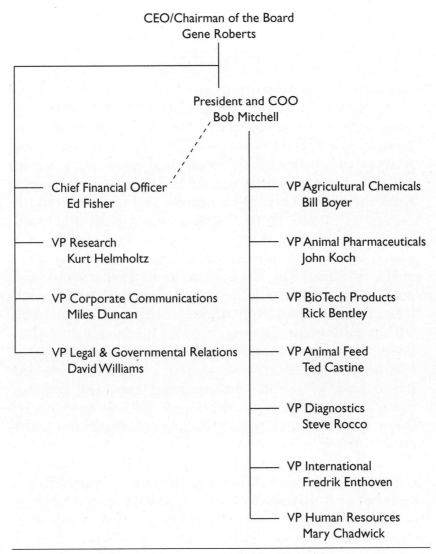

Figure 9–1. Organization Chart—Pharmco

the OpCom meetings with Roberts' people in attendance (see Figure 9–1).

Pharmco: Part I

As discussed in Chapter 1, Bill Boyer, one of the divisional VPs, had complained bitterly to Bob Mitchell about his frustrations with Gene Roberts and the company's operating committee (OpCom), of which he was a member. To Boyer, the CEO was an interfering, arbitrary manager who made the meetings of the OpCom a disaster.

Bob was disturbed by the problems cited by Boyer. He too was dissatisfied with the way things were going for the company and for him personally. He believed that Boyer's complaints were justified: the OpCom was more of a discussion group than a problem-solving team. And Gene Roberts, despite his contributions and creativity, was part of the problem. Meetings ran better when he wasn't there. Even though Bob set up an agenda and tried to hold the group to it, Gene felt free to explore any path that interested him. Bob would try to gently steer him back to the main point, but often without success. Yet if Gene was not at the meetings, there was little point in discussing important topics, since he would override decisions at will. If Gene was upset with a manager, he would badger him with relentless questioning.

But Gene wasn't the only problem. The five line divisions operated independently and competitively. Rivalry between Boyer and John Koch was causing constant sniping. Boyer's agricultural chemicals product line represented the original business, but Koch's had steadily grown to the point of being its equal in profit contributions.

Rick Bentley's genetically engineered product line area was also a sore point. When Gene acquired that division, he separated it from Agriculture, knowing that Boyer's people would feel threatened by its very different approach to product creation. Their rivalry nevertheless worked against the company.

Each of the line divisions was fully integrated, with its own sales, marketing, production, finance, and research functions. So several sales forces called on the same customers. Agricultural and Biotech weren't above undercutting each other in an effort to boost their own chances to make a sale. There were also rivalries between animal health and animal feed. Mitchell believed that interdivisional competition was unnecessary since the divisions could nicely complement each other. Also, the rise of organic farming created new possibilities for market segmentation.

The International group was primarily sales and marketing, and handled foreign sales for all of the line divisions. There were constant battles from the divisions to receive more share-of-mind from the sales force. To date, International had not been a major contributor to the company. Yet there was great potential for growth.

The company's multiple research organizations were yet another source of conflict. The line divisions were mostly interested in applied work and saw little short-term value in Kurt Helmholtz's basic research operation. Thus, each of the five divisions went its own way, causing considerable duplication and too little investment in fundamental research. Gene had little faith in formal product development research anyway, so these conflicts went unchecked.

Ed Fisher, the VP of finance was another source of difficulty. Because Gene used Ed to find out what was going on, Ed was viewed as the carrier of bad news upstairs. The divisional VPs instructed their finance people to delay telling Ed of any problems until they had time to try to clean them up. This only fed the CEO's suspicions that bad news was being swept under the carpet. Bob Mitchell, however, had no difficulties with Ed, who always made himself available when needed.

These many factors seriously limited individual and organizational performance, making OpCom meetings unproductive. Bob Mitchell recognized how they contributed to the team's difficulty in addressing major organizational problems. The whole company was stumbling because of the team's ineffectiveness. For example, the diagnostic equipment business had not taken off as expected. Steve Rocco claimed the equipment division was the poor stepchild of the company and did not receive the development money it needed.

Mitchell wasn't sure of the cause of Rocco's problem, but he was certain that it and other fundamental strategic issues weren't being aired during OpCom meetings. Companywide expansion was just one of those issues. Everyone knew that Pharmco had to grow or it would be reduced to a bit player in an increasingly competitive market. One option was to expand the range of Pharmco's product lines within the dominant geographic market (the Americas, especially the United States). Moving into new markets was an alternative strategy. The latter seemed especially appealing, given high potential sales in Asia.

Geographic expansion had major organizational implications: the company could add a VP of Asian Sales or pull all domestic sales and marketing out of the line divisions and integrate them with the international Sales and Marketing function. Mitchell knew that Boyer and Koch would certainly fight any move that would diminish their turfs.

For Mitchell, Pharmco was struggling through a sea of storms: He saw problems with his boss and squalls involving the division chieftains in whichever direction he looked. He saw himself at the center of these storms and the only one capable of keeping the company on course.

Pharmco's problems caused Mitchell to reflect on his own future. Gene had hinted that he would be his successor "when I am ready to retire." Gene had just turned 66 and was talking about spending more time at his ranch in the Rockies. But would he ever really let go? Mitchell remembered reading a book about founders, which concluded that the transition was rarely easy. "They either have to die or be fired," the author stated. He knew that he and Gene couldn't continue down this same path much longer.

Three forces converged to prompt Bob's desire to change to a new form of leadership. First, Bob, Gene, and the members were all increasingly dissatisfied with the way OpCom meetings were going and with its inability to resolve the difficult strategic choices that the organization faced. Second was Bob's personal frustration about his blocked career. But the third pressure came from below. Bob had been introduced earlier to the post-heroic leadership model by the director of training and development, who was enthusiastic about introducing shared leadership as the basis for a new training program for middle managers. Bob had approved because this approach to leading fit his values. The program had been so well received that many of the participating middle managers had begun to question why senior executives in OpCom dealt with each other in ways so at odds with a training program that stressed openness, shared responsibility, teamwork, and mutual influence.

All this came to a head after the meeting in which Gene had cut off Bill Boyer and trashed his idea. Boyer's subsequent complaints about Gene's behavior and the failings of the OpCom set the subsequent change process in motion.

Discussions with a Consultant

Bob Mitchell decided that he needed to move forward. He had informally discussed many of these issues with his direct reports one-on-one. Each had provided a useful perspective, but always from his or her own vantage point. Nor was Bob certain that they were being direct. "After all, I don't always tell them everything I think." He held back some of his concerns for fear of demoralizing his troops. "So why should I expect any more from them?"

Bob Mitchell realized that he needed to talk to someone with whom he could be totally frank. He immediately thought of a management consultant named Lincoln (Linc) Turner. Turner already had good working relationships with many senior executives because Pharmco had used him over the years as a development coach. Furthermore, Lincoln had helped develop the middle management training program so was knowledgeable about the new post-heroic leadership model. Mitchell had personally made use of his services once before, in that case to sort out some problems he was having with Bill Boyer. Mitchell contacted him and set up a meeting.

The meeting took place at Bob Mitchell's house the following Saturday. Mitchell laid out his frustrations with Gene, with the team, the organization, and with his own future. During a 15-minute rant, he placed most of the problem on Gene's doorstep, all the while claiming that he was "loyal to Gene and did not want to lead a revolt."

"Look, Bob," the consultant responded, "Gene's behavior is certainly a major issue, but aren't you also part of the problem? In defining your role as a buffer between Gene and the other OpCom members, you are keeping them from raising their concerns with Gene directly. Are you protecting your troops from unreasonable attacks, or are you just avoiding conflict?"

Bob responded defensively, pointing out how difficult Gene could be when anyone disagreed with him. He added, "Besides, I don't want him to feel attacked." After a pause, he confessed, "And I really feel immobilized not knowing if I'm ever going to be made CEO."

"Bob," Turner said, "You have two challenges that until now you have avoided: First, you need to confront Gene about his disruptive behavior—and you need to do this before the team will be able to do it constructively. And second, you have to find out where you stand on the issue of becoming CEO."

"I think I can do the first one, though I wasn't raised to deal with conflict openly," Bob responded, "But the second is easier said than done. It's a really difficult conversation, and what if he gives me the song-and-dance about how 'It's likely, but the board isn't sure yet.' If he tells me that, I'll be no further ahead than I was before."

"Sure, it's going to be tough confronting him, Bob, but you need to expand your leadership repertoire beyond what you were raised to do. You need to find out what his concerns are with you and negotiate some agreement. At 48, you are at the prime age to take a CEO job, but if Gene strings you along for another seven years, which he could do, then getting another job will be problematic. If the CEO job at Pharmco isn't in the cards, isn't it better to know now?"

Bob grudgingly conceded that Turner was right.

"You also need to use every opportunity to act as Gene's partner and demonstrate that you can deal with the tough issues. Each of the problems you've told me about—fighting among the VPs, the decision about expansion strategy, even Gene's intrusive behavior—is an opportunity for you to demonstrate your toughness. Avoiding these just confirms to Gene that you're not a peer, not presidential, that you're not up to the job as he sees it."

Turner told Mitchell that his preference to "work around problems" by dealing one-on-one with Gene or with a particular divisional VP wasn't the right way to build a team. "The only way to get a strong team is to get the team involved in making the big calls. Let *them* join you in wrestling with the big decisions. There'll be fights, maybe even screaming and yelling. But in the end whatever you decide *as a team* will almost certainly be better than anything that you and Gene decide in his office. Let's face it, Bob, these people have insights and information that you and Gene, smart as you are, can't know about! You need them."

Mitchell agreed with the consultant, but confessed that he wasn't sure how to raise these issues with his boss. Turner suggested, "Even though you need to be direct and not beat around the bush, you'll be more effective if you frame them so that they speak to Gene's best interests and not yours alone."

A natural opportunity for Bob Mitchell to begin some team building was close at hand—an off-site strategic retreat. The official purpose of the retreat was to respond to recommendations about Pharmco strategy from a large consulting firm hired several months ago to study options. Bob knew that the recommendations would be far-reaching and controversial; if the team didn't improve its ability to function, it would be paralyzed by the decisions required. If it could improve its way of operating while making the tough decisions, that would help the team and the organization start to share the leadership in important ways. The retreat was also an opportunity for Bob to start a different kind of relationship with Gene Roberts, the company's powerful CEO and founder.

Bob had the rest of the weekend to decide how to proceed.

MEETING WITH GENE

Gene and Bob met every Monday afternoon. On Monday morning, Bob stuck his head into Gene's office to say that he was concerned about the organization's ability to deal with the recommendations in the strategy report. "Can we put these on our agenda this afternoon?" Gene nodded but didn't seem surprised. "I wonder if he has the same concerns," Bob mused as he went around the corner to his own office.

Bob didn't get much else done that morning; he was preoccupied with playing over in his mind how best to approach the situation. By the time the meeting rolled around, he was ready.

"Gene, we've both seen the preliminary consulting report. They have shown clearly that we have no overall strategy, only a collection of separate strategies for each division. I think you would agree that what we decide and our ability to execute will determine whether we grow or stagnate."

Gene was surprised by the forcefulness of Bob's statement, but nodded in agreement.

"My major concern," Bob continued, "is with our ability—or should I say inability—to work as a team. Our OpCom meetings are largely a waste of time. We don't deal with important issues and people play it close to their chest."

"Damn right," Gene thundered, "that's the problem with all this groupy stuff. They are more concerned with looking good and having safe relationships with each other than in facing the tough issues. Leadership, Bob, requires getting to the bottom of things quickly."

Bob tried not to respond defensively. "Gene, it sounds like that's why you probe so hard when you think there is a problem."

"Of course. If I didn't, people would just talk in circles."

Bob had clearly touched one of his boss's hot buttons. "Bob," Gene continued, "We're losing our entrepreneurial edge. Pharmco is turning into a sluggish bureaucracy where highly paid people are more concerned about defending their turfs than in getting the job done. I see it every time I sit in on one of your meetings. They're all talk and no action."

"Gene, I agree that we need to be tougher and I haven't done my part. I have acted more as a protector than as the COO. But to turn things around I need some things from you."

"Like what?"

Bob took a deep breath and plunged in. Part of the difficulty, he told Gene, was that everyone was caught in a vicious circle. The more that Gene played "prosecuting attorney," the more that others acted to protect themselves and, in turn, the more that Bob tried to smooth things over. And, of course, the more Bob and the managers withheld, the more Gene probed. "Well, if you didn't hold back—if your meetings weren't such gab-fests—I wouldn't need to push," Gene replied, obviously intrigued.

"Fair enough," Bob responded, "but if we get someone to take the initiative and raise a tough issue, can you keep from nailing him?" Dubious, Gene asked, "How are you going to get them to do that?"

Bob responded that he wanted to build a strong team, tough enough to be able to share responsibility for crucial strategic issues. "And I want to use the strategic report, and the way we deal with it, as an opportunity to build just such a team. That way everyone will be contributing and not just taking up space."

Gene was visibly skeptical, but considered Bob's points. They talked about how a team could actually work, the type of core problems the group should deal with, how to get members to take ownership for the company and not just push their own areas, and the implications for Bob's and Gene's styles. Bob then shifted gears. "As long as we're talking turkey here, Gene, I need to tell you this: If you want me to be an effective COO, finance should re-port to me."

Gene balked: "You're asking me to let go of the best lever I have over this group with no evidence that your scheme will work? Those figures tell me what's *really* going on. I don't have any assurance that you'll keep me on top of things."

Bob countered that the problem was that Gene used the figures to jump into line management, undercutting his po-sition as COO. "I'm supposed to be the COO, remember? But you get into managing down the line, and I'm left looking like a puppet, and a limp one at that." The two argued about their respective roles, but eventually arrived at a compro-mise. Fisher in finance and Williams in legal/governmental relations would have a solid-line (direct) reporting relation-ship to both Gene and Bob. Also, Gene would check with his COO about any issue deeper in the organization, giving him the option of being the one who followed up.

Emboldened by his progress, Bob turned to his own future.

"Gene, before this is all over, I need to know whether I will be the next CEO; if it's never going to happen, I need to look elsewhere. If you have concerns about my abilities, it's time we put them on the table."

Gene seemed relieved that this difficult subject had been raised. He confessed to concerns about Bob's lack of decisiveness and toughness. "I'm afraid that we will lose the entrepreneurial spirit that got us this far. I don't want to see us with nothing more than a feel-good atmosphere. But if you come through in the ways you have been talk-ing about this afternoon, I will be much less worried."

They ended the meeting with a number of agreements: Bob would take on a more problem-raising role and be less protective of his team; Gene would not interfere with op-erational meetings; Bob could confront Gene whenever the CEO hounded one of his team members; and each would publicly point out any violations of those agreements.

Back at his office, Bob reflected on the meeting. It was one of the most difficult he had ever been through. Being that direct made him uncomfortable, but he felt good about the outcome. "It cleared the air," he thought, "and even better, it feels like we have changed the nature of the relationship." The trick would be to stick with it under fire. Bob had to explain these agreements to the OpCom and figure out how to turn intentions into action.

MEETING WITH THE OPCOM

Tuesday morning was the regularly scheduled OpCom meeting. Bob began by describing the challenging organizational problems they would be facing over the next six months. Then he dropped the bomb.

"I am dissatisfied with the way this team has been operating, and I know that many of you feel the same way. This has to change. We have to start pulling together. Everyone has to be more up front, and more willing to put aside parochial concerns. Otherwise, we'll never find workable solutions to the problems that will come our way in the months ahead."

The people at the table could feel a change in the air. Several of the team members had been so discouraged about the team that they had once before raised similar points, but had given up when little had changed. About all they had ever accomplished was the introduction of the "shot pot," a jar into which anyone who took a cheap shot at another member would have to contribute $10. That had made the meetings more controlled, but no more honest or effective. They were glad that Bob was now at least acknowledging the problems. Gene liked what he heard.

Bob then briefly reviewed his agreements with Gene, and their expectations of each of the people sitting around the conference table. He noted the look of surprise on their faces. Several glanced sideways to gauge Gene's reaction, which was deadpan. Bob then laid out his expectations for the group.

"Here's the news, folks. From now on we are going to share responsibility for managing Pharmco. What does that mean for you? It means that you will continue to represent your areas—marketing, research, and so forth—but you will also have to do what's best for this organization. In my book, doing what's best for Pharmco means being open about our individual problems, helping each other out whenever possible, and holding each other accountable to high standards of performance. Each of us will still be able to fight for what we believe to be right, but that fighting can't be motivated by one-upsmanship or nasty intentions. Going at it must serve a higher purpose: to get the best results for Pharmco and this entire group."

Bob then returned to the agenda. As the meeting went on, he thought that his pointed speech had done some good; the OpCom was operating with a little more candor and less guardedness. Gene seemed to be involved, but without having to control everything. At the meeting's end, Bob reminded the group of the upcoming retreat.

"We are going to have some tough issues to handle. It isn't reasonable to expect that we can be a top-notch team overnight; we will need some help. I propose that we add a day to the retreat and bring in Linc Turner to help us with the team-building."

This was met with loud protests. "We have been through these sessions before and we don't need any more 'lost-on-the-moon' exercises. They don't lead anywhere." Bob felt blocked.

Mary Chadwick finally jumped in, "Can't we do our development while we struggle with the strategic issues? Let's have this be a work session, but bring in Turner as the consultant to help us identify when we get stuck, and do short training bits that help us over the rough spots. Then if this works, we can do more; this won't be the last retreat on strategic issues." The group reluctantly agreed, but was adamant about not adding another day. Feeling that half a loaf would have to do, Bob conceded.

"We will start Friday noon with a presentation from the strategy consultants. Each of you will receive a copy of their report next Wednesday. As you read it, try not to respond from the perspective of your individual areas but from the Pharmco-as-a-company viewpoint that Gene or I would."

In the week that followed, several OpCom members came by Bob's office to get a better sense of what was going on. Was he really serious about sharing responsibility? How would they deal with all the subgroups and covert battles? What would make them like each other any better? Did he really think Gene could change? There was some enthusiasm for the possibilities inherent in the new arrangement. Mary Chadwick from HR, and another manager strongly supported Bob's effort to work out a new role, and offered to help. Bob was relieved that "at least I'm not going into this alone."

PREPARATIONS

At Bob Mitchell's request, Lincoln Turner met with Gene. His objective was to better understand the CEO's views and prepare him for the upcoming retreat. In Gene's view, there needed to be even more clarity and specifics about his and Bob's roles, "not just written down, like now, but in practice, so we don't have two COOs." He believed that they lacked a common vision they could all follow. He thought the company was "dead in the water" if the management group didn't pull together. Gene clearly wanted tougher management and had serious reservations about Bob's willingness to push lagging performers.

"Do you think that Bob will succeed in getting the OpCom team to start taking responsibility and to work toward your goals?" Turner asked the CEO. "I wouldn't bet my ranch on it, would you?" he replied. Nevertheless, he recognized that his behavior at the retreat would play a part in the success or failure of Mitchell's efforts and he grudgingly agreed to be supportive at the retreat. "I hope that he makes it work," Gene said. "I have outside interests I'd like to pursue, but I really can't until Bob can take charge of the company."

Bob and Turner met later that week to work out the retreat agenda. Turner agreed with Mary Chadwick's suggestion to integrate team-building with task work. They decided to start on Friday afternoon with the strategy consultants' report. This would be more comfortable for the managers. The strategy recommendations were something that the group could wrestle with and would provide fodder for subsequent discussion of how they would work as a team.

Like his boss, Bob had doubts about the likely success of his plan. He worried about whether Gene would ever back off, and that even if he did and a cohesive OpCom group really took ownership of the key issues, Gene might see Bob as being weak and losing control. If that happened, Gene would step in and take over. The OpCom members themselves were another concern. They were more skilled at jockeying for position than collaborating. If he encouraged discussion of the really tough problems, would his well-planned retreat turn into a brawl?

Linc tried to reassure Bob that nothing would be worse than continuing along in the same ineffective ways.

The day prior to the retreat, Bob stuck his head in Gene's office and asked how he was feeling about the upcoming meeting. Gene shrugged noncommittally and said, "I just don't want it to be a waste of time. My daughter's coming to visit this weekend with the grandchildren, so let's hope something good happens at this retreat."

"Both of us might be getting some hard-to-hear feedback from the group," Bob warned, but again Gene expressed little reaction. "Better than tiptoeing around" was his only response.

ISSUES IN THE PHARMCO CASE

With a situation as blocked as the one at Pharmco, what can a leader like Bob Mitchell do to unclog the system? Where can he start? How can he create a more effective partnership with the team members whose cooperation he needs and with a boss whose instincts take him in an opposite direction?

Bob has a dilemma. He knows that a series of crucial strategic decisions have to be made, but he also knows that they will be worthless if Gene and the members do not endorse and own them. He needs to arrive at an accepted vision for the company, but that is impossible without a team that knows how to agree. He has to influence the team members to give their all, but he cannot influence them without first overcoming their skepticism about his leadership.

Bob also recognizes a second layer of problems: The company lacks an effective problem-solving, decision-making system. People are not aligned around a common direction, they do not speak out openly and constructively, they do not work together to improve the business. So he must set a vision—shared leadership—for how the team will work and then must focus on implementing that. To build such a system, Bob has to gain commitment to this vision of how to operate, has to build a team invested in this new way, has to use influence to get Gene to cooperate, and even has to get the team members to put in the time at the strategic retreat.

The shared responsibility team will be the vehicle for creating the fundamental conditions for mutuality and partnership in achieving better business decisions.

Seeing the Organization as a System

The first step in creating shared responsibility is to diagnose the situation objectively. To do this, you must detach yourself and view the organization as a system in which all parties are connected. The interlocking patterns of behavior must be identified. In the Pharmco case, Bob is both a leader and a follower. Creating a new leadership system will certainly require him to change his behavior in some ways, But he should also understand how others in the system—both above and below—must change. To alter his relationship with Gene and win the autonomy he desires, Bob will need considerable cooperation from the team members. Bill Boyer's complaints to Bob helped launch the change process. The team will have to work together better and make team meetings action oriented. If they won't change, Gene won't care that Bob is behaving more decisively.

Gene also must change. The OpCom members will only become more collaborative and company-minded when Gene changes his behavior and stops interfering, but his new behavior will only persist if they do their part. Gene must also learn to accept his new role and not view cohesion between his COO and the OpCom as shutting him out of company management.[1]

Overcoming Ambivalence

An earlier chapter described the ambivalence of leaders and members toward really dramatic change. Greater experience with post-heroic leadership reduces that ambivalence.

One of the dilemmas leaders face when they want to create a new leadership system is the personal investment they must make. It's not possible to purchase a shiny new leadership system and have it installed on Tuesday; the leader is part of the system and must be deeply involved. The leader will be watched closely for signs of low commitment, insincerity, or unwillingness to change in line with the new culture. Lukewarm commitment is a prescription for failure.

On the other hand, deep commitment to something new and beyond one's experience is not easy. The leader needs to do some testing, think through the likely consequences of plunging ahead, and develop a phased plan adding modifications as necessary to achieve genuine commitment. The ambivalent leader should wade in when taking a full plunge would be too risky. This can be accomplished through a task force or through a unit in desperate need of change. Either of these can serve as a "test bed" for the new system. In general, it is better to do whatever you can to assure that early change experiments will be successful, but when that isn't possible, untested innovative approaches may still carry the day.

Bob Mitchell's conversation with Lincoln Turner, who was willing to challenge Bob about his assumptions and behavior, helped to move Bob past his ambivalence. Mitchell was definitely part of the problem as well as a critical part of the solution, and nothing could go forward until he was comfortable with the direction and concepts.

Tying the New Leadership to Important Decisions

Bob Mitchell's decision to use the upcoming strategic planning retreat as a vehicle for engaging people in the new leadership was risky but wise. Leadership ideas are meaningless if not tied to critical managerial decisions; they are part and parcel of daily business life, apparent in the tough decisions, how they are executed, and how people work together.

Mitchell's linking of team development with front burner strategic issues undercut any suspicions that this would simply be fun and games, as so often happens. The risk was that things would explode: Either the team wouldn't buy it, decision making would be paralyzed, Gene or Bob would return to their old habits, or the Pharmco people wouldn't have the skills to make post-heroic leadership work.

Doing It for the Right Reasons

The risks Bob Mitchell was taking were only justifiable if commensurate rewards were available in terms of better business results. The reason for adopting a post-heroic leadership system is performance improvement. Too often, advocates for changes in relationships justify the costs and risks of change efforts on the basis of team solidarity and good feelings. These are valuable, but no changes last for long if they do not produce better results. And there is ample evidence that good feelings do not necessarily lead to better performance, although they often follow it.

There is a danger that people with high affiliation needs will latch onto the ideas presented here and become advocates for the wrong reasons, turning off hard-nosed managers who need the new ways. Tough managers often growl that business isn't a lonely hearts club, and they are right. Work can be deeply satisfying, and fun, and a source of genuine connection, but these should be by-products of work, not goals. Great results are their own justification.

Changing Expectations

It is generally best to prepare the turf outside your unit before launching any change: Talking about your goals with your own manager, showing the benefits to the company, informing other leaders, prepping colleagues as to what they might expect, lining up resources, and so on.

It isn't always necessary for one's manager to change his or her own style to accommodate the change desired, but you at least want to reduce apprehension, misunderstandings, or opposition. Be sure your leader knows what is being attempted, what impacts it might have, and how the results will satisfy his or her true business interests. At Pharmco, Gene was a key person, and Bob had to prepare him for the feedback that he would be hearing. In addition, Gene needed to understand that Bob was willing to move early on difficult performance issues, even though his way of addressing them might be different from Gene's. If your boss has a highly traditional view of leadership, and wants to see you leading in the same way, you need to spend time to negotiate some latitude, as Bob did with Gene.

Change Can Begin Anywhere

Because every part of a system is interconnected, change in any one part will produce changes elsewhere. Thus, the leader need not be the prime mover of change. Bob's boss Gene could have initiated change; so too could have any OpCom team member. Any one of them could have raised questions about the way they were failing to address Pharmco's critical issues. Bill Boyer did, although his attacking style made him less effective than he could have been. Had he been more skillful in talking to his boss, as was the consultant, Bill could have gotten Pharmco moving in the right direction sooner.

Initiating change and sustaining it, however, are two different matters. Anyone in the Pharmco case could have gotten the ball rolling, but no one—not Gene, Bob, Bill Boyer, or the consultant—could have kept it rolling without the support and collaboration of others who must also change.

BEYOND PHARMCO

A shift from heroic to post-heroic leadership, like that at Pharmco, requires all the elements of a major change effort. Such changes take time, especially if there are expectations of transforming the total culture of the company. Champions of major change must:

- *Anticipate resistance.* It doesn't matter how wonderful the new world will be, no major change will win more than a small percentage of instant converts. People resist change for all kinds of reasons: fear of the unknown; knowledge of how change will affect their future, their relationships, or the work they have been doing; past negative experiences with similar changes; an inability to imagine the new state or how to get there; a lack of implementation skills; and so on.

- *Be persistent and flexible.* Without persistence, organizational inertia will carry the day. Organizations can be remarkably resilient in bending but bouncing back to their basic state. Sticking with the goals of the change are critical. At the same time, drivers of change have to learn to be flexible, adjusting as they encounter resistance, discover new data, and learn from their experiences early in the implementation cycle.[2]

- *Hold up an exciting vision of what will be possible when change is accomplished.* Little significant change is likely without an exciting vision. People need to see that change will be worth all the effort. Sometimes that can be accomplished by a vivid description of the desired future state; in other cases those who are supposed to implement changes need to see people in other organizations actually living the new behavior in their day-to-day work. It is difficult to visualize interactive changes in the abstract.

- *Identify clear pathways.* Similarly, the pathways for arriving at the new state must be visible and the possibility of mastering them credible. If people cannot see a way to a different state, change will stall, even if they are excited about the prospects. They need to understand the roles, structures, teams, agendas, and skills required and how to acquire them. The idea of flying is inspiring, but a simple directive to "Leap tall buildings in a single bound" will leave everyone stuck on the runway. High flyers need to know the specifics of how to get off the ground.

- *Align practices and policies with desired outcomes.* Take a systems view of things. If you want the organization to reflect a mind-set of shared responsibility, you'll eventually have to change practices and policies that stand in the way such as traditional measurement and reward systems, career paths, and reporting relationships. Though a lot can happen before all accompanying changes are implemented if there is good will and trust, to sustain change these subsystems must be aligned and in tune with the future you aim to create.

Readiness for Change to Post-Heroic Leadership

The prescriptions just described apply to any situation in which broad-based change is the goal, Pharmco being just one. Others are more specific to the organization that aims to change to the post-heroic model. If you are the leader of that change, here are a few questions to ask yourself:

- *Is the post-heroic style appropriate to the situation?* Shared responsibility leadership will not cure every organizational disease. It works best when:

  Tasks are highly interdependent.

  The environment is complex and rapidly changing.

  No single person, including the leader, has almost all of the needed expertise.

  Team member and leader goals and values are basically aligned.

  Outstanding performance is needed and desired.

  Absent these conditions, heroic leadership can get decent results, with less strain, since heroic assumptions are so widespread and die hard. (At Pharmco, each of these conditions was present.)

- *Do people feel the need for change?* Major changes seldom are undertaken without strong needs being felt by key players in the organization. Bob Mitchell felt the need to make difficult strategic choices, overcome dissatisfaction about the way the team operated, and gain some clarity about his career future.

Crisis is another motivator of change, galvanizing people to action. New competition, declining market share, a key player leaving, an impending merger or acquisition, loss of major customers, labor unrest, sharply declining profits—something cries out for not doing business as usual. But crises pass, allowing everyone to slip back to the old ways of leading and following. Sustaining behavioral changes usually requires more than a response to current crises; if there is no passion for extraordinary performance, the perceived need for change may fade. This is where the articulation of the post-heroic leadership system, a clear picture of what it looks like and how it would work, is as necessary as tangible vision about products or strategy. It is hard enough to change behavior when it is clearly specified and near-term, like quitting smoking; it is less probable that people will embrace the painful journey of change without a clear picture of the promised land. If you are the driver toward changed leadership practices, you need to spell out what kind of organization you are striving for—and why.

NEGOTIATING WITH THE BOSS

Here is a final piece of advice about changing the leadership system: Get the boss on your side. It is much easier to create change from the middle of the organization when you have a leader who will support you and provide resources. The boss's approval may not be necessary if you are already a star, or can obtain quick results, but it is still desirable. Managing post-heroically, however, does not require that your boss become post-heroic. Leaders who share responsibility can and do operate with heroic bosses. It is important that your boss feel comfortable with your preferred management style. Here is how to gain that comfort without forcing your boss to change style.

Negotiate Means, Not Ends

To achieve freedom to manage post-heroically with a heroic boss, negotiate autonomy on stylistic means in exchange for agreed-to goals. Be certain that you understand the outcomes and measures that matter, and commit to achieving them. Your commitment should be explicit: "These objectives, in this order of priority, by these deadlines, are what you want. That is what I will deliver." Having agreed to your boss's goals, and having committed yourself to them, you should be able to negotiate the means to those ends. "I need to manage in ways that fit my style. To deliver on these goals, I need discretion on how I manage." So many subordinates try to weasel out of accountability that most (heroic) bosses will be sufficiently pleased with your commitment to allow you the flexibility to manage as you see fit.

Understand the Boss's Concerns

If your boss is reluctant to agree to the bargain just described, don't jump to the conclusion that he or she is rigid, a control freak, or stupid. Instead, look for an unspoken concern. Is your boss afraid that an emphasis on groups will retard decision making, produce mediocre compromises, or cause you to give away the shop? Does he fear that the emphasis on vision will produce nothing but vapid slogans? Does she simply not understand the new leadership approach? Once you have found the underlying source of the boss's hesitance, you have a much better chance of finding a way to deal with it.

The greatest concern of almost all bosses is that a system of shared responsibility will result in no one taking responsibility. You can counter this concern by stressing that nothing in your style will ever lead you to pass off your own responsibility and accountability; in the final analysis the boss can and should hold you accountable for your unit's performance.

Use the Boss's Language

Managers desiring change often forget the first lesson of selling any idea: Frame it in language that is compatible with and familiar to the audience. People who have not been immersed in your ideas may not understand its particular jargon, or they may have negative associations with certain words. Traditional managers may associate the language of post-heroic leadership—words like collaboration, sharing responsibility, peer control, and consensus—with soft-headed management and "touchy-feely" psychology. Post-heroic leaders can use tougher language to express the same ideas. They can talk about "moving away from hand-holding," "demanding more from subordinates," "treating them like adults," "getting people to pull together, or to open their kimonos." Some organizations tend toward military metaphors, which can be as heroic as "command and control," or "following orders," but as supportive of collaboration as "foxhole buddies," "storming the hill," "listening to the troops," or "not letting down your comrades in arms." The issue is not deception but clear communication—when in Rome, speak Italian.

Link with the Organization's Goals and Values

Every organization has a set of core values, whether or not they have been made explicit. For some, it is customer responsiveness; for others, it is technical innovation or entrepreneurial spirit. Many organizations are facing the need for major readjustment—a shift in strategy, reenergizing of the product line, or adaptation to restructuring. Since the essence of managing post-heroically is focusing all members on joint ownership of organizational goals, it is essential to link your managerial aspirations to the goals and traditions of the organization. Doing so will make the shift in management style seem less like wild horses running off in their own direction and more like an innovative process to achieve mutually acknowledged objectives.

The way to deal with a heroic boss is to *find the core objectives or values and show how your new way of leading will help achieve them.* By focusing on core objectives or values, the post-heroic leader can do what traditional managers cannot, get subordinates to pull together toward goals that the boss supports.

ROLE OF THE TEAM MEMBERS

Leaders and managers aren't the only ones who can create change in the system; members can help to both initiate and support change. As at Pharmco, it is possible to raise concerns about the consequences of current leader practices. Often, the leader too has been concerned, and is grateful that others have noticed.

When team members and leader share the same diagnosis of team problems, both are more willing to risk major changes, even if they have not agreed on exact solutions or how to proceed. Those who raise the issues no longer need to feel "crazy," odd, or isolated.

Team members can do other things to help raise the leader's felt need for change, including:

- Initiating an employee survey.
- Documenting customer dissatisfaction.
- Benchmarking.
- Getting the leader to talk to counterparts at other organizations.
- Making the leader aware of books or consultants who address the perceived problem.[3]

Surfacing Concerns

Team members may have plenty of ideas for change, but they may be buried under the leader's own approach to handling group interaction, as the following case indicates:

Example at Spreadsoft Incorporated

When he was CEO of "Spreadsoft Incorporated," Mort Berger tried to use a combination of external threat and internal dissatisfaction to get his executive group to change. The company had a somewhat protected market niche, but Mort knew it was just a matter of time before the dominant player, Lotus, would move into its area. Mort was also disappointed by the negativity he felt in executive team meetings; they took the pleasure out of building the company. He wanted the others to feel the same keen sense of pride that he did and to embrace the strategic issues that would shape the company's future.

Eventually, Mort expressed his concern to the assembled company executives. In the ensuing discussion, the head of software development angrily declared:

"The reason I act negatively is because you quash any discussion of problems. I know you came from marketing, Mort, but this pressure to always be upbeat means that we can't legitimately raise our concerns. You move too quickly into having us say 'What are we going to do about it?' before we can really explore the problems. That's why I'm so negative."

Other members echoed this sentiment. Seeing their point, Mort promised to restrain his natural impulse to move quickly from problem identification to problem solution. The quid pro quo was that members would take greater responsibility for finding practical solutions. The team agreed and decided to set up a strategy task force to explore options to counter possible threats from Lotus, the dominant player they feared.

Supporting from Below

It is easy to forget that even strong, hard-driving leaders need occasional support, especially when they are introducing a controversial new way of doing things. As clear as Bob Mitchell became about going ahead with the move to post-heroic leadership, the support of Mary Chadwick and another manager made a big difference. It is hard to sustain any change effort if no one else seems to think it is a decent idea.

Members can also help by giving feedback to leaders when their behavior is inconsistent with their message. At Biotekk, the management council had announced the need for cost reductions and made a big deal of the discipline required. When the yearly budget review sessions actually took place, however, the management council went easy on the division managers, fearing that the cuts would cause too much conflict. At their next meeting, the division heads discussed what happened. It eventually came out that no one had spoken up at the management council meeting, because they each hoped to get away with their request intact. After heated discussion, the division managers decided to go to the management council and face them down: "What's going on? Do you mean it or not? If you let some of us get away without seriously addressing cuts, the whole effort will go down the tubes. We're grown-ups; if there is real need, then stop fooling around and hold us to what you said is needed. If not, then stop pretending! We think you need to set up a cost reduction czar if you want adherence to cost cutting." The management council talked it over, thanked the division managers, and put a czar in place. It worked—and everyone benefited.

Once the leadership change is launched, there is still a great deal to do. Chapter 10 describes how Bob Mitchell and his colleagues moved Pharmco forward.

10

MOVING CHANGE FORWARD

Once an organization launches change, it is necessary to keep momentum going. Resolution of successively tougher issues is a practical approach to doing this and can advance the change quite rapidly. The challenge, however, is to change the *entire* system; this usually requires changing many things at once. While one or more key leverage points beckon leaders to "Start here!" it is necessary to begin on several fronts at once since all parts of a system are interrelated.

In the initial Pharmco operating committee session described here, the team begins to work on tangible vision; members then move to addressing touchy issues of interpersonal influence, explore leadership practices, and begin to make decisions about the organization's purpose and direction. Both the leadership system and a series of strategic questions are on the table at once. The leader uses strategic discussions as the vehicle for continuing to change the leadership assumptions of key managers.

Pharmco: Part II

Bob Mitchell, Chief Operating Officer of Pharmco, was determined to use the strategic planning retreat to advance the creation of a shared responsibility team among the company's top managers. With the help of consultant Lincoln Turner, he had made careful preparations for the meeting. As he drove to the meeting site, Bob mused on his prospects for success. "Will Gene stick to his promises and really change his behavior? What will I do if he starts to take over our meeting? He did agree to let me call him on that, but what if he won't listen? Can I count on any of the team members to back me up? They might just sit on their hands and leave me twisting in the wind. They've got some strong feelings about Ed being Gene's operative. If he gets attacked, will Gene rush to defend him? What if we end up in a war between 'my guys' and 'Gene's guys?'"

Suddenly, Bob realized that he was pulling into the resort. He would know the answers to his questions soon enough.

The Retreat

The session began Friday afternoon with the strategy consultants giving a brief summary of their findings. The main issue concerned growth. If Pharmco wanted technology to be more than a stepchild, significant infusions of R&D money would be required. That would cut into the resources available to extend existing product lines or to expand into Asia.

The afternoon was spent discussing the pros and cons of the company's strategic options. As the session wore on, Bob saw that even though members struggled to take the corporate view, there was no general agreement on what Pharmco stood for or where it was going. In the past, strategic decisions had been made separately and opportunistically without benefit of a commonly accepted vision.

Determined to keep the meeting focused and moving forward, Bob huddled briefly with Lincoln Turner, then suggested an agenda change to the group. "We've done some excellent analysis this afternoon, but I think it will be difficult for us to make a quality decision unless we agree on what Pharmco is. Otherwise, it will only degenerate into horse-trading or compromise. I suggest that we temporarily put discussion of the specific strategic issues on hold until tomorrow and use this evening's session to begin exploring our collective vision of Pharmco and what it should become."

John Koch, VP of Animal Pharmaceuticals responded, "That sounds appropriate, but can we avoid it becoming one of those blue-sky fantasy discussions of vision? We need to be grounded in practical plans."

Koch's request was seconded all around. Lincoln Turner suggested a framework for them to think about the future of Pharmco.

"First, using the strategy report, keep key customers and Pharmco's core competencies in mind. That will form the basis of how you can differentiate yourselves from competitors and add value. Finally, do some thinking about what it will take to make this organization a place in which work is exciting, productive, and fun."

Guess Who Isn't Coming to Dinner

There was general agreement with Turner's suggestion and the afternoon session ended with a universal feeling that progress was being made. As the group broke for drinks, Gene pulled Bob and Lincoln aside and said: "As I mentioned yesterday, my daughter and new granddaughter are visiting us this weekend. Since you are going to be driving this company in the future, it ought to be more your vision than mine. Would you mind if I ducked out this evening? I will agree to whatever the team comes up with as long as it continues our past entrepreneurial culture."

That sounded reasonable to both Bob and Lincoln, so they agreed. The CEO's absence was noted by several VPs later, during dinner; they nodded noncommittally at Bob's explanation.

When the members reassembled that evening, Bob noted that they seem subdued. "It's been a long day," he thought, "hopefully that they'll get their energy back for this session." As he opened that session, Bill Boyer, VP of Agriculture, abruptly interrupted.

"Bob, before we start, I have to say that I am royally pissed at what you and Linc did." The room went silent as all eyes turned toward the combative VP. "You said that this would be a shared responsibility team, and yet you guys just made a side deal with Gene Roberts. He always pulls us off one-on-one to get what he wants. That undermines the group. Why the hell did you do it? Is this our group or your group?"

Bob immediately protested: "There was no deal, Bill. Gene simply wanted to spend the rest of the evening with his family. That, to me, is a reasonable request. He thinks this is our future; we can develop the vision we want without him."

Lincoln Turner broke in at this point. "Bob, are you feeling defensive about this?" Bob acknowledged he was. Turner pointed out that while Bob's and his own intentions may have been benign, it was important to understand the reactions of others. "It's going to be tough for us to hear this, but we need to explore what happened."

Two issues emerged from that discussion. First, there was a general suspicion that Gene would eventually pull the rug out from under them. As one member put it, "What if we put all this effort into developing a Pharmco vision and Gene says no?" The second issue was Bob's playing middleman again between the team and the CEO. "Just as you protect us from him," Bill Boyer stated, "you also protect him from us. If we are going to be a team, we need to take him on directly."

For Bob Mitchell, the remarks of his team were difficult to hear. The fact that he agreed with many of them made him feel disloyal to his boss. Also, he felt unappreciated for the efforts he had made to smooth troubled waters.

What was also hard to hear was that smoothing was as dysfunctional as it was useful. With Turner's urging, he expressed these reactions as well as his sense of helplessness about what to do next.

John Koch offered a solution: "We need to be the ones who confront Gene on this tomorrow."

His suggestion made sense to Bob, but it also put him in a bind. "Look, if I don't warn Gene, he'll feel blindsided by me. On the other hand, if I do warn him, you people will nail me for playing the go-between. This suggestion puts me in a no-win situation."

The team saw Bob's dilemma and suggested that he and Turner give the CEO a short briefing before opening the next day's meeting.

With that business settled, the team turned back to the question of Pharmco's vision. Though the hour was late, there was enough energy in the room to take a first cut at the items suggested by Lincoln Turner. After identifying present and potential clients (and how Pharmco's core competencies could add value), all agreed that the best way to strengthen the company's competitive advantage would be to expand into new geographic markets. Although they would need to continue development of current product lines, the marketing of existing products (and product line expansion) in new markets could fuel the growth of the company for many years.

Turner reminded them that while they were getting clear on their strategic direction, they also needed to do some work on how they wanted to operate as a team and organization—the values that would support this vision. But the hour was late, and that would have to wait.

After the meeting closed, Bob and Lincoln adjourned to the bar, where they debriefed the day's events. Bob felt badly about their having unilaterally agreed to Gene's request, but the consultant pointed out that it turned out well: "Look, if the goal was to have the team feel ownership, that helped. Maybe the only mistake is not acknowledging

one's mistakes!" Bob grudgingly admitted that the end results were good, depending, of course, on how Gene would
take the news in the morning, but that he still didn't like
having goofed.

A New World Dawns

The next morning, Bob and Lincoln Turner intercepted the
CEO in the parking lot. They explained to him what happened the previous evening. "There is a lot of heat about
what you did, and about our decision to agree," Bob said
apprehensively.

"Well, we'll just have to deal with it," was Gene's unper-
turbed response.

Bob started the second-day session by saying that he
had briefly filled Gene in, and then threw the matter open
for discussion. Without being punitive, the group expressed their difficulty with Gene's interactions. "You and
Bob make side deals that cut us out. That makes it difficult for us to influence what goes on, and makes us dependent." Others raised the issue of Gene's floating in and
out of meetings.

Gene was silent and poker-faced as these comments
were made, but eventually responded. "To me, it didn't
seem crucial that I be there last night, even though the
subject was important. I really needed to see my daughter.
I knew that I could buy into your decisions about vision,
which will be Bob's to implement. And I figured it would
be less disruptive if I just slipped away. I guess I sent the
wrong message." Again, it was Bill Boyer who made the
telling comment, saying emotionally, "Gene, we realize
how you feel about your daughter, and it's great that you
are so attached. We would have gladly agreed to your leaving had you asked us. But your making a side deal kept us
from giving that 'gift' to you." Gene choked up. His style
had been so gruff and arm's-length that he rarely saw
the genuine affection that many members felt for him.
This time, their caring had found a voice, and Gene was
touched.

In the end, Gene promised to bring issues to the group and Bob agreed that he wouldn't collude in any more side deals. More in sorrow than anger, he said to Gene, "Now you can see what you do to me all the time." This was the first time he had ever criticized Gene in front of the team, and it helped reinforce a new level of openness. Team members, in turn, said that they wouldn't sit on their frustrations, but would express dissatisfactions as they arose.

As the group took a mid-morning break, Turner huddled with Bob and Gene to propose a change in the agenda. Instead of moving into a review of the previous night's work on strategic vision, he suggested that they follow up on the interpersonal work of the morning. "We have experienced the benefits that come from opening up role-related issues, and we have some momentum; let's give people an opportunity to deal with tensions they have with each other." Bob worried that those tensions would get out of hand, but deferred, as did Gene, to the consultant's recommendation.

Lincoln Turner started the next session by saying that he wanted to suggest a modification in the design. "In order to build on the good work we have just accomplished, I propose that we do another cut at clearing away the interpersonal underbrush that makes it hard for us to work together. If you would be willing, I want to give a 15-minute talk on effective feedback. I'll then lead you through an exercise that will provide a chance to practice these vital skills."

Members weren't sure what this meant, and struggled with whether they were willing to open up Pandora's box. After vigorous discussion, Turner asked, "If we can't deal with issues here, when will we be able to?" Finally, they said they were willing to give it a chance.

After a short lecture on behaviorally specific feedback, Turner asked each person to write down the names of three others on the team with whom they had difficulty working. "Then, for each person, write down *exactly what that person does* that is bothersome, and how you react.

Stay on your side of the net," he warned, "stick with your reactions, not their motives."

After about 10 minutes of intense writing, they were asked to stop. "Now," he said, "I want you to pick one of your three names, pair up with that person if there's a match, and spend the next 45 minutes discussing the problems you noted in work with him or her. Talk over the things that bother you, and see if you can agree about ways to improve your interactions. I'll roam around the room and help anyone who gets stuck."

With some apprehension, the members paired off. Koch and Boyer paired up; Ed Fisher, the CFO, grabbed Bob Mitchell; Mary Chadwick, the HR director approached Gene Roberts; everyone picked a tough match. Lincoln Turner walked around in search of anyone who needed help, but all were so busily engaged that he quietly listened.

Just prior to the lunch break, he called the group together. "Well, how did it go? Any death threats to report?" All laughed. In fact, everyone was pleased with the feedback exercise and admitted it wasn't as bad as they had expected. "Remember that each of you has two other names on your list. Sometime in the next couple of weeks, make appointments with those individuals and repeat the feedback exercise you did here this morning."

Back to the Future

After lunch, the team returned to Pharmco's strategic vision. The previous evening's work had been built more on perceptions and intuitions than on hard data. In this session, they checked their initial thoughts against the facts and also explored the future implication of competing visions. They discussed the data they needed to make a final decision and identified questions that required thorough research such as the consequences, in terms of market penetration, of divesting the equipment unit; what it would take to make it attractive to a buyer; the advantages and disadvantages of an integrated sales force. These questions were prioritized, with assignments given to individuals and subgroups.

At the end of the day, team members were satisfied and slightly amazed at their progress. Turner suggested that they plan for another meeting, since they had only laid the groundwork and had a great deal more to do. There was grudging agreement: "Well, if we can be as productive as this one was . . ." Another three-day retreat was scheduled a month in the future.

"That will give us time to do the analysis on the strategic issues we've identified," Bill Boyer volunteered. The team also accepted Turner's proposal that he send out a questionnaire for each to fill out on the others that could be the basis for more systematic feedback on each person's leadership style.

Bob and Gene Follow Up

At the next regular Monday meeting between Bob and Gene, the bristly CEO expressed satisfaction with the recently concluded retreat. "It went well," he told his COO. "You seemed more in charge, more assertive. That's what I've been hoping for. Saturday morning was a little hot—not something I anticipated—but it turned out well. But now we do need to get the real work done, wouldn't you agree?"

Bob echoed his sentiments about the success of the meeting and the need to make tangible progress. Then he raised the other issue that was on his mind. "Gene, in the past we've discussed our respective roles—what each of us should do and where the boundaries are. Given the progress we made last week, we ought to revisit those issues. We need to be clearer about who is running OpCom and what your role will be."

To Bob's surprise and delight, this request initiated what proved to be the most open and useful discussion of the years of working together. For the first time, Gene talked about what Pharmco meant to him personally. "I look at Pharmco as my baby. And like a father, I'm obliged to see that it grows strong and able to fend for itself in a tough world. Once I see that, I'll know that its time for me to move on."

Gene went on to say what he expected from Bob. "I want you to be more aggressive—bite the bullet sooner—especially on personnel issues. It bothers me when I see people not performing and you not doing anything about it. I don't want to manage the day-to-day stuff, and when I see you take hold of things, I feel better about letting go."

The two men agreed that OpCom had to be Bob's meeting and that Gene wouldn't interfere as long as he had an opportunity to make his views known. That was fine with Bob, but he asked how willing Gene was to be confronted if he led the discussion off track. "Look, you should have learned from last week's retreat that you can take me on—just do it directly and don't beat around the bush." They also agreed that Gene's habit of bullying individual managers did not fit with the new leadership model they sought to achieve. "Bob, I'll try, but kid-gloves isn't my style. So, if you see me acting inappropriately, just tell me. But I've got to be able to express my opinions when I have big-time concerns."

Bob responded, "We need your input, but it's the way you put things that's the problem. Why don't you use Lincoln Turner. He's serving as a coach for several of us and it has been useful." To Bob's surprise, Gene agreed. They decided that Turner should occasionally attend OpCom meetings as a catalyst and observer for Gene. At the meetings, Turner would sit next to Gene and nudge him when Gene began diving too deep into the details. The two executives also agreed that Gene should take on a more visible symbolic leadership role, both inside the company and in the outer world of lenders, shareholders, and customers. Bob explained, "I want you to be more active in telling people about where Pharmco is going, our aspirations and plans. And you need to be the spokesman with the industry groups, so that we can help shape regulations and policy."

Pharmco Issues—The Interrelationships among Vision, Team, and Mutual Influence

The Pharmco retreat, which addressed both company strategy and interpersonal relationships, was extremely useful in moving people toward shared leadership and its responsibilities. Bob's insistence that they tackle the strategy consulting firm's report, and not back away from addressing the team's way of working, has started to alter his boss's and the team members' acceptance of responsibility for success of the company.

Before the retreat, Bob had spelled out his expectations for everyone and his desire to move to shared leadership. This is a critical step, but to make it real and likely to stick, specific actions are needed. Without concrete action, members are inclined to treat the expectations as another set of fancy words to be waited out.

Attempting to build a team is not new, nor is the attempt to set out a fundamental direction for the organization. And there have been many attempts by Bob, Gene, and the members to influence each other, usually accompanied by considerable frustration and blaming. What is new is the desire to tie these all together to create collective psychological ownership of the team, and by implication, the company. There are numerous hurdles:

- *Leadership commitment.* Team members have to know how committed the leadership is to this new approach. Is it only for the good times, or for those occasions when the team is going in directions that the leader desires? Bob was directing the retreat (with the consultant's help), and he acted to take the discussions deeper at several key points. When he too quickly acceded to Gene's request to leave for the evening, his response to the group's anger was very important. He did not abandon ship, nor did he continue to protect Gene as he had in the past. For his part, Gene took the team's pushing on him well and did not retaliate or give off signals that he resented their increased directness. The credibility of Bob's desire for engaging the team increased. The way he involved them in struggling with the strategy dilemmas was another indicator that he meant it.

- *Justification for risks.* Without clear reasons for taking the risks of sharing responsibility, team members are likely to hold out or give up quickly, as had happened in the past. The implications of the strategic choices to be made were an unmistakable stake that provided ample reason to wholeheartedly join in decision making. The risks of not sharing in the decisions were at least as high as those of full engagement.

- *Agreement on vision.* To make wise decisions about critical issues, however, there has to be at least a measure of agreement about the vision of the unit—where it is and where it is going. That is why the team needed to defer discussion on strategy for a while and turn to work on the team vision. Bob Mitchell, who insisted on this, had the foresight to know that quality decisions on core issues can't be made in the absence of agreement on overall direction ("what the company stands for"). It isn't necessary to have the vision resolved before starting to discuss these issues. In fact, the process of addressing strategic choices helped clarify where the disagreements were and just how useful vision agreement could be as a guide to decision making.

- *Mutual influence.* One of the necessary conditions for sharing responsibility in making critical decisions is the ability to work with and learn from the diverse expertise of the team members. Mutual influence is the process that enables give-and-take. This too has begun, especially in the push-back from the team. They tell Bob they are unhappy with the way the evening meeting decision was made, and stick with it until he sees why they are upset, and can join with them in determining compensatory actions. The symbolic power of the team confronting Bob and then helping him invent reasonable action is far greater than the actual decision. It was an important demonstration that Bob would listen (and then that Gene would listen), but also that upward confrontation did not automatically mean the whole place is in revolution or irresponsible uproar. Everyone learned from this.

The interplay among influence, team, and vision work illustrates that moving toward shared responsibility is not about plowing through the three elements in sequence. There is a flow back and forth as needed. Issues are touched but will need to be revisited at a deeper level. Vision setting, like strategic planning, should be an iterative process that works back and forth from concrete issues to abstract principles. Neither makes sense without this interplay.

The Pharmco team has started work on vision but will need to test it against hard data. It is difficult to make crucial vision or strategic choices if the team is undeveloped and unwilling to collaborate; conversely, the increased willingness to put the real issues on the table and to wrestle with different points of view that have no obvious right answers moves the group along. They are making progress as a team but still have to work through major conflicts as they encounter them. They started increasing their influence with one another over the tough interpersonal style issues but will need to take a more systematic look using leadership questionnaire data.

Pharmco's work on team process evolved out of task needs. They decided to build a team because critical organizational/strategic decisions were at stake; they discussed vision because those decisions couldn't be made without agreement about direction; and they couldn't deal with the vision questions until they cleaned up feelings about Gene and Bob's collusion.

Too often, work on group process or team dynamics is done in isolation from task decisions. Not only can that fail to produce commitment ("we are only doing exercises that have no relation to the real work"), but it prevents transfer of what is learned back to the organization. Discussions usually have to be embedded within genuine task work to have a lasting effect.

It isn't always necessary to deal with all three elements of shared leadership at once; teams vary in their readiness and can make great progress if one or two of the elements builds a sense of ownership. Eventually, however, vision, team development, and mutual influence will all come into play if full shared responsibility is to be achieved.

Finally, in spite of all the good planning done by Bob and the consultant, it was an unplanned mistake that had the most potent impact on the OpCom's development. Imagine how different the outcome of the retreat would have been had the members concluded that "nothing has changed" and gone underground with their irritation or if Bob and Gene had responded defensively and punitively. In either case nothing would have changed. Bill Boyer's emotional outburst over Gene and Bob's presumed side deal had unwittingly saved the day. Thus the success in moving forward is due as much to the team members as to Bob or Gene, though their open, learning-oriented responses certainly helped.

BEYOND PHARMCO

The Pharmco experience provides more detail about how a group can be developed into a shared responsibility team. Here is a reminder of the progressive stages that teams go through on the way to full collaboration:

1. Membership.
2. Subgrouping.
3. Conflict.
4. Individual differentiation.
5. Collaboration (shared responsibility).

Return to Early Stages of Group Development

Prior to its retreat and the attempt to alter the team's way of working, the OpCom had been operating somewhere between Stages 2 and 3. No members felt committed to full membership or to working through their differences and problems, and in the words of one member, "We don't like each other very much." Factions were jockeying for position, but not really addressing each other. At least one member wanted to discontinue the group, and the CEO viewed it as a waste of time. Bob Mitchell, the person charged with running its meetings, did not know how to make the OpCom's work more productive.

When trying to move a team to the post-heroic leadership system, it will inevitably revert to Stage 1 as the terms of membership change. Initially, members will ask, "How committed do I want to be to this new way of operating?" "Will it be worth the effort of becoming personally invested?" "Is the leader really committed?" At Pharmco, they were asking, "Will Bob really stick with the new way of operating? Will Gene allow it to happen, or leap in the first time he has strong views and destroy all progress?" Some situations demand no more than superficial commitment, but no group can reach Stage 5 without team member willingness to invest.

Moving through the Early Stages of Group Development— Leader Actions to Build Commitment

In this early stage, the leader has three primary objectives:

1. To clearly state and reinforce expectations of what the team should be like.
2. To demonstrate leader commitment to the new post-heroic model.
3. To directly help members become committed to the group.

As we have stated, members will be more committed when they see that there are significant benefits for the extra effort that shared responsibility demands.

Expectations of the Team Members and Their Roles

The greater the clarity of the leader's expectations, the more chance there is that members will come to accept the obligations and begin to make the needed commitment. Especially when what is wanted sounds so similar to, but is so fundamentally different from, what people have become used to, guideposts are important. Clarifications about such fundamentals as altered leader and member roles, what is supposed to be discussed and decided in the team meetings, and how disagreements are to be handled, can help eliminate needless confusion over what the leader wants. Merely specifying new behavior will not instantly produce it, but articulation of what is desired and how it differs from business as usual clarifies the transition.

This doesn't mean that team members will automatically agree. If they have doubts, it is best to encourage them to raise their reservations. This not only clears the way for a fresh attack on the old ways, but can lead to valuable modifications that improve the plans of the leader. In the process of going forward, there will be numerous opportunities to revisit and reinforce what has been said up front, as members come to situations that they can't quite interpret through the new system. Few people can alter their behavior through hearing a concept once and then instantly using it everywhere; experiences throw new doubts or new light on the idea.

Demonstrate Leader Commitment

Any one or a combination of the following five approaches can demonstrate the leader's personal commitment to shared responsibility and thereby foster member commitment:

1. *Dealing with the core issues.* As noted in Chapter 6, there is frequently a discrepancy between the issues that team members know are critical to success in the next 12 to 18 months, and what is on the agendas of their meetings.

Moving from discussions of trivialities to grappling with core, central issues is the most fundamental way to build commitment to shared responsibility.

2. *Deciding on appropriate decision-makng styles.* Ownership also increases when the toughest, most critical issues are decided by consensus, not just by consulting with the leader. But not all decisions require consensus. Table 10–1 shows an exercise that helps teams learn when to use which form of decision making.

3. *Linking with other major organizational changes.* In a fast-paced world, organizational members can barely keep

Table 10–1. The Decision-Making Styles Exercise

- Discuss with team the four decision-making styles, autonomous, delegated, consultative and joint.
- For next meeting, each person lists 7–10 recent or upcoming decisions, and how each should be made.
- At meeting, pairs reach agreement on their lists.
- Post large sheets of paper with one style at top of each sheet.
- Each pair places its choices on the appropriate sheet.
- Team discusses differences and reaches agreement on how it will decide various matters in dispute.

The resulting discussion, in which members often will disagree about the desirability of a certain style for a particular decision, does several things at once. It:

- Helps the team understand the new post-heroic model.
- Gains agreement about how to handle important upcoming issues.
- Demonstrates that not all decisions should be made by consensus.
- Legitimizes those times when the leader should make a decision autonomously without undercutting the principles of shared leadership.
- Provides a living forum for practicing coming to consensus (about when to come to consensus).
- Gives the leader a chance to join the discussion as both an advocate/ guide and a full-fledged team member who is open to discovery and new agreements.

up with daily job demands, so are reluctant to climb on board with any new initiatives until it is clear that they will last. Too many organizations have moved from the disliked flavor of the month to the dreaded 28 flavors of the week. In this context, it is easier to build commitment if the move to post-heroic leadership is tied to other change initiatives underway. Can shared responsibility help the company go global, implement quality, speed the product development cycle? Making the connections and showing how to get two or three payoffs from the move to shared responsibility adds more credibility to the effort.

4. *Developing a tangible vision.* The link to other organizational changes can increase the manifest need for a clear vision. Why bother with something that takes energy to implement in the absence of a compelling goal that makes the risks worth taking? The discussion earlier in this chapter shows there is no prescribed sequence for the elements of shared responsibility, and it may be necessary to move back and forth among the elements in iterative fashion. In those situations where it is possible to articulate and begin to use a tangible vision, commitment can be enhanced. When team members understand and accept the higher purpose for the unit, they are more likely to see why they should invest themselves in all that shared responsibility demands.

5. *Addressing operating styles.* Working on leadership and interpersonal issues is another way to demonstrate leadership commitment and develop member ownership. One powerful way is to utilize some form of leadership style data collection from team members (and the leader's leader, as well as colleagues if possible, so 360-degree feedback is available). The way that the leader uses the data tells a great deal about how things are now supposed to work. We have found it most effective when the leader shares the summarized data with team members and invites them to help interpret the data and then set leader priorities. Then they are asked to assist the leader in making these agreed upon changes. Although so much sharing of data and responsibility for improvement at such an early stage can be

threatening, all of this conveys powerful messages about not doing business as usual. Would a heroic leader take the risk of making partners of team members in his or her attempts to be a more effective leader? But then, if the leader really means it, who can be more helpful than the led in monitoring progress, giving feedback, and providing continuing support for learning?

Dealing first with interpersonal tensions is most relevant for existing groups in which there are unresolved interpersonal issues that are blocking real work on business issues. In many traditional groups, such difficulties rarely are openly discussed. If they haven't been resolved one-on-one outside the meetings, they just grow and fester. With a new set of expectations that legitimize open and direct communication, what was suppressed and tolerated before can now be resolved.

For other groups, jumping right in with discussions of personal or interpersonal issues can be too uncomfortable. Tackling business problems, on the other hand, can seem more objective and more "arm's-length," and so can serve as a safer way to know and be known. Backing in to discussions of relationships only when they are getting in the way may be less threatening.

The most potent demonstrations of the seriousness of leader intentions are those that happen during regular meetings and discussions. Leaders can stay tuned to skepticism about their commitment and encourage it to be openly expressed when it is only being revealed indirectly or in a guarded way. Organizational members everywhere devise disguised tests of leaders who want to implement anything new, probably because so many hot new ideas die a natural death soon enough anyway. The leader can remain alert to the opportunities to show that it is okay to challenge whether the leader is really committed this time.

Another opportunity arises whenever the leader is excited about some business solution and senses that some team members may be less than enthusiastic. A simple question about what else hasn't been said yet, or what the leader is missing on the issue, can dramatically demonstrate a new willingness to treat the team members as partners and not just obstacles to overcome.

In ways major and minor, the leader needs to set the expectation that this is the team's team, and not just the leader's. In the early stages, members will be watching the leader closely (even if sometimes pretending not to) for signs about what is really valued and what will please the leader. Evidence that the leader is concerned with each member and the team's collective effectiveness will go a long way in helping the team move forward.

All these ways of building member commitment tap the three core elements of the shared leadership system. Vision is at work, making it worth investing. The team is the setting for decision making and is being developed as the work goes forward. And there is increasing mutual influence as members speak up, and leaders learn how to push without shutting members down.

In all five approaches, the leader must do more than go through the motions. Letting go of hands-on control so that the team can take ownership is essential. We observed the sad case of "Ken Kreiger," a large company divisional president who truly believed that he would get better results from having his executive team make the most important decisions together. But he was so used to figuring things out ahead of time and then presenting his solutions for ratification that he couldn't stop himself. Struggling valiantly to change his style, he managed to avoid starting discussions by presenting his ideas about the solution to big issues, but would sit in the meetings and try to steer the group to arrive at what he considered to be the best decision. Even when the group called this to his attention, he blocked them from freewheeling discussions, and tried to be more subtle in his backseat driving. After a few attempts, the team gave up and reverted to their advice-giving ways, leaving the responsibility with Ken. When he retired 18 months later, the new divisional president, chosen in part for his commitment to building shared responsibility, was quickly able to engage the team as partners.

Team members also play a vital role in building a post-heroic system. They need to be willing to risk speaking out on leader behavior and style, verbalizing what they actually see instead of only what they think is acceptable. Easy for us to say? We're no more fond of career-limiting moves than anyone, but know that if team members promote mutual influence it is often safe for them to say more than might have been thought possible. The core challenge is to point out inconsistencies in support of the leader's underlying intentions. The object is for team members to join their manager as a partner, providing needed information for that beleaguered person to be more effective, not punishment for failing to be perfect. (For more on how to push bosses in their own interests, see Appendix A, "Power Talk: A Hands-On Guide to Supportive Confrontation.") There is no better demonstration of shared responsibility than actions members take to be responsible for the development of the team.

During the early stages of development, teams can get meaningful work accomplished, but it will require extra effort and attention from the leader in managing the problem-solving process. The leader will have to be certain that the team clearly and correctly identifies the problem, does ample diagnosis, and generates reasonable alternative solutions. As the team progresses, members will increasingly be able to manage that process and monitor each other. But the latter isn't easy when members are still trying to determine where they stand with the group around acceptance, influence, and role.

Members become committed for different reasons. For some, it is the excitement of the task; for others, it might be the opportunity to have greater influence; and for still others, it might be the opportunity to belong to a high-performing team. Whatever the basis for commitment, in this period the leader is working to link individual needs with the team's objective and helping members connect with each other by showing commonality of interests.

All of this prepares the team for dealing with the critical issues likely to create conflict and dissention. Chapter 11 reveals how the Pharmco team handled that challenge.

11

ADDRESSING CONFLICT

Movement toward a shared responsibility system is bound to bump up against conflict. At times, it will appear that things are falling apart. There will be disagreements about strategic direction, who has influence, and many specific implementation decisions. Interpersonal tensions increase. These differences can either block movement toward collaboration or release energy and allow change to move forward. The leader must recognize the value of conflict and set up processes that turn its energy toward productive purposes. Unless the organization can resolve differences, change will stall. Similarly, management teams need to find ways to work through emerging conflicts. This allows for more open, direct discussion and enables the team to address increasingly more central issues.

The operating committee (OpCom) at Pharmco had begun a major strategic planning and transformational team-building effort aimed at creating shared responsibility. With the help of a strategic consulting firm and an organizational consultant, Lincoln Turner, it had completed a first off-site meeting and worked through some difficult relationship issues involving the CEO, Gene Roberts, the team, and the COO, Bob Mitchell. Team members had come away with assignments to investigate some of the strategic options that had been discussed, and had agreed to ask their direct reports to complete a leadership style questionnaire for the next off-site meeting.

Pharmco: Part III

The Month before the Second Pharmco Retreat

Team members reported that the weekly OpCom meetings were now far superior to previous sessions. They dealt with more important issues and communication was increasingly open although not entirely candid. Gone were the put-down jokes that had been used in the past to convey loaded messages. Members were still cautious about confronting Gene, but since his behavior had decidedly improved, there was less felt need to do it.

During these intervening weeks, OpCom members dropped by Bob's office. Sooner or later, the conversation turned to Gene. "He has changed, but how long do you think it will last? Do you really think he is committed to this new way of working? Will he really let go of making the minor decisions? You know how he hates groups, will he really buy into *our* making the important decisions?" As these conversations repeated themselves with different members, it dawned on Bob that they were also implicitly asking another question: "Bob, are you going to change *your* way of managing and confront him if the 'old Gene' emerges?"

Bob realized that even though OpCom had asked to be empowered, members were highly skeptical about the results. They wondered whether he would act on his intentions.

Preparations continued for the second retreat. Those who had been given assignments were busy collecting the necessary data. Lincoln Turner and Bob met to design the session. Three factors stood out. First, the emphasis on members taking the larger perspective might not be sufficient to keep them from responding primarily to their own needs in discussions of reorganization and possible downsizing. Everybody had to know that they would be treated fairly if their own job was eliminated. Bob decided to ask Mary Chadwick to develop a safety net for these cases.

Second, it would be necessary to change how they made decisions. As a science-based company, Pharmco managers tended to study things to death. This drove Gene up the wall, confirming his fear that Pharmco was losing its entrepreneurial spirit and causing him to jump in with hasty decisions. In this meeting, they would have to learn how to find a balance between doing sufficient analysis and making rapid decisions.

The third factor was to continue the process of increased collaboration in OpCom. Even though significant progress had been made in dealing with interpersonal problems at the initial session, Bob and Linc agreed that many deep-seated antagonisms remained. Linc suggested that the Leadership Questionnaire results could be the vehicle for surfacing the issues. All members were already scheduled to get summaries of their own results and meet individually with Linc before the retreat to discuss the findings. This would form the basis for their personal development plans. Members would also be asked to prepare a summary of strong points and areas for improvement to be publicly shared at the second off-site meeting. Bob proposed this plan at the next OpCom meeting. Members were apprehensive, but agreed.

In the meantime, Mary Chadwick completed her work on the early retirement package created to make it easier for team members to think objectively about organizational needs, without undue worry about their future roles with the company. The team was pleased at the generosity of the proposal, and after discussing a few minor modifications, gave their endorsement.

The Second Off-Site

Bob started by stressing the importance of everybody taking the company perspective. He reviewed the preliminary vision work that had been done at the previous off-site meeting and linked that with the strategic issues to be decided. He continued, "We need to move beyond our silo orientation that caused us only to take care of our own areas. Can I have your agreement to do that?" He looked around the room to make sure that all were on board. He then concluded with a reminder about their personal futures.

"As you know, we will be considering reorganization or consolidation, which potentially means downsizing. In order for us to make these decisions as objectively as possible, and not in terms of our personal financial needs, we have to be secure about our futures no matter what the outcome. That was the point of the early retirement package for anyone who is asked to leave. With that in place, we can make our decisions on the basis of what's best for the organization."

Next, Lincoln Turner led the group through an exercise in which each person posted on newsprint what he or she "tended to do that could sabotage teamwork." The very act of identifying potential problems decreased their occurrence; "violations" could easily be handled by jokingly pointing to the item.

The group reviewed the preparatory work that had been done. They went over the financial projections, market conditions, and competitive positioning, and taking account of the identified core organizational competencies, explored possible areas of growth. They decided on the criteria for reorganization; the company should be more market focused, present a more integrated and coordinated sales face to the customer, and develop a lower cost structure and streamlined operations. All of this took the first morning. Members broke for lunch feeling good not only about the areas covered but about the team's interactions. The old territory-defending behavior had been largely absent. Also, members were enjoying their interactions; it was now becoming fun to work together. But Bob and Linc anticipated more tension as they moved into decision making about investments, divestiture, and reorganization.

After lunch, the group focused on the results of their leadership questionnaires. Each person was asked to write on a newsprint sheet the highlights from the questionnaire and a summary of the areas that the person wanted to work on. Everyone moved around the room and read the posted newsprint, with clarifications taking place as they proceeded. This process legitimized discussing each person's style, made it possible to get clarification about what behavior caused the responses, in turn clarify the reasons for the behavior so others could see that the intentions weren't malevolent, and begin planning corrective action where appropriate.

The tension built as they moved along toward Ed Fisher's summary. On his newsprint sheet was the statement, "Too concerned about pleasing his boss." John Koch took a deep breath and said, "that is why we can't trust you. We withhold financial information because at the first sign of bad news you run to Gene, and then we have to battle him as well as try to resolve the problem." Several people chimed in that they really resented being treated as if they were trying to get away with something.

Ed complained that he was in an awful position, "Look, I don't want to be seen as a spy, but how am I to respond to Gene when he inquires about bad numbers and missed targets?" As Ed spoke, he got increasingly emotional and was on the edge of tears. He turned to Gene and said, "This is the bind you put me in!"

The resulting discussion made the group realize that they had a distorted view of Ed as being personally sneaky and political, and members expressed greater willingness to deal with his role if he would agree to come to them first with problems in their areas. They urged Gene to trust them to deal with poor results since they certainly did not want to ignore important data or perform poorly.

The feelings about Ed's relationship to Gene aroused more complaining about how difficult it was to disagree with him. Gene responded, "Look, we've been over this already. I've already asked that you take me on directly. When you've done that, I haven't bit your head off, have I? Let's keep it moving, and just let me know if there are problems." Sheepishly, members pledged again to be more direct and to give him a chance to respond to their views of him.

After dinner, the team reviewed the day and identified the topics they wanted to address the next day. Everyone agreed that the new way of operating was producing a far more effective and satisfying meeting.

The next morning, the team returned to more strategic questions. The discussion of company core competencies and possible alternate scenarios was heated and uncomfortable. Several members argued that the weakest fit for the company was the diagnostics equipment area, since it required considerable capital in an area where the company had little unique advantage. Steve Rocco, the diagnostics VP, insisted that those arguing against the equipment investments were shortsighted, failing to recognize the massive potential in his program. Steve was one of the most well-liked team members, and his vigorous defense of the equipment area made others uncomfortable. No one wanted to offend him or push him out, but the logic of the situation argued against his area in terms of risks and rewards. Everyone tried hard to understand Steve's views, but couldn't keep from raising objections to his arguments.

Finally, David Williams, the legal VP, said, "I really like and respect you, Steve, but we can't mix personal feelings with business considerations. I want you to be around, but I haven't heard compelling arguments in favor of our continued investing in equipment, given the opportunities available from geographic expansion of our other product lines." After a long silence, several others acknowledged their agreement with Williams, and the team decided, with Steve abstaining, that divestment of the diagnostic equipment division made the most sense.

As soon as this decision was made, the members asked Steve Rocco if he wanted to stay with the division when divested, or take another position within Pharmco. He explained that even though the way they were now operating made staying more attractive, he was deeply committed to the technology of his division, and preferred to go with whichever company bought his division. That led to a request from the team that he figure out how to cut costs and make the division more attractive to a buyer; he accepted the assignment, with much relief all around.

Given the consensus that the company should concentrate its strategic thrust on moving existing product lines into new geographic markets, a series of organizational issues had to be tackled. Should they go it alone in Asia, or joint venture with a Japanese company that already had established distribution arrangements? Should the research labs be located closer to the two main product lines? Did it make sense to have separate sales forces for each division or to consolidate under a VP of Sales? Should a comparable choice be made for marketing?

The group brainstormed a list of these issues and then decided on several of the most important. They agreed to explore a joint venture with a Japanese company, and assigned Bill Boyer the responsibility for investigating possible options to bring to the team.

During this discussion, it also became clear that it would make sense to integrate the biotech division into the agricultural chemical division, again necessitating complex transfers and responsibility shifts. They focused on determining the appropriate structure, and postponed to a future meeting the question of who would lead the combined division.

Toward the end of the day, the team returned to a discussion of a vision for the company. What did they want the company to be? By this time, there was growing trust of one another, and enthusiasm for a new era of working together. The animated discussion evolved into a common understanding of the unity they desired. John Koch summed it up by suggesting that the vision statement should be "One Company, One Stock, One Geography." The team agreed to that, and decided to introduce it to the rest of the company in a subsequent meeting.

The team was now in it together, coalescing around both the strategy and a new style of sharing responsibility. It was ready to tackle something much more controversial and loaded with potential conflict: overall company structure that went far beyond integrating two line divisions. The implications of fundamental reorganization—however handled—were clear to all concerned. Some people's jobs would be eliminated and existing jobs and reporting relationships would be altered. The status and fortunes of some might be advanced while those of others might not. To make the discussion as unrestricted as possible, the team agreed to spend the next day discussing a new company structure without reference to who would fill the resulting positions.

There was a charged atmosphere at the start of the next morning. Opinions on possible reorganization were predictably divided. One group argued for reorganization along geographic lines. Another group, believing that Pharmco's future depended on the development of new products, wanted to combine existing divisions and place research under them. Each group was convinced that its solution would help the company grow faster.

The team decided to attack the reorganization issue by having each group go off to develop the case for its point of view. As expected, when these groups reported back, there were more disagreements than common ideas. Team members could not reach consensus. If there was an opportunity for the new system of management to go up in smoke, this was it. Faced with an apparent deadlock, many wondered if Bob or Gene would make the decision. They did not. Instead, Lincoln Turner, the consultant, offered an approach to breaking the impasse: each person was to pair up with someone who held an opposing view, then talk about the *drawbacks* of his or her own position and the *advantages* of the other's. Each pair would then seek a solution that combined the best ideas of the two participants.

Two pairs suggested a matrix organization, with four geographic sales areas—the Americas, Asia, Europe, and Near East (including India and Africa)—and two main product lines. The reorganization would pull all the sales forces together, out of the product lines, under a world-wide VP of sales. The sales force would be matrixed to the product lines. In turn, some other functions could be matrixed, especially research.

A spirited discussion ensued about the difficulty of implementing and managing a matrix organization. Was this team ready to deal maturely with the resources and priorities conflicts that a matrix would create? They concluded that the organization could now handle the challenge: The matrix required the same orientation as shared leadership, taking into account the interests of one's area and the wider organization. Many members were pleased with how people with opposing viewpoints had been able to argue productively over a difficult set of ideas.

A second major decision would be to fundamentally change the function of the animal feed line. It would move from its current focus on marketing and sales of existing products to becoming a source of major growth. This would require a focus on new product development, strategic alliances, and acquisitions. A critical question was who could best lead this refocused division, but that would be tackled at another time.

After lunch, the meeting turned to a discussion of ways to reduce the size of the OpCom, which all agreed was too large to be effective as a decision-making body. The agreed sale of the equipment division would eliminate one position. The proposed combination of chemicals and biotechnology would eliminate yet another. And if corporate communications were to give up its seat on the OpCom, which all deemed a good idea, membership would be reduced by three.

All of this restructuring would require complex, delicate decisions about who would fill the new roles. The group, however, still did not feel ready to make all the resulting personnel decisions together. But they did not want to revert to just passing the job up to Bob, so they asked him to spend the next month talking with them individually about possible assignments, and then bring his recommendations to the next retreat. Then they would make joint decisions. There was still a great deal to do to align the elements of the organization.

PHARMCO ISSUES

The OpCom members have demonstrated an increased willingness to share responsibility. They have spoken up about their views and concerns while taking the corporate point of view, insist on high standards from each other, are increasingly honest about awkward feedback, and participate fully as partners in making critical decisions.

Again at this meeting, the team worked on all three elements of building shared responsibility: vision, team development, and mutual influence. The process is iterative, progressively deepening and reinforcing commitment. The team is taking greater ownership, with more of the initiative coming from the members. The authenticity of what can be discussed is steadily increasing.

Vision was used, tested, and deepened by the discussions, with their prior general agreement about it first serving as a framework for decision making. Then they built understanding and commitment through direct discussion, and finally the summary statement of vision emerged. "One Company, One Stock, One Geography" could be a cliché if members had not evolved it through intense discussion. Instead, it was shorthand for a set of complex assumptions about what the company stood for and how they were to deal with each other.

Mutual influence was also increased. Sharing their leadership questionnaire results set a tone making it legitimate to discuss interpersonal style. There was powerful exchange about Ed's behavior and role, with resulting demands on Gene for autonomy and trust, but accompanying requirements for the responsibility that goes with privilege. The team more directly challenged Gene, and in turn he pushed back on them. He was direct in telling them he preferred to be confronted openly, which also demonstrated that leaders can set norms that increase the level of openness and honesty. Everyone was readier to talk straight and respond to confrontation, so that instead of turning a dispute into a win-lose contest or a weak compromise, they creatively resolved it.

Because of the agreement about vision and the increased ability to influence one another, the team was able to deal with increasingly central issues, taking on delicate relationships, divestiture, organizational structure, and membership in the top team. Each time they resolve one of these tough questions, they solidify their ability to take on even more critical issues.

It would have been easy for the team to let Bob and Gene play referees and make the call when they were deadlocked about organizational structure, but they came up with another way to think through the possibilities and make the decision together. Although the team was not yet ready to make joint personnel decisions, they did not abdicate their responsibilities, and asked Bob to come back to them with recommendations, rather than the final decisions. They did not try to pass the decision upward and then blame the leader for not taking all factors into account.

STAGES OF GROUP DEVELOPMENT

Movement between stages of group development is never as orderly a progression as any model implies. The upcoming second retreat brought back some vestiges of the membership stage, and they had to clean up the residue. There was shared skepticism about Gene's commitment—and Bob's ability—to change. The confrontation of Gene at the first off-site had been liberating to the team members, and they were able to resume their regular meetings with far greater readiness to work. As the second off-site approached, however, with the hardest strategic decisions coming, Gene and Bob's commitment was again questioned. The answers to these questions would determine how much commitment the team members' wanted to make. Why invest in sharing responsibility if it wouldn't be sustained? Was the early conflict resolution a fluke? When they were satisfied that shared leadership was for real, they could invest more.

Rapid Move through Subgrouping

The strategic questions were posed so clearly by the original strategy consultant's report that the real differences among subgroups were immediately flushed into the open and became a direct source of conflict. The underground feelings about Ed surfaced relatively quickly, helped along by the individual data-sharing process adopted for the off-site. The group's history had already helped everyone find allies, so that wasn't an issue. Finally, the use of the retreats and a consultant legitimized direct disagreement. For all of these reasons the team moved rapidly through subgrouping into conflict. In short order, the team began to deal with conflict over style, structure, and strategy.

Teams can stall over task disputes or personal/interpersonal dominance, but more often there is an interpenetration of both. Differences about basic direction get identified with the individuals and subgroups who are most passionately divided over the future, and it can be hard for the players to separate the issues from the individuals. But the Pharmco team was able to stop to work on relationships when that was blocking progress, as with Ed, and then continue back on clarifying responsibilities and other tasks.

In this period, they moved easily back and forth between work content and process, discussing difficult issues, examining the way they were working, and then improving decision making. For example, they managed to separate their liking Steve from prioritizing the organization's goals. They have determined how to face basic differences wherever they occur.

BEYOND PHARMCO

Because conflict is so problematic in so many organizations, the balance of this chapter will focus on it. It will be extremely difficult to develop full shared responsibility if the organization is unable to accept the inevitability and desirability of conflict, and is unable to work through it.

The Pharmco team has moved beyond the subgrouping stage into conflict, and is learning how to handle it productively. In today's organizations, conflict is both inevitable and healthy. It should be embraced, not avoided or suppressed. In an increasingly complex world, correct solutions are rarely knowable in advance. Differing views have to be raised, defended, and questioned.

Dissension was less crucial in the past. When problems are simple, and someone knows the answer—especially the boss—just let that whiz make the decision. Today, it is rare for a single person to have all the right answers to questions about emerging markets, global competition, technological innovations, impending obsolescence, new forms of cost reduction, areas for continuous improvement, or breakthrough products. So team members' best ideas, opinions, and hunches need to reach the surface and then receive critical testing to arrive at solutions with the highest probability of success.

Contention can:

- Sharpen issues, saving time.
- Force everyone to think through their positions and do their homework, so the one who argues loudest doesn't automatically prevail.
- Guard against groupthink, an inadvertent condition where members too readily agree with one another to avoid unpleasant disagreements.
- Clarify where people stand.
- Energize, generating interest and investment.
- Develop more creative solutions.

- When resolved, strengthen relationships and build commitment to solutions.

Post-heroic leadership and shared responsibility make open conflict more likely, since everyone is encouraged to invest in the team's success and take responsibility for overall results. As at Pharmco, the more a team is asked to deal with fundamental strategic issues, the greater the likelihood of disagreements. And when the leader is committed to sharing decision-making responsibility, strong feelings and opinions are less likely to be suppressed.

COSTS OF POOR CONFLICT-RESOLUTION MECHANISMS

The mere presence of conflict does not guarantee high performance. When a team cannot deal effectively with their differences, meetings are spent in unproductive fights that never seem to get resolved. The goal of winning supersedes any concern for quality outcomes.

The alternative trap is extreme politeness, carefully avoiding controversial topics and skirting around hot issues to avoid real or imagined danger. Guerrilla warfare and backstage maneuvering make meetings cumbersome. Groups stuck in this stage snipe endlessly but never directly deal with the differences, or have ritualized meetings in which all important subjects are avoided for fear of explosion. Meetings resemble tea parties (but watch the sugar).

There is a big difference between the heated discussions of a team that is stuck in the conflict stage and of one that is developed to the point of having healthy disputes over genuine business issues. In a team that is stuck, there will be attempts to win at all costs, domineering behavior (often the boss's), battles over turf and personalities rather than over issues, endless recycling of the same arguments (only louder and angrier), and comments meant to wound.

Whether the team avoids open conflict or is stuck in attack-one-another mode, the consequences are negative. The members' energy goes outside the group, often into behind-the-scenes lobbying or internecine warfare, wasting enormous amounts of time and ensuring that there is too little benefit from having team members' involvement. Decisions are needlessly delayed, but even when they are made, it is difficult to get members to invest energy in implementation, since they have not collectively committed to the decision.

FEARS OF CONFLICT

If conflict is so important, why is its direct expression so rare in most organizations? Many people have been raised with the notion that conflict is bad. This may come from early family experiences or cultural socialization. Some may have grown up in households with a high degree of unresolved parental conflict. For others, it may be mother's voice saying, "If you can't say something nice, don't say anything at all." Some cultures place a premium on being rational and view strong feelings as a sign of immaturity. One of the authors consulted with an insurance company whose top management team almost botched a bet-the-company decision because the leader had so clearly signaled his discomfort with strong disagreement that members neither spoke up nor understood each other's concerns. Although team members had strong opinions, since this big decision would have dramatically affected their departments, no one wanted to become the leader's "poor team player." Staying on the kindly president's good side was more important than making a critical decision with all the analysis and passion on the table.

Part of the resistance to conflict may come from the leader's fear of losing control. After all, if different viewpoints are passionately expressed, who knows how it will turn out? Heroic leaders, who think they must be responsible for determining outcomes, try to maintain control of all important issues.

Team members may also work under heroic assumptions, and be reluctant to engage their colleagues or boss in open disagreements. For them, it's simply too risky. They worry that the venting of differences might lead to hurtful accusations that they will later regret. They might say something that would create an enemy, reveal an error, disclose a lack of preparation, or threaten one of the boss's sacred cows. So members and leader often collude to keep conflict under wraps.

Some managers give conflict a bad name. We have been present when the general manager of a billion dollar division screamed, "That's the dumbest idea I've ever heard," and "I can't believe that in this whole group of overpaid executives, not one of you can do an analysis!" It isn't hard to guess how creatively or effectively his team attacked cost-cutting when the economy slowed and business declined 15 percent. That he only lasted two years in his position was little consolation to the poor souls who tried to defend themselves. They did not learn to value conflict.

Another fear is that people might get locked into their positions, feel inhibited, or hold back anything but unassailable hard data. Without agreement on a vision for the unit, there is no agreed-on basis for making decisions, which can make conflicts hard to resolve.

But probably the greatest fear is that *task conflict will degenerate into personal attacks.* Many managers agree that spirited discussion is appropriate in today's organizations, as long as such disagreements are about difficult tasks. But how can these disputes be contained? What if the discussion degenerates from "Should we move aggressively into South America" to "You are pushing to build up your territory because you like to control and show off how powerful you are"?

We observed this escalation during a meeting of the top management team in the French subsidiary of a packaged food company. They were struggling to address performance problems by becoming more of a team, and groping for ways to address the long-standing coordination breakdowns. The logistics manager, encouraged by the well-meaning but unskilled leader to express her views, tried, with a sweet voice, to challenge the sales manager about the inventory and forecasting problems arising from his failure to convey sales information using the approved requisition forms. She was so unpracticed at confrontation that instead of explaining the costs to the company, she put the problem in a way that implied that the sales manager was not smart enough to follow the rules. Wounded, he screamed at her that she was "an idiot and imbecile." The resulting eruption of angry and hurt feelings, "proved" to the group that it was better to speak in allegories or avoid anything but abstract, intellectual debate. The dispute was quickly closed down and the team retreated to its safe but indirect and ineffectual mode of interacting.

While the probability of personal attacks can be lessened, there is no guarantee that they can be avoided entirely. Many of the actions that managers take to prevent these from occurring block the productive use of other forms of conflict. They disparage dissenters, saying things like "We'll discuss that off-line" or changing the subject just as real differences are about to emerge.

If a manager is afraid of conflict, the move from being a traditional team to a shared responsibility team will be difficult. The team will be stuck in subgrouping and never work through to the genuine collaboration of Stage 5.

RAISING AND RESOLVING THE CONTENTIOUS ISSUES

In making the most of conflict, it helps to recognize that there are three forms of conflict: task, role-related, and personal. Task and role-related conflict are both inevitable and necessary for high performance; personal conflict—which can be difficult to distinguish from role-related but is fundamentally different—is not necessary and should not be tolerated:

1. *Task conflicts* involve disputes about what should be done. "Should we expand into new product lines or stick with our core business?"

2. *Role-related conflicts* are about how the other is carrying out his/her job. "You aren't meeting your obligations." "Your repeated focus on tiny details drives me crazy."

3. *Personal conflicts* are attacks on an individual's character. "You are an insincere, selfish, and power-hungry person."

These three forms of conflict often follow one another in sequence. If conflicts over tasks are not resolved, (for example, whether or not to launch a marketing campaign in China when the market is ripe but the distributor/dealer network is not well developed), over time they lead to interpersonal conflicts between disputants: "Your typical caution about launching doesn't fit the risk-taking demands of a developing market." "You are being far too optimistic yet again." If these interpersonal conflicts are not resolved, they can become personal: "You are uptight and don't have an entrepreneurial bone in your body." "Well, you're so ambitious you wouldn't bother to do a painstaking analysis if your life depended on it."

The challenge is to raise and respond to legitimate disagreements about work sufficiently early and clearly so that they do not cause role-related disputes or descend rapidly into personal attacks. It isn't that there won't always be legitimate interpersonal conflict, or that it all can be avoided, but it ought not to arise from ineptness in resolving task disagreements.

Dealing with Task Conflicts

The first step in promoting healthy conflict is to expect it and insist on a full airing of views. Subgroups must be encouraged to state their positions clearly on core issues. Here, the leader may have to listen for underlying but unexpressed disagreements. Unless members are used to surfacing conflict and are comfortable with it, the leader may have to take the initiative in bringing disagreements out in the open. Alfred Sloan, the legendary head of General Motors in its glory days, was a master at this. Peter Drucker tells the story of what Sloan did when no disagreement was expressed on a complex proposal:

> *Garrett's proposal was so well prepared that everybody supported it; and it was also suspected that Sloan was heartily in its favor. But when everybody thought the proposal had been agreed upon, the old man switched off his hearing aid and said, "I take it all you gentlemen are in favor?" "Yes, Mr. Sloan," the chorus came back. "Then I move that we defer action on this for a month to give ourselves a chance to think"—and a month later the proposal was either scuttled or drastically revised.*[1]

This response differs dramatically from that of the typical leader, who on hearing no sign of a contrary view breathes a sigh of relief and quickly checks off that agenda item.

There are other devices for generating appropriate conflict over important tasks:

- List pros and cons on an issue. This forces full consideration.
- Appoint a "devil's advocate" (preferably rotated, so no single person is discounted).
- Watch closely for non-verbal signs of unarticulated feelings, and inquire about what isn't being said.
- Support the expression of minority opinions.

The key to preventing task disputes from bogging down into role-related battles is the use of such effective problem-solving techniques.[2] While many individuals are good problem solvers, they aren't so skilled at collective problem solving, where everyone's contributions must be valued and integrated. Frustration over progress on tough issues turns people against each other.

Recent research on management teams concluded that six tactics helped to prevent task disagreements from degenerating into interpersonal conflict. Team members:

- Conduct fact-based, information-rich discussions.
- Enrich debate with multiple alternatives.
- Agree on goals.
- Use humor in decision-making to relieve tension.
- Preserve a balance of power among members, not letting the leader or members dominate.
- Seek consensus, but accept leader decisions when it isn't possible or is bogging down.[3]

These approaches are highly compatible with post-heroic leadership, although they can lead to a slide back into heroic assumptions. It isn't far from "accepting leader decisions when consensus isn't possible," to the leader heroically making all decisions by consultation, allowing participation but not demanding shared responsibility. And humor can be double-edged, softening tension, but also subtly putting people in their place by put-downs or sniping. Most important, the emphasis on managing and avoiding interpersonal conflict implies that it is never legitimate, and only the result of poor management of task disagreements. But interpersonal conflict can be a product of natural differences in relational style, as well as task disagreements, and the best results come from being willing to address it openly within the team.

Interpersonal, Role-Related Conflicts

None of these techniques for surfacing task disagreements are difficult in themselves, but many leaders hold back because they realize how readily such arguments can turn into interpersonal conflicts. Conflicts about how team members perform their roles are harder to predict or control. But such conflicts will and should arise because complex work that requires interdependence must accommodate differing work styles. Besides, since no one is perfect, irritating mistakes will happen. Like task conflicts, interpersonal conflicts can have positive consequences. Thus, addressing these role-related conflicts is a necessary part of building results-oriented shared responsibility.

Moving from a heroic to a post-heroic system, is likely to unearth pent-up feelings that previously were not allowed to be worked openly, as happened at Pharmco with Ed Fisher, the CFO. Furthermore, as work proceeds, differences over tasks generate three kinds of interpersonal, role-related conflicts.

The first follows from heated arguments, where two or more people see things differently and fight for their convictions. Since the toughest decisions are those where results will be known only in the distant future, requiring faith without indisputable proof that one's projections are accurate, there is ample opportunity for smart and competent people to be convinced that they are right and the other(s) are wrong. Will the public want rounded car shapes in four years? Will it be possible to drive reliability up and costs down on large, active matrix monitors? Will personal picture phones ever catch on? When one person or group is convinced that the opportunity is gigantic, and another thinks it will dwarf the failure of the Edsel, discussion can get heated. That is entirely appropriate, but too often the heat turns to interpersonal fire, with negative assumptions about the abilities of the person(s) with opposing views. After a while, neither party has a clear view of the other, and believes that it is difficult or impossible to work with such incompetents.

A second source of interpersonal conflict is found in the connection between task effectiveness and the person assigned to carry out the tasks. Any solution is only as good as its implementation. Thus, the discussion of the pros and cons of alternatives to a task links the fit of existing abilities to tasks of those carrying out the requisite roles. Deciding whether to move into Argentina must take into account Paul's ability to establish local connections, to recruit and hire local employees, and the ability of his staff to handle this new challenge. Such issues generally are not ignored in a discussion, but they tend to be dealt with indirectly, if at all: Many conversations seem to be carried out in code. "Paul, do you foresee any problems in hiring locals with the needed qualifications?" may stand for, "Because of the problems you had in Mexico, I am concerned about your ability to succeed in Argentina."

The third source of interpersonal conflicts arise from differing work styles. Each person has his or her own way of getting work done. Jane likes to plan carefully before acting, whereas Jim likes to experiment early on to collect preliminary data. Diane relies heavily on quantitative analysis to determine the right answer, whereas Dane places more value on hunches and intuition. Sandra likes meetings that encourage open-ended problem seeking, whereas Sam wants crisper sessions that focus on making decisions. Neither approach will always be more appropriate, and both may be needed at different times, but the differences can be a potential source of conflict. The person who wants careful analysis can drive the "let's-try-it-out" experimenter crazy (and vice versa).

The feelings from these differences can and should be raised and resolved. Having team members with diverse work styles is crucial for today's complex organization. New problems that require new solutions may demand multiple problem-solving approaches. Can members capitalize on their differences without working at cross-purposes? If they can, not only will more be brought to resolution of problems, but individual members will be stretched and learn. Working through interpersonal conflict is highly developmental.

Surfacing role-related conflict also allows members to explore whether organizational factors are causing the problems. Is the conflict between Hank, from production, and Mona, from marketing, due less to personality or work style and more to the pressure from the requirements of their jobs? Is he basically a conservative person or just rewarded for keeping costs down? Could her desire to try new approaches be work-driven?

Personal-Related Conflict

Conflict that addresses another's skills for the job is difficult, but once that genie is out of the bottle, it is easy for
things to turn ugly. What may have its source in legitimate
differences or concerns can escalate into personal attacks
on the motives, intentions, innate abilities, or character of
the opposing person. These personal attacks can damage
relationships.

Role-related conflict that deals with *how* people carry out
their work responsibilities is far less damaging than conflict
that attacks the other's character. Saying, "I don't have confidence that you will come through in that assignment" addresses a legitimate performance question, whereas "You are
an irresponsible person and cannot be trusted" attacks the
person's character. Saying, "You repeatedly attack those who
disagree with you" deals with job-oriented behavior, whereas
"It's because you are basically insecure that you lash out at
others," questions the person's motives and inner psyche.
Doing so fuels personal enmity without doing anything to
resolve conflict.

Because the recipient of the role-related comment may not
be able to differentiate between performance criticism and
personal attack, "I have concerns about your ability to succeed" may sound like a personal condemnation. Many people
have hair-trigger readiness to perceive potential insults,
which explains why so many people shy away from direct
talk; they fear being misinterpreted, or worse.

It is nevertheless vital to make this distinction between
role-related and personal conflict, since differences that
arise from carrying out work must be dealt with to achieve
outstanding results. The team can only move through Stage
3 if it experiences successful resolution of the difficult task
and interpersonal issues.

Resolving Interpersonal Problems

The challenge, then, is to find a way to raise and work through
disagreements without having openness or directness

interpreted as personal attack. Resolution must avoid the dangers of holding back as well as the dangers of escalating to the personal level. If there is a way to make work disagreements explicit and have that result in creative resolutions and better relationships, unnecessary pain can be avoided as the team moves toward greater shared responsibility and higher performance. Interpersonal disputes are as important to managerial work as disputes over strategy, numbers, or products. A powerful leadership contribution is to legitimize open exploration of these disputes while minimizing blame-seeking, establishing that developing skills in this rich but dangerous territory is a vital part of each manager's growth and development.

Focus on Behavior

A key to resolving interpersonal problems is to separate behavior from motivation. Confine remarks to role-related behavior and avoid any references to character or motives. Be specific and avoid sweeping generalizations. (For more on how to do this, see Appendix A, "Power Talk: A Hands-On Guide to Supportive Confrontation.") Remind the involved parties that they must "stay on their own sides of the net," confining their comments to what is observable about the other's behavior. Don't be afraid to rule out of bounds any negative character interpretations.

Planned and Unplanned Opportunities

If the leader has been encouraging regular times for examining the group's working processes, these can serve as natural opportunities for getting disputes on the table. If the team is suppressing disagreements, the leader (or any interested member) can ask individuals to rate the freedom they feel to express their views, then discuss the results. Another way to get at the differences is to ask members about the atmosphere of the group, and to examine it if it isn't completely open and freewheeling. Direct questions such as "What can we do to make the discussions more open?" or "What are the issues we need to discuss more directly?" can help unlock the team.

Alternatively, the leader can use the work processes examination time to identify specific issues that the team seems to shy away from, and request that members discuss them at a meeting in the near future. Leaders can help legitimize dissent by placing controversial interpersonal issues on the team's agenda and reminding members that these matters cannot be resolved except through honest discussion. The Leadership Style Questionnaire was used this way at Pharmco.

Conflict erupts, or peeks through, at unexpected times. If it has been suppressed out of fear, it can be magnified when it does emerge. A teasing remark that would usually be ignored suddenly evokes a sharp reaction. Members begin to bicker over an insignificant issue. Unanticipated conflict is the most feared since it is least controlled. Nevertheless, the leader who wants to encourage the team to address conflict, can help bring it into the open by calmly asking for more comments: "There seem to be strong feelings here. Let's get them on the table," or "What is behind that remark?" or in some other way indicating that the team need not fear more open expression of anger or dissent.

In-Meeting or Off-Line Discussion?

The first inclination of most managers is to take interpersonal conflicts outside the group, especially when they are accompanied by strong feelings and attributions about the other's character or motivation. Fear of escalation prompts the leader to step in and smooth over differences, call a break, or say "We'll deal with this after the meeting."

There are times when it is desirable to work issues one-on-one, in private. This makes sense when the team is just starting its development, the individuals involved are too volatile, or are too locked in to listen while others are present. If it is a boss-subordinate conflict, the subordinate may not wish to discuss the issue in front of colleagues perceived as potential rivals.

It is preferable, however, to deal with and resolve such conflict in the group. This strengthens the group as its members learn to handle touchy issues, and increases team and member learning. The Pharmco team reaped great benefits by involving everyone in the conflicts relating to Gene, Bob, and Ed. It takes a group setting to bring out the various points of view. The goal is to provide different slants on the issue, not to take sides.

Marie and Jeremy are colleagues having trouble with each other. If Marie's critical style in meetings is bothering Jeremy, are others bothered as well? If that is the case, she can't just dismiss it as "Jeremy's problem." But if others aren't disturbed, Jeremy must learn why he is getting so upset. The challenge is to bring out these issues without assigning blame.

The first step is for the leader to legitimize the dispute as a discussion item. Doing so may require nothing more than saying, after Jeremy has accused Marie of shooting down all his proposals, "this feels important, what's going on here?" Such a comment is likely to increase the conflict as both sides defend their positions. At this point, it could be useful to turn to others for their perspectives. This complicates the discussion, as each is likely to have a slightly different view. Some might say that Marie is a sharp critic of new proposals, but differ as to whether her criticisms are excessive or personally motivated. Others might say that Jeremy is too sensitive to criticism, which has caused them to treat him with kid gloves. The advantage of this complication is that it breaks down the polarization between Marie and Jeremy. There is more involved than "which one is right," and recognizing this opens the door to problem solving.

What If the Conflict Becomes Personal?

But what if problem solving escalates to personal attack? Suppose Jeremy barks, "It's just because you are insecure that you attack others' ideas," and Marie returns in kind by accusing Jeremy of being so insecure about his masculinity that he can't stand questioning from a woman! Is all lost? Not necessarily.

Here, members can come to the rescue, especially if they have accepted responsibility for shared management. In

that case, the leader has to make sure that member involvement works toward resolution rather than smoothing
over the dispute.

What should the leader do when help is not forthcoming?
First, indicate that personal attacks are not legitimate and
have no place in the organization. Second, legitimize the importance of this issue (but not the way it is being expressed).
Third, shift the discussion back to the role-related level on
which the attack was based. A statement such as the following one accomplishes all three requirements:

> *"Jeremy and Marie, these personal attacks have no place
> here. However, they indicate an important problem in the
> way the two of you are working together. What's going
> on?"*

That kind of straightforward comment should help. But
suppose that this duo continues slinging mud:

> *"She never listens and doesn't give a damn for what oth-
> ers say."*
> *"Well, if you had something of value to say, Jeremy, I
> might actually listen!"*

Once the conflict shifts to intentions, motives, or personality, each party must be dragged back to opposite sides of
the net—moving discussion back to specific behavior.

> *"Jeremy, you don't know Marie's deep motives about
> domination or anything else, and even if you did, that
> isn't relevant. What is important is the behavior that is
> bothering you. What specifically does she do that gets
> you so upset?"*

This focuses the discussion without closing it down.

Returning to specific behavior takes some of the sting out
of differences, and makes it possible to examine that behavior objectively—to be certain that the perceived behavior

actually took place, and that the reactions to it are not necessarily universal but particular to the reactor. If others in the group react in a similar way, that is also useful information, and makes it more possible for the person receiving the feedback to take it without wanting to pass blame back across the net. But even if the reactions from one member are totally idiosyncratic, sticking to the behavior and its impact reduces defensiveness and makes exploration more possible.

Reciprocal Reinforcement

Another useful addition from the leader (or a member) is to raise the possibility that the "problem" is not in one person or the other, but in the *interaction* between the wants, values, and behavior of one, and those of the other. Regardless of which one initiated the pattern, both keep it going. And either one of the two can stop it. A neutral attitude and willingness to push for understanding rather than blame can help break the tension and move the discussion toward problem solving—figuring out how to end the mutual negative reinforcement and promote a more favorable cycle of behavior-reaction-behavior.

Reaching Resolution of the Issues

Focusing on behavior and its impact encourages the team to get into problem solving. The leader, or any member, can start exploring what new behavior can improve the situation: "Jeremy, how can Marie raise her concerns without your feeling attacked?" Each combatant should state what he or she needs from the other and then negotiate a pact, with specifics, including what they will do if either party regresses to the old behavior.

Learning

Raising and resolving role-related difficulties can be a source of learning on multiple levels. For the principals involved, there is personal learning about the impact of their behavior. That is important in every career path. Some of the greatest learning can be about how to resolve problematic interpersonal conflicts. The issue is immediate—not something that is discussed abstractly in a training program or long afterward in a performance appraisal. The feedback tends to be richer and more complex coming from all the members and not just from the leader.

Other group members can also learn. Since interpersonal difficulties often are reciprocally sustained, members can see their own behavior in the problems between contending teammates like Jeremy and Marie. Furthermore, they increase their skills in giving behaviorally specific feedback.

Finally, there is learning at the group level. Most people think that raising role-related conflict in a group is only an excuse for sharks to go after the bleeding victim. Instead, people learn how effective collective problem solving can be. They see that individuals, relationships, and the team not only survive but are strengthened through conflict resolution.

RESOLUTION OF STAGE 3

Once a team has resolved one or more serious conflicts, it is prepared to move beyond Stage 3 to the later stages of group development. Members are able to pursue the team's business with a new sense of confidence that future conflicts can be faced and overcome.

When the resolution of conflict settles the fundamental direction of the team, then members will accept the overall organization's tasks as being equally important for them to accomplish as those of their individual subunits. If members really agree on the overarching goal, reference to it can generate their willingness to explore differences rather than to insist on winning every argument. (This is analogous to the negotiation concept of exploring interests rather than fixed positions.)

If interpersonal differences are raised and resolved, then members can feel that their psychological needs for acceptance, influence, and freedom to be themselves are likely to be met. In either case, the team will be greatly relieved that conflict is not going to tear the team apart, and they can get on with the team's work. Furthermore, once there has been success in dealing with interpersonal conflicts, everyone learns more about how to deal with the inevitable future conflicts so that they do not become personal and destructive.

Even when the fundamental issues have been resolved, conflict will arise again, as new strategic issues get on the agenda, the environment changes, members leave or join, or working styles begin—or continue—to create friction. The good news is that these conflicts will be the result of issues, not uncleared interpersonal underbrush. In fact, it is important for the team not to become so giddy with relief over resolving a first major conflict that it ignores or avoids other unresolved conflicts to avoid spoiling the new cooperative atmosphere. It is tempting to want to preserve good feeling by pretending that every point of contention has now been taken care of or by tacitly agreeing to overlook disagreements that can be worked around or tolerated in an era of good fellowship.

When a conflict has been satisfactorily resolved, it is worth the effort to inquire whether there are other unresolved issues that the team needs to address, and to watch carefully for signals of strong feelings below the surface that may need a bit of coaxing to elicit. There are times for celebration (which can serve a healing function), but these good feelings should not block raising other difficult issues. The way to preserve good feeling is to keep doing good, hard task work, successfully tackling the business and relationship conflicts that other teams shy away from.

The Value of Examining Process

A group should periodically review its decision-making/discussion process; doing so will help members understand how they have been working. Periodic review should take place at every stage, though it is most useful in earlier stages when members are still learning how to work together in new ways. Whether the team uses a questionnaire of some kind to collect data, an open-ended set of questions, or simply a discussion at the end of meetings, the processing of experience is a corrective device, a preventive tool for making changes before there is major damage, and a facilitator of group learning. Don't leave home without it.

What Members Can Do

Our discussion thus far has focused more on what the leader can do to help the team effectively deal with conflict. Most of these same actions, however, can be taken by members. Members can support the expression of minority opinions, see that disagreements are cleanly and clearly stated, and provide new alternatives that can move the contentious sides from their entrenched positions. This will prevent the papering over of real disagreements to achieve a false peace. Members can also help set norms and encourage the group to examine its own process.

Insofar as people feel accepted and valued, they feel safe in bringing their individual energy and an enlarged range of ideas to the group. They will be prepared for the more advanced stages of individual differentiation and collaboration. When collaboration is achieved, it is possible to spread the shared-responsibility system throughout the organization.

12

ACHIEVING COLLABORATION

Changing the leadership system in an executive team is hard work, but it helps immeasurably when people work through conflict and learn to pull together. Much more must be done, however, before true collaboration becomes the way of life. The team has to make tough decisions together and solidify the new leadership assumptions as it does so. It must also extend the new beliefs and the new mode of operating throughout the organization. Otherwise, backsliding toward the traditional heroic system will be inevitable.

The Pharmco operating committee (OpCom) had made great progress in resolving disputes about the company's direction and strategic choices. Working together at their second off-site retreat, committee members had accomplished a great deal: They would divest the equipment division, consolidate two line divisions, fundamentally refocus a third, and set up an integrated sales operations. In doing so, they had begun to see the benefit of confronting each other directly on important issues, including finally addressing long-festering antipathies toward CFO Ed Fisher. But many organizational issues remained to be settled. A key issue was who would head the new divisions. Bob Mitchell had been talking to each member individually about their self-development plans and who might fill jobs. There was a sense that momentous decisions were in the offing.

Of all the personnel decisions, one of the toughest had to do with leading the animal feed division. Because the focus had shifted from sales and marketing to spearheading new product development or acquisition, the question was whether anyone at the company could handle the ambitious new goals for this division. Bob knew that Ted Castine wanted to stay in the feed division's top job, where he had been an effective sales and marketing manager, but Bob had his doubts about whether Ted had the appropriate skills for the newly focused division. Bob couldn't bring himself to recommend that Ted leave, and decided to give him the benefit of the doubt. He planned to begin the retreat with the proposal that Ted take the position.

Pharmco: Part IV

The Third Pharmco Off-Site

Bob Mitchell opened the meeting by reminding the team that they were still to take the larger view and that they had created the early retirement plan as a safety net so that no one need worry about his or her personal future as they contributed to the discussions. Now they had some difficult personnel decisions to make. The team had asked him to talk with everyone about their futures, and he had done so. "I appreciate the candor in all of our conversations," Bob told them, "but unfortunately, that doesn't always lead to easy answers about who should do what. We need to think this through together."

He suggested that they start with the VP of Animal Feed position, and recommended Ted for the job. Everyone understood the critical nature of the position being created, and wanted it to be filled with someone suited to it. Ted Castine was certainly interested. But was he the best candidate?

After some awkward moments, several individuals began to talk about the administrative skills needed for building a new products organization. They did a thorough job of specifying the talents and instincts needed. Though it wasn't easy to say, they concluded that these were not

Ted's strong suit. They saw him as a person phenomenally skilled at selling, but not a great organizer or business builder. "Ted, you should work from your strengths," one person suggested. Others concurred. There was no political jockeying for position, since no one else in the group personally wanted the job. This made the feedback particularly powerful.

Debate over the pros and cons of Ted Castine's fit with the job while he sat among them was uncomfortable for everyone. Tension in the room was thick. Eventually, Ted broke the tension. With a quaver in his voice, he said, "I'm going to take myself out of the running. I can see that I am not the right guy for the job. And since I don't see another place for myself in the new organization, it's best for me to leave the company."

A long uncomfortable silence followed. Everyone realized the full potential of jointly tackling delicate issues and not backing off to spare feelings. They felt badly about how things had turned out for Ted, despite the assurances of the new retirement plan. Yet they stuck to their guns because they had determined the criteria for success, which didn't match Ted's skills. Bob Mitchell was struck by how decisively and objectively the team had acted. It had gone further in addressing a difficult decision than he would have and had handled it extremely well.

More Decisions

Other tough personnel decisions remained. If not Ted, who should run the new products division? Second, who should head up the newly combined agricultural chemicals and biotech division? And who should be in charge of the new consolidated world-wide sales division? Convinced now that the team could handle these decisions, Bob asked them to proceed.

The team started by summarizing their previous discussion about the characteristics needed to lead the new products division. Consensus emerged that Rick Bentley was the person best suited to head it. But Bentley resisted:

"Thanks, but new products has always been a suicidal job in this company. It never gets the support it needs to be successful. Taking the job is, in my opinion, a death sentence."

"What would it take to change that, Rick?" asked Bill Boyer. "What would it take in terms of budget, staff, and facilities to make new products a success?" Bentley offered his opinions and the rest of the OpCom team joined in. Eventually, they reached agreement as to what a new products division needed in order to flourish, and Bentley agreed to take the job on that basis.

After lunch, with the Bentley appointment settled, the other positions were addressed in turn. The discussions were hot; the line divisions did not want to give up control of sales without being sure they would get the right levels of service from whoever ended up with the world-wide sales job. There was equal wrestling over who the leaders of the combined divisions should be. But they were able to manage the anxious feelings and examine individual skills and competence in the light of position requirements.

As a result, they identified that Bill Boyer would fill the top position in the newly combined agricultural chemical-biotech division, and Fredrik Enthoven would retain international sales. But since all the domestic sales functions were to be pulled from the line divisions and placed under Enthoven, there was extended discussion about how to prevent jockeying for his attention. He said, "I need a process so that I don't get hammered by each of you." They agreed to create a task force to work out procedures. It made sense to let the managers below get familiar with the problems and opportunities created by so much organizational reshuffling before making appointments at the next few levels, so they agreed to tackle that after the dust had settled.

The afternoon ended with agreement to set the next day's agenda and then enjoy dinner together. The agenda would include alignment of the bonus system to reinforce collaboration. The group also wanted to decide how to carry the new leadership ideas throughout the organization. Gene and Bob reported that the Board of Directors were less than enthusiastic about what they had heard about this new approach to shared leadership, and that needed to be addressed.

After dinner, Ted pulled Mary Chadwick aside and asked whether he should not return for the next day's meetings. "After all, the issues don't really involve me and I'm a lame duck." Mary encouraged him to come back. "In the past you have been seen as taking a partisan perspective; here's a chance to practice being a statesman by using your knowledge of the larger context. You can help the team as a totally detached observer." He agreed, and when he walked into the meeting room the next day, he was greeted with spontaneous applause. Ted was an active and insightful participant for the remainder of the retreat.

Think Inc.

The morning meeting began with the need to align the reward system with the new commitment to shared leadership. OpCom members had discussed their commitment to working together and summed up the need to do so by coining the term "Think Inc." But the current compensation plan weighted bonuses heavily on the performance of each executive's subunit. Mary Chadwick proposed that a new bonus plan be developed to make all executive bonuses dependent on overall company results. This would require a major change in investment from members who had previously been in competition with one another. "I can't think of a better way to express our commitment to shared management of Pharmco," said Ed Fisher, "than to link rewards with companywide results." Several others seconded his statement.

Chadwick was assigned to spell out the details of the plan and to bring it back to the next OpCom meeting for discussion and endorsement.

Expanding Involvement

Stopping to reflect on its many decisions, the team decided to make everything provisional, pending the reaction of the next two levels of company managers, 125 in all. They realized that middle management had information that would be useful for making appropriate plans and overcoming obstacles to implementation. There had been meetings with the lower levels in the past, but these had mostly been used to make announcements, do new product rollouts, and conduct state-of-the-business updates. OpCom members were apprehensive about whether middle management would buy into the strategic and organizational changes. Would an open meeting expose the OpCom too much? To facilitate a new, more interactive approach, two OpCom members were given the task of planning a two day retreat to explain this new strategic thrust. The objective was to create more of a partnership by soliciting feedback from the managers before finalizing all the decisions.

The board of directors also needed attention. They were concerned about Gene loosening things when the business was not growing. Bob and Gene were asked to think through an approach and prepare a report for the next meeting of the Pharmco board of directors. The retreat had ended with the team making suggestions for the presentation, including that the board be sent *Managing for Excellence* "to show them what post-heroic leadership is and how managers plan to use it in running the company."

PHARMCO ISSUES

The Pharmco Operating Committee was increasingly able to function as a true team, collectively making difficult and far-reaching decisions. These decisions could readily have evoked self-promotional behavior among the members. Reorganizations and reassignments inevitably lead to shifting power and status, and alter the fit of some individuals with the new roles. Nevertheless, there was little maneuvering and posturing. The retirement package made it easier to be objective, but would not by itself have induced such organizationally oriented discussion. The team was able to balance organizational requirements with individual needs.

The OpCom's new collaboration started with a sense of shared responsibility and shared leadership. The most important elements of the new leadership system had been developed:

- High *commitment to the organizational vision*, to the concept of shared responsibility and to the growth of Pharmco all were in place.
- High *mutual influence;* allowed the directness between the members and Ted Castine about his strengths and weaknesses, and allowed Rick Bentley to make his requirements clear for accepting a new position.
- Experience in *working through conflict* allowed team members to address both task and role disagreements directly without fear of harming personal relationships.

The team could value a high-quality decision ahead of the preservation of good feelings, avoiding the trap of saying only nice things to Ted. Earlier success in facing and resolving the awkward relationship issues involving Bob, Gene, and Ed had moved the team forward, and made it increasingly possible to share responsibility for deciding such delicate matters as who should be on the team, remain with the company, or fill new roles. Each decision made the next discussion more open and authentic, enabling members to cope well with difficult decisions.

As the OpCom team continued working together on important issues, its members became more skillful at assuming the managerial tasks previously reserved for Gene and Bob. A driving entrepreneur, Gene had many reservations about collective management, but he was pleased to see his senior managers stepping up to the plate and taking responsibility. Entrepreneurs typically worry about whether their "babies" will be properly looked after, and many of them can never let go because no individual looks strong enough to them. He was reassured that the spirit of the company he had founded would not follow the slippery slope into bureaucratic inertia.

In making difficult managerial decisions, the team practiced mutual influence. Here, the power of straight talk was demonstrated. Making a shared responsibility team sing takes agreement on a tangible vision, mutual influence, and the willingness to talk both tough and supportively to one another. This is at once easy and extremely difficult.

Beyond Pharmco: Advanced Stages of Group Development

Once a team has worked its way through several major conflicts, the atmosphere changes. Suddenly, everyone has found his or her place in the team. Discussions are heated but reasonable, task focused, and free of sniping. Alliances that emerge do not impede consensus-building because boundaries shift as new subgroupings arise and dissolve with different issues. Each member can be counted on to do what he or she promised. Meetings are efficient workplaces. Members, for the most part, enjoy dealing with each other.

Does all of this sound like Nirvana? Organizational life would be vastly improved if all teams could at least get to Stage 4, individual differentiation. Yet, the payoff for moving beyond Stage 4 is high. Bathing in good feeling is a legitimate reward for hard work, but the leader (or some responsible members) must be ready to push the team into new territory.

Critical Issues to Be Resolved during Stage 4

Stage 4 has several limitations that stand between the management team and the full potential of shared leadership.

- *A tendency to back off.* Members may participate in discussing important issues, but too readily back off when they sense that the boss has a strong opinion, irrational attachment to a person or solution, or a blind spot. "The old man is dug in on this one," they reason. "It's safer to defer to him."

- *Consensus is seen as the only way.* Once people get a taste of consensus decision making, they tend to think that it is the only way to deal with problems. When this happens, meetings become longer and more frequent as even trivial decisions are massaged to death; any other form of decision making is viewed as a regression to "the old system." But autonomous, consultative, and delegated decisions all have their place too. The team needs to determine when to use each kind of decision making, so that it can become comfortable with individuals and subgroups acting on behalf of the team when the contributions of all aren't necessary.

- *Major issues are avoided when the peace is threatened.* When members have broken through the confrontation stage and find that their working relationships with other members are still intact, their relief can create a honeymoon period in which everyone is afraid to lose these new good feelings. Important but controversial subjects that could rock the boat are avoided and the team slides back into mediocrity. There is a reluctance to take on issues likely to disrupt established power balances and personal relationships. Even when a loaded issue is raised, colleagues may "agree to disagree," since courtesy allows everyone to dodge the tough problems. Meanwhile, there is always enough other work to do to keep the team from seeming idle.

- *People are too accepting of mediocre performance.* Out of good personal feeling, long history, or inertia, the team will not insist that all members be first-rate. "Oh, that's just Paul's way" can be an excuse for allowing someone to be charming about an inadequacy that everyone else has to work around. We do not intend to sound cruel, or to insist that any performance slippage deserves immediate firing, but there is nothing about post-heroic leadership that implies merely adequate standards. If extraordinary performance is not the goal, it isn't worth bothering with this demanding form of leadership.

It takes real courage to say to a peer, "You have been a valuable member in the past but conditions have changed. What can we do so that you can find productive work inside or, if necessary, outside the organization?"

- *Lack of real collaboration.* Members don't go the extra mile in supporting each other. They accept each other's idiosyncrasies and autonomy, but do not rush to support team members when they need help. "Each person stands on his own two feet" is the watchword.

It is very difficult for a heroically led team to break through the limitations of Stage 4 into the more fully collaborative and creative Stage 5. The assumptions of heroism continue to reinforce an individualistic way of operating. As much as the heroic leader may talk about collaboration, there is still a premium on self-reliance. Asking for help is seen as a sign of personal inadequacy.

MOVING THROUGH STAGE 4 INTO STAGE 5

Full shared responsibility involves genuine commitment to the overall goals of the unit and to the success of the other members. All members share with the leader in the management functions, making the decisions on critical issues by consensus. The powered up organization concentrates its energy on getting the important work done. Freed from traditional role boundaries, team members can be full contributors, with individuals and the team delivering more than they had thought possible. People fill in for each other as needed, and support each other's growth. Rather than the team being no stronger than its weakest link, it is energized to be stronger than its strongest individual member. That requires sharing decision making in areas typically thought of as the preserve of the leader. This is rare enough to be worthy of note, as when a management member of the wildly

successful Burlington Northern Intermodal Team compli-
mented their leader: "I never worked *for* Bill Greenwood . . . I
worked *with* Bill Greenwood."[1]

Central to the transition from Stage 4 to Stage 5 is the
degree to which critical, strategic tasks are tackled and decided by the team, especially those issues involving task interdependence among members. These particularly difficult
tasks include:

- Allocating scarce resources, such as budget, staff reduction, capital expenditures.
- Setting individual as well as team goals and objectives
  for the year, as well as career planning.
- Determining a strategic shift in product mix.
- Implementing a new set of work processes, such as
  reengineering, rapid prototyping, or decreased cycle
  time.
- Giving feedback on personal performance, including
  what each member does/does not do well, should work
  on, does to lose influence with other members.
- Making hiring decisions.
- Changing team composition.
- Allocating bonuses (or annual pay increases) for
  members.

Although these topics are loaded, and usually cannot be
attempted until the team is quite well developed, they can
accelerate team development in the middle stages. And once
the team has started to tackle the developmental plans of
each member, the leader does not have to rely on personal
one-to-one meetings with each person. Some explosive topics, such as allocating bonuses or determining membership
in the team, should be reserved for relatively mature teams.

A final difference between Stages 4 and 5 is the extent to
which members are connected and committed to one another. This goes beyond tolerance of ineffective behavior
and socializing with each other outside work. It is about

genuine concern and investment in one another's success and growth.

A Note of Caution

Close relationships usually work best when they flow from the ability to accomplish outstanding work. Teammates who are friends do not necessarily deliver high performance; high-performing teams, however, tend to end up liking each other since the ability to do winning work makes other team members look good.

It is also true, however, that close relationships can help members get past issues on which they strongly disagree, allowing them to fight hard but not lose their willingness to continue collaborating.[2] When there is a strong level of personal support, people are more willing to acknowledge learning needs and to talk about personal needs and difficulties. Closer relationships make it easier for the team to examine its processes whenever something is impeding work. Any team member will feel free to stop the action to clear up a problem.

Thus, in Stage 5 the team finally takes on equal responsibility for the development of its members as well as the management functions that it shares with the leader. Members both support and confront one another, demand high individual and collective performance, and provide the support to achieve it. That is what is required to make full collaboration work.

We do not know if there is a stage beyond full shared responsibility, but we do know that reaching Stage 5 is not the end of the journey. Teams do not automatically stay forever in a developed state, with all members fully competent and fully sharing responsibility for the unit's success. Even if the membership stays intact over time, which seldom happens, there is always backsliding, the temptation to coast, or new strategic challenges that can upset a hard-earned and satisfying status quo. Teams need not invent new difficulties to keep their competitive edge because the external world does quite nicely at throwing new challenges at any team and organization. Perhaps it isn't necessary to run faster to stay in place, but the team and leader must be alert to signs that the team is not stretching or using its full capacities.

Pharmco: Part V

Larger Organizational Transformation: Pharmco Powers Up

The middle management retreat, intended to engage middle managers as partners in the strategic planning and implementation process, started with Bob Mitchell explaining the new strategic direction and the rationale for the restructuring decisions. He went on to redefine the role of OpCom and of groups below. "Too many decisions have been shoved upstairs in the past," he told them. "We want the decisions to be made where the expertise resides. OpCom will set the strategic direction and lay out the parameters, but you will be responsible for figuring out how to carry them out. You know more about that than we ever could. As a start to this new way of operating, we want your reactions now to the changes in direction that we have posed."

The middle managers were then organized into cross-functional groups, each joined by one member of the OpCom. For the remainder of the morning, the groups explored the new strategic thrust Mitchell had described. Each group closely questioned their OpCom member about the objectives and priorities, and then identified parts they wanted clarified by OpCom. After lunch the teams reassembled without the OpCom member. Bob asked them to now react to the strategic thrust. "We are partners in this so we need your thoughts about whether we have left anything out. Now that you understand what we are trying to do, let's have your reactions. Are there actions we can take to accelerate movement? Barriers to remove?" The day adjourned with all of the suggestions put forward, from the trivial to the profound. To provide rapid reaction, the OpCom met until midnight to determine their responses to each of the suggestions.

The next morning, Bob went through the decisions made by the OpCom. He was crisp and clear about what they planned to change, what they would reconsider, (the emphasis on geographic expansion over product development) what they wouldn't, and why. "We are going with the matrix organization even though we agree with your concerns that this will be harder to implement. We are going to stay the course on this one." This was a marked change from past OpCom waffling and reversals, and demonstrated that real changes were underway. Even those who did not agree with all the decisions were pleased by the new decisiveness. For the first time, the middle leaders could see that they were having real impact on the strategic plans of the company. Bob Mitchell actually got a standing ovation at the end of his presentation. Later an attendee recalled, "It was amazing. We were so excited about being genuinely included that it was like the whole room was levitating."

For the rest of the day, departmental teams met to examine the implications of the new directions for their department's priorities, activities, and operating style. To what extent was their behavior reflective of the new values OpCom had called for? What practices would have to change?

All Aboard

The next scheduled board meeting followed the third OpCom retreat in a matter of weeks. Gene and Bob had developed a complete presentation of the team's plans and decisions. The board was surprised by what it learned: the tough issues that had been addressed, the OpCom's bold plans for reorganizing and staffing, and Bob Mitchell's new assertiveness. They were concerned about whether the new matrix structure would slow down decision making, whether post-heroic leadership fit the company, whether responsibility could really be shared, and whether the new divisions and roles were workable. One whispered to another: "Is Gene losing his grip?"

The CEO and his COO took turns detailing each of the OpCom's decisions, answering questions, and surfacing concerns. Even the doubters could not withhold approval. After all, each of the issues had been objectively examined, thoroughly debated, and was supported by managers at several levels.

Pharmco had come a long way. The OpCom was functioning well, major decisions had been made, the board had approved of the changes, and many of the leadership relationships and assumptions had been worked out. But organizations are complex systems, and changes in one part will lead to required changes in other parts. OpCom had tough decisions ahead. The spread of the post-heroic leadership system was only beginning.

Reducing and Reshuffling Staff

After reorganization of the functions, it became clear that some organizational fat required trimming and that not all the right people were in the right positions further down. In response, OpCom set a target of an overall 10 percent personnel reduction, but agreed that this should not be an even, across-the-board slice. The wisest cuts would be adjusted to each unit's needs. While the personnel reductions would eliminate redundant or overlapping functions, the individuals affected would be assessed for skills that might be valuable in other spots, necessitating personnel cuts in those areas. Since OpCom members had been working together much better over the intervening months, they decided that an extended staff meeting at the office would be sufficient to make the difficult decisions, and that they could handle this without help from Lincoln Turner, the consultant.

Everyone was asked to propose more cuts than were needed in total. On the first meeting day, team members put their proposals on the table for general discussion; in some cases colleagues said that the proposed cuts were too deep and would affect the business negatively, while in other cases they confronted members about not thinking boldly enough or cutting sufficiently. After spirited discussion, they made tough decisions on which functions should be reduced or eliminated.

Discussion on the second day was to focus on which individuals at the next few levels would be assigned to the roles shifted by reorganization and cost-cutting. Bob and Gene had to miss this day to appear in New York City before the financial analysts who followed the company's stock. They told the team to go ahead and make the decisions without them since "You are the ones who know the people and your needs; any decision you come up with and can agree on, we can live with."

Mary Chadwick, VP Human Resources, ran the meeting. Each member was asked to arrive with recommendations about who should fill the new roles. To block the natural tendency to push their own area and candidates, they were split into subgroups of three to identify names of candidates two levels down. Then each member was to reverse roles and argue for someone else's options. This worked better than anyone expected; soon members were developing arguments to support the candidates of other members, looking at who would be good for the organization. When a member appeared to be arguing solely for the interests of his own area, others protested, and stopped the partisanship before it accelerated.

To keep discussions on track, the team assigned one person each half day to be the process observer and to lead a discussion of the group's process at the end of a session. This worked well in several ways. Team members became very conscious of having to take the overall company point of view, and for the most part, they did so. The rotating assignment raised awareness and dramatized team ownership of the way they worked. And in two instances, the team review led them to change an earlier decision, as they identified places where they had missed data, not fully explored implications, or failed to see better alternatives.

Bob and Gene had said that they would live with any team outcomes, but they couldn't refrain from calling in a few times to see how it was going. They did not, however, change any of the team's decisions.

Follow-Up Middle Leadership Retreat

With people in place and a new, collaborative leadership style, Pharmco was making good progress. But better teams did not automatically mean that there was full cooperation across the organization.

At a subsequent meeting of the 125 middle leaders several months later, Bob Mitchell started by reiterating that strategy implementation was their responsibility, and that their job was to "make the matrix work." The focus was on breaking the silo mentality and working horizontally with each other. Each department identified the interdependencies among the different functional areas of Pharmco. Representatives of different departments described where they had problems, where they needed help from others, and what they could offer in return. Lincoln Turner, the consultant, gave a brief lecture on exchange and reciprocity, showing how to influence those one can't command by making win-win exchanges between departments.[3] The various departments were expected to use exchanges of what each needed from the other to directly negotiate agreements for more effective collaboration. OpCom declared, "As long as you are within strategic parameters, you don't need Bob or Gene's blessings, or OpCom's approval." The rest of the day, departments sent emissaries to other departmental groupings, negotiating a new way of collaborating so that each would benefit. Agreements were made public, to reinforce their use.

Over time, the 125 participating managers had opportunities to practice what they learned. Most organized meetings in their own departments aimed at deepening the use of the new leadership. This built on the previous middle management training in post-heroic leadership that had helped spur Bob to bring the new leadership system to the top. Shared responsibility was becoming ingrained as a philosophy and set of practices. At last there was consistency in the leadership philosophy throughout the organization.

Bob and Gene Deal with Succession

With the reorganization and 10 percent downsizing taking effect, the OpCom realized that the organization was top-heavy. It didn't need both a CEO and COO. Gene could remain Chairman of the Board but move Bob into the CEO role. OpCom members first discussed this among themselves, then one-on-one with Bob.

At an OpCom meeting from which Gene was absent, the team began to push Bob about his relationship with the CEO. They encouraged him to keep making it clear to Gene what Bob wanted, and what the group needed to keep developing. Team members felt strongly that they should set their own cost-cutting, down-sizing example for the rest of the organization. Bob was hesitant to push Gene for clarification on their respective roles because he didn't want to be seen as self-promoting, but the team stressed that this was for the good of the organization.

Bob scheduled a meeting with Gene to "determine what Gene wanted to do in the company." The first steps in planning and negotiating the succession process had begun. Bob asked Gene to write out his desires as preparation. Gene declared that he wanted to cut back to three days a week, with the balance of his time reserved for philanthropic and personal activities. He wanted to be involved in the following four areas:

1. *Carrying the Pharmco flag.* Using his position as Chairman of the Board to further work his contacts with other companies and leaders of customer groups.

2. *Governmental affairs.* Managing a small staff group to deal with regulatory issues that impacted the company.

3. *Strategic thinking.* Heading a small ongoing task force of key OpCom members and staff to blue-sky new possibilities. They would also help plan OpCom retreats dealing with strategic issues.

4. *Business development.* Exploring new possibilities outside the current line organizations.

Gene agreed that with this setup and with the CFO reporting directly to Bob, he could let go of the ongoing financial oversight of the company. He was now confident that Bob would stay on top of the financial health of the company.

Bob was thrilled with Gene's plan and his continued involvement, and began to act far less ambivalent about becoming CEO. He raised this issue with Gene. Board members supported Bob in this effort and also put some pressure on Gene to move up. After a period of personal indecision, Gene agreed, and six months later, Bob was made CEO.

Outcomes

"OpCom is 85 percent there," reported Mary Chadwick a few months later. "The process is highly collaborative, and our key issues, especially on the reorganization, were jointly determined. Decisions are timely, and by and large are of high quality. Some of them are made a bit too hastily, and will have to be reexamined, but we can do that without finger-pointing."

Other team members commented:

"During the past five months, OpCom made use of floating task forces, so that the strategic process was speeded up without anyone forming entrenched positions. In fact, there were a lot of individual shifts in beliefs. Increasingly, we are building on to a larger company goal rather than arguing only for our own areas."

"We do need some more work on the decision-making processes, especially on which issues should be jointly decided, and which we can let go of because they are less consequential. We need to prioritize and see which items need our full attention and which can get done at just an 'OK' level."

"Bob is stating his position more and more openly and not waiting to see how Gene or the group feels."

"Our middle managers are now more aligned with the company's strategy, and they have finally learned not to run to top management with every problem. They are increasingly willing to cross departmental lines and deal directly with each other."

Company profits soared, and the stock price began to climb, as Wall Street noticed that the company finally had its act together.

PHARMCO ISSUES AND BEYOND

In most organizations, the heroic mind-set causes leaders to take on too much responsibility, and results in team members taking too little. A similar cycle governs traditional relationships between top management teams and the departments below. Leadership teams tend to take on too much responsibility for assuring that all decisions are made right and that there is proper coordination and control. In turn, middle teams push their interests, which increases executive team certainty that they need to coordinate and decide everything important. The middle teams tend to delegate tough issues up, so that many decisions are made at too high a level, where the expertise does not reside.

At Pharmco, the planned changes in patterns illustrated by the two middle leadership retreats resulted in shifts between levels similar to the shifts between Gene and Bob, and between them and the OpCom members. The establishing of a strong strategic vision allowed the middle managers to have more than the usual input on direction and implementation. They were treated like junior partners—middle leaders—and urged to take the organizational perspective. Mutual influence was established between levels, on operating style as well as task issues. Although the middle leadership groups didn't as fully share in the management of the organization as OpCom members shared in their team's work, they were given management responsibilities for dealing with each other and working out the horizontal coordination. A long period of passivity and frustration was broken, and more initiative began to be taken.

All of these changes enabled middle managers to become middle leaders, and enjoy greater autonomy from the top, without the organization sacrificing necessary coordination and control. That meant the top group did not need to intervene often, reinforcing the responsibility of those in the middle. The post-heroic leadership system was embedded throughout the organization.

PRESERVING A ROLE FOR THE LEADER

In earlier chapters, we noted how heroic leaders worry that letting go of the usual responsibility and control will leave them with nothing to do. The events at Pharmco should put this fear to rest. Bob Mitchell had plenty on his plate; in addition to his own need to learn new skills, he had the demanding task of building a shared-responsibility system. He initiated strategic change; sought new behavior from his boss; worked with his team to get them to take more responsibility; monitored the team's progress; did his share of homework for the team; helped deal with and sell his boss's boss (the board); provided direction and symbolic leadership to the troops below; and in general worked at getting members to share responsibility.

Post-heroic leadership does not put leaders out of business; it just fundamentally changes their role. And building the system is never finished. As members start to pick up more of the responsibility, the leader has more time and energy for long-term strategy, implementation, alignment, and renewal.

COLLABORATION ACHIEVED

The way events played out at Pharmco should encourage every company and every manager who can see the flaws in traditional organizational leadership. People have changed; the conditions of competition have changed; and leadership must change in turn. For most organizations, the old way simply won't do.

Pharmco extended the new leadership through the organization in less than a year. Where there is strong need and determination, progress can be rapid. Note, however, that offering managers below the top the chance to take more initiative was both welcomed and resisted. It wasn't enough simply to create the opportunity; *leadership* was required including a dramatic raising of the stakes. But leadership is not just about spurring subordinates to do more; the subordinates also need to exercise leadership, which includes the extension of their vision, team, and influence skills to their colleagues, and back up to their own leaders. Post-heroic leadership is essential at all levels of the organization, and can spread throughout after starting almost anywhere. At Pharmco, one of the pressures for moving to shared responsibility leadership came from middle managers exposed to the ideas in their own training. But then when top management adopted it, there was still work to do in extending it back down the organization.

Any individual at any level can become a post-heroic leader, working first to gain the cooperation of direct reports and then bosses and colleagues. Entire organizations, too, can become post-heroic through training and planning. Any move to the new system of shared leadership begins with the same two sparks—a desire to change for the better, and the courage to act.

CONCLUSIONS

Creating the post-heroic leadership system; there's nothing to it—and everything to it. Just think about leadership differently, bring your colleagues along with you, and extraordinary outcomes await you. But it isn't quite that easy.

In terms of daily work, we have set out a difficult path. It requires courage and skill to share responsibility, commit to a vision, trust team members to identify with overall goals, talk directly and respond non-defensively to straight talk from others, and encourage and work through conflict. When the post-heroic mindset is fully internalized, none of this feels as if you are working uphill, but skill and courage are required for those in leadership roles to be tough enough to be vulnerable, open, and truly collaborative.

Yet there is another area where courage is required. The managers we work with frequently tell us, "shared responsibility leadership is a great model, and it fits me well, but I have to wait until my boss is willing to let me manage this way, and the conditions are right." Throughout the book we have consistently argued that the leader is also a member to some other leader(s), and that leadership extends in all directions. It is too narrow a definition of leadership to focus only on managing down. Everyone will have to manage sideways and upward.

We discussed in Chapters 5 and 9 how to build a post-heroic unit even when reporting to a heroic boss. But we now make a bolder claim: *it is possible to be a post-heroic team member in a heroic organization.* It is possible to make contributions to effectiveness from whatever position you are in, with almost any boss. It isn't necessary to wait for your boss to be struck with a sudden conversion from heroic to post-heroic assumptions. You can create *power up.*

How is this possible? Remember that the core of post-heroic leadership is to feel responsible for the success of the larger unit as well as the one you head. You can do that on your own; no permission is needed to change your attitude. You can help surface the important issues that are not being fully stated. You can think about what is missing from the way your boss's team works that would make it better at problem solving. And you can provide information—off-line if necessary—about the effect of others' behavior that they need to know to achieve the results they want. Make yourself valuable by determining what needs to be done to make your boss and peers more effective, and do it to help them reach their goals.

This kind of positive initiative was illustrated by John Gardner, one of the most thoughtful scholars and practitioners on leadership, in the example he told us about being the beneficiary of leadership from below. When John was head of Common Cause, one of the more challenging groups he had to manage was its Board of Directors. The Board was large and mainly composed of citizen-activists who held strong opinions and definitely felt free to express them. Getting the group to move through the agenda and reach agreement was often a difficult task.

The late Michael Walsh (then a 30-year old Federal Attorney in San Diego, and subsequently the CEO of Tenneco, which he built into a very successful corporation) was the most junior member on the Board. But John Gardner observed that Walsh played a key role in helping to make the meetings successful. John explained:

> *In running these meetings it dawned on me that Mike was rather consistently helping me to move the business along. Over and above what his views were, he was trying to get things done—which was what I was trying to do. When the Board had talked a subject to*

death but couldn't let go, Mike would say in a helpful, non-confrontational way, "have we talked about this enough?" and suggest a motion that captured the essence of the discussion. If two sides were unable to agree, he would likely propose a compromise that would bring them together. He was also helpful in achieving closure by a summary comment like, "it seems to me that what we are trying to say is . . ."

We never explicitly talked about this, but I thought it was a great example of someone participating in the leadership function. I didn't feel threatened at all, because both of us wanted a quality outcome. His timing was very good in that he was able to capture the moment when people wanted to be moved. So even though he was the junior member, others didn't resent his taking up this function.

As the head of an organization committed to improving the workings of democracy, John Gardner did not operate from heroic assumptions, but even the most heroic leader wants to have effective meetings, anticipate and head off problems, please higher-ups, make great decisions, and respond to the extraordinary demands wrought by the competitive and changing economic scene. In heroic organizations, keeping quiet and playing it safe has almost never been the path to great advancement. Remember in Chapter 7 how the top managers at TPG&E all marveled that despite the clear, conservative rules of the organization, they had not themselves followed the keep-your-nose-clean route to get to their present positions. While it isn't possible to successfully violate rules without performing in other ways—and like Chapter 4's John Sloan, you can violate them so severely that your job is threatened despite good performance—pushing upward isn't only risky; it is also often the best formula for personal success. Bringing unusual contributions to your boss's team, helping make the organization work better, speaking the unspeakable truth in a supportive way, seeing how to get the most from people, all are valued, and all can turn career-limiting moves into career-enhancing ones.

As you set out to transform your organization through shared leadership, whether you are sharing responsibility with those who report to you or those to whom you report, we wish you the power to stick with your convictions and to keep learning from your experiences.

APPENDIX A

POWER TALK:
A HANDS-ON GUIDE
TO SUPPORTIVE
CONFRONTATION

When people work together and depend on one another for success as they create shared leadership, disagreements and disputes about task issues or work style are inevitable. As these arise, colleagues, direct reports, and the leader must be prepared to change their views, decisions or behavior. To create a shared leadership system each person—leaders and team members alike—must be willing to state their views fully and be open to the influence of those who disagree with them. In order to make it possible to settle contentious issues, resolve inevitable interpersonal tensions and stimulate continuous learning of personal skills, postheroic leadership requires a level of openness and honesty rarely found in traditional organizations.

The term *supportive confrontation* describes the *power talk* that enables leaders and team members to influence others and to resolve interpersonal disputes. Power talk is potent and direct, not diplomatic or sugar-coated. This Appendix explains supportive confrontation and shows how to use it to address task differences without creating battles for dominance, to make disagreements explicit without increasing defensiveness or resistance, and to raise concerns about colleagues without inflicting personal harm or damaging the relationship.

FOCUS ON BEHAVIOR

The most difficult and potentially divisive disagreements involve the pattern of *behavior* of some other person, either a colleague or boss. These conflicts about operating styles can come from ways of doing work or interpersonal habits; whatever the source, they can be annoying and disruptive of work. Jen focuses on the big picture but Jon relishes the details; Michael focuses on problems while Michelle revels in accomplishments; Chris is laid back, but Christine is a go-getter. There is nothing inherently superior about one style of behavior or the other; in fact, diversity is required for high performance in a complex, interdependent world. One style can be useful for some problems and limiting for others. Nevertheless, it often drives a worker to distraction when colleagues don't behave "the way that I do—the right way."

How can team members address differences that reduce performance without making matters worse? Can they do it without causing defensiveness, denial, or retaliation? It is difficult because many people can't distinguish between criticism of specific *performance* and general disapproval or dislike of the *person.* Well-intentioned comments can tap feelings about being devalued or rejected, especially when the comments are delivered by someone unskilled at making the distinctions.

THE PROBLEM OF AVOIDANCE

Just about everyone who has moved through the supervisory ranks has studied the rules for giving and receiving feedback, but casual observation in almost any organization reveals that many interpersonal problems are neither directly discussed nor resolved.[1] Fearing an explosion, people hold back their true feelings or beliefs and leave these relationship problems to fester, in the vain hope that they will go away. They may toss out hints, but so indirectly that the true depth of the impasse remains hidden.

Yet, when team members fail to confront problematic behaviors early and directly, resentment at the colleague simply grows, and pent-up irritation puts a trip wire on the situation that may sabotage even innocuous events. Before long, annoyance with someone's behavior takes the form of disdain and of attributions about that person's malignant motives, incompetencies, or poor character. And once defective character becomes an issue, future interactions are likely to be adversarial. In this context, the sensitive trip wire can trigger explosions. This is what happened to Andy, who lost control and erupted at his boss. Here's how he explained the situation.

Andy's Investment Banking Explosion

As a third-year analyst in the New York office of a major investment banking firm, my work was exciting and challenging, and I was doing well. I reported to Jack, a senior partner, who thought highly of me. I was pleased when he asked me to work on a new Eastern Europe venture. If successful, this would be a significant stepping-stone for my career. The project would operate out of London. Unfortunately, Sam—another senior manager—had primary responsibility for the project; Jack would be in New York and only tangentially involved.

Sam had the reputation of being a nightmare boss. He was abrasive and would embarrass people in public. On the other hand, if he liked you, he could be your best champion. But no one knew the code for winning him over, and you didn't want to be on his bad side. I sensed that I would be strongly tested when I heard that Sam had asked Jack, "And who is this fair-haired boy you're sending me?"

Sam had served in Vietnam and had a dagger on his wall; that said it all to me. He used military terms in conversation, like "nuke the enemy," and "out-flank them."

This wasn't my style, but I minded it less than his way of putting people down in a public setting. When this happened it was usually over something petty. He really knew how to damage a person's self-confidence. And he often set people up. Here's an example. Sam and I discussed how we should analyze the data for a meeting of the general partners. We agreed on one approach, then he casually speculated, "I wonder what would happen if we analyzed it in a different way?" But he added, "Oh, never mind, probably it wouldn't make any difference." Then at the meeting, he turned to me and said, "Of course you've run the other analysis, haven't you?"

I felt caught in a trap. In investment banking, hierarchy is respected. It seemed inappropriate to take him on publicly. I think he would have denied our previous conversation. But I was concerned that the other partners would view me as superficial, something you *cannot* be in this business.

Sam was tough to take on. He is very tall, towering about a foot over me. He had a strong temper and would intimidate by screaming and cursing. It was so distasteful to confront him that people let him get away with these games. He also sent mixed signals. He could be charming, especially with clients. In our private meetings, he would be very positive, so I always kept guessing about where I stood with him. If I were to complain about how he treated me in public, I was afraid that he would put me down and make me feel like an idiot. I could imagine him saying, "Lighten up, Andy. You're just too sensitive. You have to be tough to be an I-banker."

About a month into the project, I encountered the straw that broke this camel's back. We were planning a conference call with New York, Hamburg, and Moscow. The meeting hadn't started, but everyone was on the line. I was the most junior person there. Sam turned to me and said, "I told you to invite Michael to this meeting; why isn't he here?" The truth is that he had mentioned "It would be kind of nice if Michael attended this session." But since this was a closed meeting and Michael wasn't one of the inner team, and not crucial, I never made the invitation.

I didn't know what to do. I bit my tongue and said, "Sorry, I guess I forgot." I offered no excuse, but took the blame hoping that it would go away as fast as possible. I was livid during the entire meeting, bitter and resentful. I thought, "I am damn good; how dare you do this to me in public!"

After the session, Sam was walking ahead of me. I followed him into his office and slammed the door so hard that the walls shook. Everyone nearby heard it. Sam's back was to me and he turned around with a surprised look. Before he could say anything, I slammed my notebook on his desk and shouted: "Sam, this is absolutely bullshit! You know that you didn't explicitly ask me to invite Michael to the meeting. So why did you embarrass me in front of everyone? You've been twisting the facts ever since I got here. I don't have to take this crap from you any more."

Before he could respond, I picked up my notebook and left, slamming the door behind me. Back at my desk, it hit me: "I can't believe that I just yelled at a senior partner." I had lost my cool in an environment where calm is rewarded. But I felt a great sense of relief—as if a giant weight had been lifted from my shoulders.

A few minutes later, Sam came into my cubicle. "Can we talk?" It was a request, not an order, and I nodded agreement. "What's going on?" he asked. I said, "Sam, you know what you have been doing, and I don't appreciate it." Sam was apologetic: "I didn't mean to put you down, Andy," he said. "I'm sorry that you took it that way." He sounded sincere. I didn't think that an apology from me was appropriate, so we just shook hands and he left.

After that incident, and to my surprise, we became the best of buddies. I became closer to him than to Jack. And Sam never pulled another embarrassing stunt again; he supported me to others and we had a great time on the project.

In this instance, an explosive attack worked. But door-slamming and shouting at one's boss is a high-risk strategy. Perhaps Andy was lucky or had picked up some signal that Sam would respect a person who could fight back. And Andy was a strong performer; if he weren't, his explosion could have propelled him from the firm.

SUPPORTIVE CONFRONTATION

Though there are times to let frustrating issues pass, and times for explosive outbursts, these two options are too extreme—too weak or too strong to enable joint problem-solving. They restrict the influence needed to make shared leadership work. There is a positive third alternative. We call it *supportive confrontation*. It is a process of giving strong feedback by talking only about what one knows, the impact of the other person's behavior. Although it is powerful because it allows a person to raise issues early in a way that minimizes defensiveness, and can be linked to the other person's interests, too few people know how to do it well.

In the conversational volley, people run into trouble when they "cross over the net," and move from their area of expertise (their own reactions) into an area of blindness (the other's motives or intentions). It is difficult to be influential when operating from ignorance. This is not about sugarcoating comments, or using the insincere sandwich technique, where any negative feedback is deliberately sandwiched between positive statements. It is about becoming more honest by staying with your reality instead of turning to what you can only infer.

To understand the concepts underlying supportive confrontation, here is a brief overview of the inference process by which people make sense of others' confusing or disturbing behavior. After the initial reaction, they interpret as best they can. They try to figure out just what kind of person the other is. This interpretive process, called *attribution*, often gets in the way of effective feedback.[2] People observe behavior, then make inferences based on their own experiences, in the attempt to understand the motives and intentions of another person. The difficulty is that their own experiences may not be a reliable guide to someone else's motives and intentions, which are never directly observable. In addition, the observer's needs and motives can become a perceptual screen and distort the attribution process. The only thing that people *can* see is the other person's ensuing behavior. (See Figure A–1.) To illustrate this, we will use a common situation involving a manager and direct reports.

Hal is running a meeting of his team. Tony and Meg are arguing about how best to market an important new product both have been working on. As the tension between them begins to rise, Hal fears that the conversation may escalate out of hand. He wants to cool things down. So just as Meg is becoming more emphatic about the advertising approach she *is sure* is right, Hal says, "This seems to be getting nowhere.

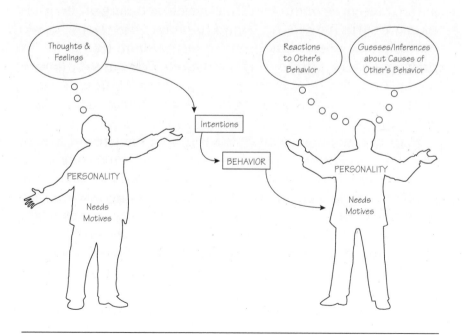

Figure A–1. Interpersonal Attribution

Why don't you two discuss this after the meeting so that we can get through the agenda?"

In this scenario, both Tony and Meg are likely to have reactions to Hal's attempt to divert the discussion, but focusing on Meg will illustrate how team members can address the most difficult interpersonal situation—changing a boss's behavior. Meg is annoyed that Hal is cutting off the discussion just when, from her perspective, they are finally getting to the key disputed points. She feels patronized, but fears what will happen if she objects, so she goes silent.

There are two differing realities in this situation: Hal's actual thoughts, feelings, and intentions, and Meg's reactions and interpretations of what he said. Both participants are knowledgeable about their own realities and unaware of the other person's. Ignorance of the other's inner feelings and motives is unavoidable; a lot of emotion is attached, making accurate perceptions unlikely.

As Meg goes silent, she doesn't stick to what she knows (feeling annoyed and patronized); instead, she begins to make inferences about Hal's motives for cutting off her discussion with Tony. *Is he trying to protect me? Does he see me as weak and needing protection? Maybe this is just a problem he has with conflict; he usually dampens it at meetings.* Then she begins to get suspicious: *Maybe he can't stand a strong woman and wants to shut me up so that Tony can win.*

With her musings, Meg is moving from her area of expertise (her reactions) to her area of ignorance (guessing Hal's motivations). Trying to determine the motives and intentions of others reflects the basic tendency of people to search for meaning in observed behavior. The difficulty arises when people move from wondering about motives to unilaterally concluding that their conjectures are facts; they then become judge and jury, convict the offender, and throw away the key.

Since Meg has incomplete information, her conclusions are unlikely to be accurate. Is it that her boss doesn't value women, or could the opposite be true, and he cut off discussion because he thinks Tony isn't fighting fair, and Hal wants to create a level playing field? Does he believe that Meg can roll with the punches, but that Tony loses control when he thinks he is losing? Does Hal want to let Meg really go at it with Tony in private, so that others will not see Tony lose face? Does Hal come from a culture where the senior person's job is to ensure that conflict between any two family members, male or female, does no harm?

Meg's attributions and inferences about Hal's intentions and motivations are, at best, only guesses. Meg has moved from her side of the court, across the net, and is playing in Hal's backcourt. Foul! Once she assumes that she knows his motives, anything she says (or thinks, or conveys by attitude, tone or body language), will produce defensiveness and resistance in Hal. This lowers the likelihood that she will positively influence his behavior. She has gone from observing his behavior and statements to invading his innards, a place most people reserve for trusted intimates only. If she openly reveals her attributions, he will feel pigeonholed or oversimplified. Few people can take feedback or learn from anyone who is being judgmental, even if it is cloaked in polite language or forced smiles. The negative judgment is what comes through. What started as a legitimate role-related conflict has turned personal.

Crossing the line between objective remarks about performance and judgments about the person is common in workplace feedback:

- "You have a poor attitude."
- "All you want to do is build an empire."
- "You are a controlling person."

Each of these statements contains assumptions about another person's motives and intentions. None address observable behavior or its consequences. The person on the receiving end of this inept feedback will naturally become defensive.

FOUR APPROACHES TO
SUPPORTIVE CONFRONTATION

This section explores four approaches to influencing another person's behavior (and being influenced in return). Each has limitations and traps. No one way works in every context. In fact, they are often most effectively used in combination. Which one to use, and in what combination, depends on the situation and the user's style. With practice, you should be able to find the most appropriate approach for each situation.

Approach 1. "This Is the Effect of Your Behavior on Me"

The simplest and most direct approach is to make clear to the other the effect of the undesired behavior. Meg can tell Hal, "I feel patronized and controlled when you interrupt." Now she is staying with *her* reality. She is not saying that Hal is patronizing her, which he could deny; instead, she is sticking with her reaction, which is indisputable. Hal can't say, "No, you don't feel that way."

Hal might respond, "I don't mean to patronize you; I just want to keep a fight from breaking out and wait for a less emotional atmosphere before we examine the arguments." His reality *doesn't negate Meg's reality*—both can be true. When each reports his or her own reality, neither has to guess the other's intentions.

This is easier said than done; staying focused on behavior is difficult. A behavior is something observable that can be pointed to, which is possible, for example, with "you interrupt," but not with "you patronize." Figuring out what behaviors have caused the interpretation of patronization is complex, and would require exploration of the language, tone and non-verbal actions that led to the judgment.

If Hal is concerned about Meg's reaction, they are in a position to move to joint problem solving. Simply knowing Hal's intention may be sufficient to prevent Meg from feeling controlled the next time. Or they may work out some mutual arrangement (e.g., Meg will agree to make her point more calmly, and Hal will agree not to cut off discussion so quickly).

This approach works only if Meg's reactions cause Hal to want to change. But something else is needed if he is defensive, and tells her, "that is your problem, not mine," or even worse, labels her as weak or over-sensitive.

Approach 2. "Your Behavior Is Not Meeting Your Apparent Goals or Intentions"

The second approach to supportive confrontation is to show the other person how the particular behavior does not help advance his or her interests. That is powerful leverage for change. Most behavior is goal directed, intended to produce a desired result. A person who is behaving in a way that fails to achieve those results is more likely to take feedback seriously.

If, for example, Hal defines the issue as "Meg's problem" she can examine the extent to which Hal's behavior is not meeting his goals. "Hal, I think you want us to disagree without getting overwrought, but when I can't express my strongly held views, I get frustrated and angry."

Again, Hal can't say, "No, you don't feel frustrated," as she is sticking with her expertise. He might say, "You shouldn't feel that way," and she could agree, "Yes, I know I shouldn't—and I don't want to—but *you* are making it difficult for us to explore the issue to the extent that we must in order to make good decisions. I don't think that's the effect you want." Does this get Meg into a guessing game of Hal's intentions and goals? Not necessarily. People often freely broadcast their goals:

- "I want programs that expand our base business."
- "We need to have people feel included and empowered."
- "We should have exhibits that draw on our core strength."

It is likely that Hal has said (probably many times) some variation of "We need to make informed decisions by considering all relevant views." Also, some goals are close to universal—wanting to be heard, wanting influence, wanting to be respected, and so forth—although these must be tested against the particular situation. Meg made this test when she acknowledged, "I don't think that's the effect you want"; this made it possible for Hal to correct her, and to express some other desire.

What if Hal's goals are unknown or unclear? Is Meg then precluded from this second approach? Not if she proceeds from the premise that Hal is acting reasonably *from his perspective* (i.e., from his reality). Instead of attributing negative motives, she should take the radical step of inquiring! (This might have been a good place to start this approach anyway.) "Hal, I don't understand why you are interrupting me; it bothers me. Why are you doing that?"

Suppose Hal is resistant, responding: "Look we have a lot to accomplish and I'm impatient with all the time we are taking." Instead of treating this as a blocking statement, Meg could hear it as information about one of Hal's goals, and link to it: "Hal, I agree that we need to move on, but each time you interrupt, it actually takes more time, because I find myself wanting to explain the point again. Can we work out a better way to deal with this?" If Hal agrees, problem solving is possible.

But what if Hal's action *is* meeting his goals (by causing Meg to be quiet, allowing him to move on to the next topic without having to deal with a possible explosion), yet his behavior is still bothering her? She still has another option that links to Hal's interests.

Approach 3. "Your Behavior May Meet Your Goals, but It Is Very Costly to You"

If another person's behavior is bothering you usually it is in some way also *costly to him or her.* These costs can be of two kinds, specific or general reactions to the other person's

behavior. Specific reactions are in relation to particular issues, such as the person being so persistent about selling
an idea that you feel unable to get your objections heard; in
response you dig in, and resist something you might have
yielded on had your objections been considered. General reactions are those that make you generally less willing to cooperate, work together or be influenced. Similarly, the
reactions of others may be costs, about a particular issue, or
more generally, about the person's reputation—competence,
style, trustworthiness, attractiveness as a colleague. A poor
reputation is very costly.

There are often more costs to problematic behavior than is
immediately apparent. If the behavior makes you feel irritated, it is natural to focus on what annoys you; stepping
back to examine the context can allow a richer assessment
of the other ways that the behavior hurts the person doing it.
For example, does Hal's behavior make Meg less willing to
see the positive sides of Tony's ideas? Does it make other
team members feel less willing to express their views? Do
people conclude they do not want to work for him? The Hals
of the world can be winning battles, but losing the war.

Diagnosing the many negative consequences doesn't require
that they all be dumped on the other person at once. It is best
to reveal the minimum number of consequences that will mo-
tivate the other to enter into joint problem-solving. But knowing many different costs provides more potential sources of
influence leverage, so one can escalate as needed.

Exploring the costs, however, can get into territory that
requires careful navigation skills. Speaking of costs is likely
to pull you dangerously close to crossing the net. Since the
costs are connected to the goals or intentions of the other
person, it is too easy to interpret motives negatively when
all you mean to do is point out the costs to your colleague.
To avoid this potential trap own any attributions as just
that. "Hal, I don't mean to play amateur shrink since only
you know your inner feelings, but it's hard not to speculate
that you can't stand conflict and will kill it as soon as you
can. I doubt that's the impression you want to give, but when

you close down discussion so fast, it's really difficult not to draw that conclusion. And it wouldn't be good for you if I just wrote off all of your comments on controversial issues because I saw you that way."

If you can stay on your side of the net and be clear that you are talking about your impressions, not your convictions, then the danger is reduced and the cost to the other person is sustained. It also allows you to be supportive and solution-oriented if the person claims that his or her intentions were quite different from your impressions of them. If Hal were to say, "No, stifling conflict is not what I want to do, in fact it's just the opposite," Meg could then respond, "So you can see that it is costly to you to continue cutting off discussion, and it's annoying to me. Can we talk about alternative approaches to resolving differences in our group?"

Many assessments of cost to a person imply that other colleagues have a similar reaction to yours. While it is useful to someone to know whether the reaction you are describing is yours alone or shared by 80% of the team, bringing in others can be volatile. Have you represented the others correctly? Will they feel that you have violated their confidences? Would they admit to having the reactions if questioned individually or in a meeting? If they would not be comfortable, yet have strong feelings (as is very often the case in organizations where openness is not well ingrained), how can you convey what the person needs to know without creating more complications?

What someone doesn't know can hurt that person a great deal. If you truly care about your boss's effectiveness, allowing a negative reputation to fester can be deeply wounding, so discovering a way to be able to inform him or her is an important challenge. Reporting the reactions of other colleagues can be helpful and motivating by making the wider costs clear, but it can also be abused if the response is a demand to know "Who else said that?"

Even if Hal were to demand to know the identities of others who are reacting negatively, Meg has possible ways of being constructive without tattling or backing off. She can say, "Hal, I can't name names, because that would violate confidences. However, I can assure you that I am not the only one who feels this way. And if the others who do won't level with you because they fear your response, that is still not in your best interest. What could we do to deal with that problem?" The challenge is to be clear that the costs are real, and allow the other person to decide if they are sufficiently high to warrant getting into problem-solving.

Each of the first three supportive confrontation approaches assumes that the problem is totally with Hal's behavior. But even if Meg stays on her side of the net—criticizes his behavior, and not his persona—Hal may still feel that he is being blamed, and by a subordinate no less. The resulting defensiveness may be minor and pass quickly, but if Hal exhibits feelings of being labeled as the one at fault, Meg can move to Approach 4.

Approach 4. "In What Ways Am I Part of the Problem?"

Conventional discussion of behavior place its causes completely within the individual, as needs, motives, drives—PERSONALITY. Everyone, at one time or another, indulges in behavior driven from within, no matter what anyone else is saying or doing. Some ineffective people do this all the time, only accidentally responding appropriately to others, like the stopped clock that is correct twice each day. But for most people most of the time, interactions with others heavily influence behavior. Hal may be partly animated by Meg's behavior and this would, in effect, make her part of the problem.

Meg should consider whether *she* is compounding the problem. She might recognize her tendency to escalate emotions by adopting an attacking tone whenever someone questions her judgment and could then approach Hal with the following admission:

> *"Hal, we often fall into a negative cycle that must be as frustrating to you as it is to me. I realize I am part of the*

> *problem. When I disagree with one of my colleagues, I
> anticipate that you will cut me short. This makes me
> tense and causes me to argue my points harder and
> harder. That must drive you nuts. Can we talk about it?"*

Talking this way levels the playing field and generally
makes it easier for the other party to be equally forthright.
People are usually willing to take responsibility for some of
the problem if others are willing to do the same. But park
the entire problem at one person's door and that person will
simply push it back to yours. If either party to an interpersonal dispute that is being mutually reinforced can identify
the pattern of reinforcement, that frees both of them to explore it. Naming it helps change the discussion from blame
to problem solving about how to halt the pattern.

This approach can make it possible to resolve disputes
through reciprocal agreements. "Hal, if I pledge to remain
calm when we explore differences, will you give me enough
time to work through my issues with Tony and other people?" This process of exchange makes it possible to influence
another person without identifying either party as the vil-
lain or the victor.

Choosing the Most Appropriate Approach

These approaches to influence have been described as if they
were separate and independent, but they can readily be combined. When should each form of supportive confrontation
be used, and in what combination?

Approach 1, pointing out the effects of behavior, is the
simplest and most direct and therefore should be considered
first. Because it lays out your needs and concerns, it makes
you vulnerable. This is actually an advantage. Expressing
the impact of the other person's behavior on your feelings
places both parties in an equally open and vulnerable position, which reduces defensiveness in the receiver. This approach works best when the other person is concerned about

you; doesn't want to have that sort of negative impact; and won't "blame the victim" by saying that the negative impact is a sign of your weakness or oversensitivity.

When these conditions aren't met, it can be useful to add the second or third approaches, showing how the undesirable behavior doesn't meet the other person's goals or is costly. These approaches explicitly speak to the other person's interests and therefore are likely to move that person, first through acceptance that there is an issue, and then into joint problem solving. Adding to rather than omitting the first approach is important, because omitting the effect of the behavior on you would withhold crucial information and would imply you are a good Samaritan, "only acting for the other's sake," when you are clearly acting *in the interests of both parties.*

The fourth approach, asking how you, the influencer, are part of the problem, is appropriate when a strong, *inter*personal dynamic has both people hooked into a negative pattern. Who started the negative pattern isn't relevant and is probably unknowable. When the other is sensitive to being blamed, taking responsibility for part of the problem reduces defensiveness, enabling the exchange of promises to change behavior in ways that benefit both parties. Because exchange has a negotiations aspect and is a less intimate way of discussing interpersonal problems, it is helpful when the other person has significant discomfort talking about interpersonal processes ("touchy-feely stuff").

CARING ABOUT THE OTHER PERSON

If you stay on your side of the net, you do not have to be fond of the other person. You are merely providing information that by and large he or she does not possess, which might allow the person to more effectively meet objectives at lower personal cost. If you do care about the person, however, these four approaches have more powerful impact, because the recipient is less likely to be suspicious of your motives, or feel diminished by having to admit less effectiveness than hoped for.

You are implicitly saying, "I am concerned that you are hurting yourself with that behavior. It's not in your best interest." This "I may be tough on you but I'm on your side" approach only works well if concern for the other person's effectiveness is genuine. It is almost impossible to fake sincerity, despite Groucho Marx's cynical gag: "The secret of success is to be honest and sincere; if you can fake that, you've got it made."

It is hard to be concerned for someone when deeply angry at him or her. That is why it is important to speak up early, before anger has built, rather than keeping book on the other's bad behavior to gather conclusive proof. You can address issues early with little danger by staying on your side of the net and sticking to observable behavior and your reactions. That way the person has not been convicted in your mind, so you really can care about being helpful and avoid creating defensiveness.

ACHIEVING RESOLUTION

Resolving difference through supportive confrontation requires three things:

1. The parties must reach the point where they are willing to engage in joint problem solving.
2. They must reach mutually acceptable agreement.
3. There must be follow-up.

Joint Problem Solving

For effective problem solving parties must be willing to engage about the problem and seek resolution. Winning—getting others to do what you want—is not the object of influence activities. Thinking of influence that way assumes both that the other person is wholly at fault, and that you already know what must be done. There is high probability that you are in part causing the difficulties you want to resolve.

Blaming is equally out of place in stimulating the other person to joint problem solving. Not wanting to be seen as totally at fault, people have a tendency to shift responsibility to others. This generates a cycle of unproductive finger-pointing. To prevent this cycle accept that there are inevitably multiple realities: "I understand how you view the situation and have explained how I view it differently; each of us can be right, since each version is real for us." This counters the unstated assumption that behaviors leading to bad results must be caused by bad intentions.

You will move toward problem resolution when you can bring yourself to accept that the other person is acting with the best of intentions. At that point, you can say, "I see what you are trying to accomplish; unfortunately, this isn't happening, so let's try to figure out why you're not getting the outcome you intend." Next you should move beyond generalizations to specifics. The other person needs to know *exactly* what behaviors have been troubling. And it is useful for you to know the other's intentions, goals, and concerns. The other is likely to openly share these ideas without your having to guess at—and probably distort—them. Just knowing that the irritating behavior was not done with malevolent intent is often enough to reduce its sting.

Reaching Agreement

Team members encounter two main traps in reaching agreement, even after people attempt joint problem solving. The first is "I am what I am. I can't change my personality." The person refuses to explore alternative behavior because what is called for seems out of character, implying that personality precludes behavioral choices. But people don't have to change personality to choose new behavior, even if it is uncomfortable or difficult. The antidote to this trap is to separate basic personality from specific behavior, not transplant personality. "The particular behavior is not a result of your basic personality, just your actions. You don't have to change who you are to change *what you do* in meetings." In most cases, you can point to occasions when the other party—operating with the same personality—behaved more effectively.

The second trap is to make what we call "toothless agreements:"

- "I'll try to improve."
- "I promise to be more considerate."
- "I will seek your input in the future."

The desire to quickly end a stressful conversation often induces disputing parties to rush to these ineffective fixes. What they lack are specifics. Effective resolutions state something like the following:

- "These are the *times* and the *areas* in which I want to give input."
- "Here's *how* you can signal me to calm down."

Follow-Up

Like any change, behavior changes require regular follow-up to avoid backsliding. Three follow-up steps help assure the improved relationship: (a) monitoring progress in repairing the relationship, (b) reinforcing changed behavior, and (c) handling regression.

In most cases, initial problem solving has a positive effect. But doubts quickly creep in:

- "How sincere was the other person in recognizing my concerns?"
- "The boss seemed to take my confronting her rather well. But has this soured her attitude toward me?"
- "Have we overlooked important points of division?"

Each party must follow up about agreements and determine whether more work, or repair work, is needed. The new behaviors also need reinforcement. As psychologists have confirmed, reinforcement is more potent than punishment in changing behavior. Even if progress is slow, saying, "I appreciate your efforts in making this new arrangement work" has great power.

Finally, some regression is probable, especially if the behavior in question has been a central part of the other's style. One discussion or agreement is unlikely to change 30 years of learned behavior. But rather than viewing regression as failure, use it to reinforce the new behavior. Stopping the action and sympathetically or humorously commenting, "Oops, what you did after Helen disagreed is an example of what we talked about," is the sort of specific feedback that can reinforce learning. Drawing attention to real-time regression works best when the parties have previously agreed to watch for occurrences. This makes follow-up less a case of "Gotcha" and more a continuation of the improvement process.

Being responsive in the moment requires tuning in to the process as it unfolds, so that when Hal blocks disagreement yet again, or Meg retreats, the other one can notice and use the incident to clarify the behavior, its consequences, or the intentions of the person who is behaving in ineffective ways. Alertness to the moment reveals how certain behavior perpetuates irritating tendencies in others.

FINAL POINTS

Resist the Urge to Attack

We have thus far focused on interpersonal problems from the viewpoint of the person who wants to change someone else's behavior. But everyone at one time or another has been the recipient of an accusation that attacked his or her motives or intentions. It is likely that the accuser has crossed over the net and imputed negative motives, making you feel defensive or misunderstood. When you find yourself under attack, the urge to defend or retaliate is strong. In this situation, the most important thing to do is to take the lead in separating your behavior from your intentions, and acknowledge—whether you are at fault or not—that you have done something that bothers the other person. Then invite behavioral exploration. Say something like, "I see that I have done something that bothers you, which is not the effect I want. Since that wasn't my intention I want to understand specifically what I am doing to upset you." Then after gaining clarity about the offending actions, you can encourage joint problem-solving by adding, "Here's what I was trying to do; how could I have accomplished it without causing these problems?" If the other person persists in imputing (and impugning) your motives, you can firmly block the attack by staying with your expertise: "Look, you don't know why I acted that way and I'm beginning to resent your claim to be able to read my mind, despite my assurances. We are going to get much further if we can stick to specifying what I'm doing that is so troubling to you and then figuring out a better way to interact."

Getting difficulties on the table in this way can have one of three positive outcomes:

1. Once you explain your intentions, the behavior no longer is so irritating.
2. Once you see the impact, you agree not to do the behavior any longer and search for a new one that meets your goals without upsetting the other.
3. If this interpersonal problem is interpersonally caused, you can enter a negotiation in which you agree to change your behavior in return for a needed change by the other person.

Any one of these is superior to defensiveness and retaliation.

Supportive confrontation can resolve interpersonal problems when initiated from either side to the dispute, and does not require that both parties be highly skilled in the approaches described. It just takes one person to hold to the model of staying on one's own side of the net to help both keep from leaping over it with flights of negative fancy.

Position Power Doesn't Matter

Supportive confrontation is *not* dependent on position power. While leaders may be better able to enforce agreements, supportive confrontation can be initiated by peers and subordinates as well. If the initiator stays on his or her own side of the net, speaking to the needs of the other person and being persistent in revealing the unwanted consequences of the other person's behavior, it is possible for anyone to confront anyone else. Higher-ups and colleagues also want to be effective.

Even when dealing with those lower in the hierarchy, there are many actions that cannot effectively be commanded. The subordinate must want to change. Speaking to his or her best interests, which is the heart of supportive confrontation, can produce cooperation rather than reluctant compliance.

Careful Approaches to Supportive Confrontation Are Not Always Necessary

There are many ways to address interpersonal problems. When the relationship is solid and there is mutual respect and concern, the supportive confrontation guidelines can be violated and people can speak to the intentions and motives of the other (usually off limits). Good friends and good colleagues can listen to each other when the dialogue is not perfect, or say "cut the crap" when the feedback strays too far from what is acceptable.

But when the relationship is strained or the behavior in question is a touchy subject, supportive confrontation is best: stick with the specific behaviors and their effects. This is the most accurate and direct way to communicate. Even with close colleagues who can usually handle the no-holds-barred communication, attribution and psychological interpretation can get in the way.

Reticence Reduces Influence

Outright warfare is less a source of influence problems than the fear of speaking straight. When people are not direct, their concerns are ignored and problems fester. Here's how one manager's reticence reduced her influence.

Catherine's Limits

Catherine was in charge of program development, while Rob, her colleague, was responsible for marketing and publicity. This was a new assignment for him; he had been recently demoted and, at 53, saw this as a last chance to redeem himself. Unfortunately, he spent most of his time on self-promotion.

Catherine rightly decided to confront Rob on this issue. She started out by saying how upset and frustrated she was about the situation, and how demotivating it was for her and her staff. She was about to describe the ways in which this self-promotion actually hurt him, when he burst into tears. "I have failed again. I am just a failure. I have a family to support. What am I going to do?" Catherine was totally taken aback, embarrassed for hurting him. She quickly backpeddled to downplay the problem. She ended the meeting by saying that she would take care of the publicity herself, when in fact, she was already understaffed.

Later, as she described this encounter with a friend, he asked, "Why didn't you use what Rob had said as a way to get him to change?"

"What could I have said?" Catherine asked.

"How about, "Yes, Rob, you *are* failing—but that doesn't make you a failure as a person. I want you to succeed. Your success will help you and help my department. In fact, that is why I am raising the issue. The question is, do you want to succeed?"

"I never could have said that," Catherine responded. "That's so direct, and he was so upset."

"Then," replied her friend, "you know who has the problem."

To what extent do needs for approval, to be liked, and to be seen as a nice person keep you from powerful talk, from using the influence tools at your disposal? Most people can be influenced *if you want to* influence them. The choice is yours.

RESOURCES FOR FURTHER LEARNING

Leadership and Influence Program, Babson College

A residential five-day executive development program, exploring vision, team-work, and other leadership competencies needed to influence at all levels of an organization. This highly experiential program is for managers who have direct reports managing others, and combines videos, case discussions, role plays, sim-ulations, and a day of outdoor problem-solving activities linked to post-heroic concepts. Participants request confidential questionnaire feedback on leader-ship style from peers and direct reports, and utilize the results at the program. With a faculty team led by Allan Cohen, the program runs twice a year and has also been customized for numerous companies.

Babson School of Executive Education, Babson Park, MA 02157-0310. (800) 882-EXEC, or (781) 239-4354.

Leadership Excellence Program, NTL Institute

An intensive, six-day residential workshop open to managers from different or-ganizations. It is highly experiential and makes use of role plays, exercises of critical management problems, short lectures, and skill practice sessions that help managers learn to:

- Build a cohesive team where members collaboratively tackle the core strategic problems;
- Develop a tangible vision that aligns individual goals with organizational objectives;
- Resolve conflict productively so that differences can lead to new creative solutions;
- Build mutual influence relationships so that all members can be more powerful, and
- Give feedback to subordinates so that performance improves and the re-lationship is strengthened.

There is extensive feedback from a questionnaire given to subordinates and peers at work, and from the other participants and staff members in the program.

NTL Institute for Applied Behavioral Science is an international leader in ex-periential learning. 1240 North Pitt St., Suite 100, Alexandria, VA 22314-1400. (800) 777-5227.

Consultation on Implementation, Strayer Consulting Group

Help introduce post-heroic leadership concepts through management consulting, executive coaching, and team-building activities. Provide organization development services to companies experiencing rapid change. Deal with strategic planning, corporation reorganization, acquisition and merger integration, and other forms of organizational change.

Strayer Consulting headquarters: 16151 Woodacres Road, Los Gatos, CA 95030. (408) 399-1500.

Leading for Growth Program, Wilson Learning Corporation

An advanced two-day leadership program led by accredited performance consultants for intact teams or for managers from different parts of the same organization. Videos of real management situations allow participants to develop their skills while gaining an in-depth understanding of post-heroic leadership.

Choosing Growth Leadership—illustrates the fundamental paradigm shift from heroic leadership to shared responsibility that the leader and members can use.

Building a Collaborative Growth Culture—teaches the skills of group development and when to use the various decision-making approaches of leaders.

Creating a Shared Vision—demonstrates how the leaders, with their teams, can develop meaningful visions.

Adopting Mutual Influence—teaches how to develop mutual influence, how to confront behaviors that interfere, and how to develop individual capacity.

Understanding the Growth Leadership Inventory—provides quantitative feedback from direct reports on six sets of leadership competencies.

The Growth Leadership Inventory, Wilson Learning Corporation

Diagnoses a leader's ability to make the transformation from heroic management to shared responsibility leadership as perceived by the individuals in the group(s) she or he leads. Measures six competencies:

Collaborative Culture

Shares Ownership: Ensuring that the group is involved in key decisions and takes responsibility for their implementation.

Integrates Differences: Challenging the group to openly discuss differences and seek solutions to address diverse perspectives.

Shared Vision

Sustains Commitment: Facilitating ongoing dialogue to ensure alignment among individual, group, and organizational visions and strategies.

Resolves Inconsistencies: Addressing systems and practices that impede the achievement of team and organizational strategies.

Mutual Influence

Accepts Influence: Openly seeking and acting on feedback from others.

Influences Others: Supportively confronting and consulting on behaviors that impede performance.

The *Inventory* is a multi-rater instrument scored by Wilson Learning and returned to the manager, accompanied by a personalized action planning guide.

Wilson Learning is an international training and consulting organization headquartered at 7500 Flying Cloud Drive, Eden Prairie, MN 55344-3795. (800) 328-7937. The website is *www.wilsonlearning.com.*

NOTES

Preface

1. John Huey, "The New Post-Heroic Leadership," *Fortune*, Feb. 12, 1994, pp. 42–50.

Introduction: A New Relationship for Leaders and Followers

1. David L. Bradford and Allan R. Cohen, *Managing for Excellence* (New York: John Wiley & Sons, 1987).
2. John Huey, "The New Post-Heroic Leadership," *Fortune*, February 21, 1994, p. 42.
3. "Continental Grain Co. No Longer Lives by Bread Alone," Scott Kilman, *Wall Street Journal*, May 21, 1997, p. B4.

2. Heroic Leadership: Where the Buck Stops Too Often

1. For richer explanation of these terms and more about the limitations inherent in each variation, see David Bradford and Allan Cohen, *Managing for Excellence* (New York: John Wiley & Sons, 1984).
2. Gary Hamel, "Strategy as Revolution," *Harvard Business Review*, July–August, 1996, p. 74.
3. Andrew Grove, *Only the Paranoid Survive* (New York: Currency/Doubleday, 1996), p. 184.

3. Post-Heroic Leadership

1. Scott Cook, speaking in the PBS production, *The Entrepreneurial Revolution*, 1997.
2. From Intuit Corporation statement on "Company Values." See www.intuit.com.
3. Personal communication from Bob Weissman.

4. Robert Howard, "Values Make the Company: An Interview with Robert Haas," *Harvard Business Review*, September–October, 1990, pp. 133–144.
5. Jon R. Katzenbach and Douglas K. Smith, *The Wisdom of Teams*, (Boston: Harvard Business School Press, 1993).
6. John Huey, "The New Post-Heroic Leadership," *Fortune*, February 21, 1994, p. 50.
7. The Bradford-Cohen Leadership Style Questionnaire©, which has 35 questions, has been used with more than 100 firms in all types of industries. Consistently ranked near the bottom when assessing leaders is the question: "Does your boss give you timely and honest feedback on how well you are performing?"
8. John Huey, "The New Post-Heroic Leadership," *Fortune*, February 21, 1994, pp. 42–50.

5.   Leader-Member Ambivalence

1. L. K. Michaelsen, W. E. Watson, and R. H. Black, "A Realistic Test of Individual vs. Group Decision-Making," *Journal of Applied Psychology*, 74, No. 5 (1989): pp. 834–839.

6.   Building a Shared-Responsibility Team

1. Donald C. Hambrick, "Fragmentation and the Other Problems CEOs Have with Their Top Teams," *California Management Review*, 37, 3, Spring, 1995, pp. 110–127.
2. Stratford Sherman, "Secrets of HP's 'Muddled' Team," *Fortune*, March 18, 1996, p. 120.
3. Stratford Sherman, *Fortune*, op. cit., p. 120.
4. Jon R. Katzenbach and Douglas K. Smith, *The Wisdom of Teams* (Boston, MA: Harvard Business School Press, 1993), pp. 20–21, 43–64.
5. Jon R. Katzenbach and Douglas K. Smith, "The Discipline of Teams," *Harvard Business Review*, March–April, 1993, p. 112.
6. Thomas M. Hout and John C. Carter, "Getting It Done: New Roles for Senior Executives," *Harvard Business Review*, November–December, 1995, p. 142.
7. Joseph Weber, "Mr. Nice Guy with a Mission," *Business Week*, November 25, 1996, p. 132.

8. M. J. Preitula and H. A. Simon, "The Experts in Your Midst," *Harvard Business Review,* January–February, 1989, pp. 120–124.

9. Eileen Shapiro's book is in press. *When the Enemy is Us,* (Oxford England: Capstone Ltd., March, 1998).

10. Hambrick, op. cit., pp. 110–116.

11. Several such models that have received attention, especially the one articulated by B. W. Tuckman, ("Developmental Sequence in Small Groups," *Psychological Bulletin, 63,* 1965, pp. 384–399) which cleverly calls its four stages "forming, storming, norming, and performing." W. Bennis and H. Shepard ("A Theory of Group Development," *Human Relations, 9,* 1956, pp. 415–437) devised the first model, but like Tuckman based it on groups that focused on group process rather than work tasks. We prefer the model formulated by Steven L. Obert, "The Development of Organizational Task Groups" (Ph.D. Dissertation, Case-Western Reserve University, 1979).

12. This model has two features that make it especially useful. Because it was derived from work teams, it matches more closely the experiences of business groups. This makes the characteristics of each stage recognizable to the organizational work-world, as contrasted with the better-known Tuckman model, (forming, storming, norming, performing), which is based on process groups. For example, the latter has "norming" defined as a separate stage even though, in reality, norms are set from the very first interactions through all stages of the group's development.

13. Edgar E. Schein, *Process Consultation: Its Role in Organization Development, 2nd ed.,* (Reading, MA: Addison-Wesley, 1988) pp. 41–49.

14. Hambrick, op. cit., p. 115.

15. For an excellent discussion of the value of contention in organizations, see the book by Richard T. Pascale, *Managing on the Edge* (New York: Simon & Schuster, 1991).

16. Hambrick, op. cit., pp. 115–116.

7. Creating Commitment to a Tangible Vision

1. Bradford and Cohen, *Managing for Excellence,* (New York: John Wiley & Sons, 1984), pp. 83–86.

2. For example, see Gerard H. Langeler, "The Vision Trap," *Harvard Business Review*, March–April, 1992, pp. 46–55, or numerous statements by IBM president, Louis V. Gerstner Jr., in *Business Week* about the need for performance, not vision.

3. The survey was called "Developing Global Capability," directed by Douglas A. Ready, a joint project of the International Consortium for Executive Development Research and Arthur D. Little, 1997.

4. "Values Make the Company: An Interview with Robert Haas," *Harvard Business Review*, September–October, 1990, p. 134.

5. R. Lacey, *Ford: The Man and the Machine* (New York: Ballantine Books, 1986), p. 93.

6. This is what happened to The March of Dimes when polio was conquered, and to NASA after it landed a crew on the moon in 1969. In the absence of comparably exciting and challenging goals, these organizations have struggled to find new purpose.

7. The distinction between task- and organization-based vision, along with more excellent work on vision, can be found in James C. Collins and Jerry I. Porras, *Built to Last*, (New York: Harper Business, 1996).

8. Terence Deal and Allan Kennedy, *Corporate Culture* (Reading MA: Addison-Wesley, 1982).

9. John D. Kotter, *A Force for Change: How Leadership Differs from Management* (New York: Free Press, 1990).

10. Tom Peters and Nancy Austin, *A Passion for Excellence*, (New York: Random House, 1985).

11. Collins and Porras, op. cit.

12. See Jay Conger, "The Dark Side of Leadership," *Organizational Dynamics*, Autumn 1990, pp. 44–55.

13. Peter Senge, *The Fifth Discipline* (New York: Currency/Doubleday, 1990).

14. Peter Senge, et al. *The Fifth Discipline Fieldbook: Strategies and Tools for Building a Learning Organization*, (New York: Currency/Doubleday, 1994).

15. This exercise is adapted from work described by L. J. Bourgeois and David B. Jemison, "Analyzing Corporate Culture," *EXCHANGE: The Organizational Behavior Teaching Journal*, 1982, VII, 3.

16. Peter B. Vaill, "Visionary Leadership," in *The Portable MBA in Management*, ed. Allan R. Cohen, (New York: John Wiley & Sons, 1993), pp. 12–37.

17. Thomas Peters and Robert Waterman, *In Search of Excellence*, (New York: Harper & Row, 1982). The term brute attention was used in speeches by Peters; in the book it is obsessive attention.

18. See Tom Peters, "Truths We Hold to Be Self-Evident (More or Less)," *Organizational Dynamics*, Summer 1996, pp. 27–32.

8. Enhancing Power through Mutual Influence

1. Chris Argyris, *Interpersonal Competence and Organizational Effectiveness* (Homewood, IL: Richard D. Irwin, 1962).

2. See Rosabeth M. Kanter, "Power Failure in Management Circuits," *Harvard Business Review, 57*, July–August, 1979, pp. 65–75, and *Men and Women of the Corporation* (New York: Basic Books, 1977), pp. 189–195.

3. The Bradford-Cohen Leadership Style Questionnaire is in David L. Bradford and Allan R. Cohen, *Managing for Excellence*, (New York: John Wiley & Sons, 1984), pp. 292–294.

4. *Managing for Excellence*, op. cit., pp. 146–154.

5. V. O. Allan and J. M. Levine, "Consensus and Conformity" in the *Journal of Experimental Social Psychology, 5*, 1969, pp. 389–399.

6. For a more complete discussion of how to influence a boss or a colleague, see Allan R. Cohen and David L. Bradford, *Influence without Authority*, (New York: John Wiley & Sons, 1989). There we show how reciprocity and exchange are the basis for influence, in which one person gives something valuable in return for something valued.

9. Launching Change

1. See Bradford and Cohen, *Managing for Excellence*, pp. 248–277, for the example of Murray, a manager who made positive changes in his team but forgot to keep his own manager in the loop, and was eventually fired.

2. Rosabeth Moss Kanter, *The Change Masters*, (New York: Simon & Schuster, 1983).

3. Many managers have told us that giving copies of one of our earlier books to their managers stimulated interest or provided an alternate model for leadership that led to improved practices. We hope that this book will be no less useful.

11.   Addressing Conflict

1. Peter F. Drucker, *Adventures of a Bystander*, (New York: Harper & Row, 1978), p. 287.
2. A useful book for help on group problem-solving techniques is *How to Make Meetings Work*, Michael Doyle and David Straus, (New York: Jove Publishing, 1986).
3. Kathleen M. Eisenhardt, Jean L. Kahwajy, and L. J. Bourgeois III, "How Management Teams Can Have A Good Fight," *Harvard Business Review*, July–August, 1997, pp. 77–85.

12.   Achieving Collaboration

1. Jon R. Katzenbach and Douglas K. Smith, *The Wisdom of Teams* (Boston: Harvard Business School Press, 1993), p. 39.
2. The authors of this book have had many battles over writing style and concepts when doing the two previous books written together. David is an idea extender and excellent organizer, who in Allan's view reorganizes too readily and often in a style that needs too much editing. Allan is an idea synthesizer, who writes seamlessly, but from David's point of view is too resistant to valuable polishing and resequencing that would give the writing more punch.

   Pride of authorship and of ideas is no small force in the world, and neither of us easily gives up. Each has been angry, and hurt, and convinced that the other is a stubborn (pigheaded) cuss, but both believe that neither of us would be as effective without the partnership. We have worked out an arrangement where we brainstorm together, David outlines, Allan drafts the text and agrees to redraft as often as David has ideas and new outlines to incorporate, thereby capitalizing on our strengths and working around each's inability to completely change individual taste and style. And our close friendship (in itself developed through years of working together) has preserved our willingness to support each other, give direct and uncomfortable feedback, and continue the work.

3. See David Bradford and Allan Cohen, *Influence without Authority* (New York: John Wiley & Sons, 1990), pp. 26–98, for a rich explanation of exchange and reciprocity theory.

Appendix A

1. Common groundrules for feedback include: be specific, be descriptive not evaluative, give it close to the event, when possible wait until it is requested, be tentative, be caring. See Charles N. Seashore, Edith Whitfield Seashore, and Gerald M. Weinberg, *What Did You Say?: The Art of Giving and Receiving Feedback* (N. Attleboro, MA: Douglas Charles Press, 2nd ed., 1992).
2. H. H. Kelley and J. L. Michela, "Attribution Theory and Research," *Annual Review of Psychology* 31 (1980), pp. 400–405, and J. Jaspers, F. D. Fincham, and M. Hewstone, *Attribution Theory and Research; Conceptual, Developmental and Social Dimensions* (London: Academic Press, 1983).

INDEX